Exploring the role of managers as employees in Britain, the United States, Australia, New Zealand, Germany, Sweden, France, Italy, and Japan, *Managers as Employees* documents the differences and similarities that exist in the employment relationships of managers in these developed countries, and identifies the forces that shape and regulate these relationships.

To many in the business world, the concept of managers as employees is a contradiction: a manager is an owner of an enterprise or an agent of the owner, and not an employee. Although this is sometimes true, contributors to *Managers as Employees* explain, most managers participate in an employee relationship that, in many countries, implies a specific legal status involving entitlements, duties, obligations, and responsibilities. From a practical perspective, however, managers are employees because they assume the role of employees in organizations: they take as well as give orders, are compensated for doing specific jobs or fulfilling responsibilities, and may be dismissed for inadequate or unsatisfactory performance. In short, managers are employees because they exchange services for pay.

In this book, editor Myron Roomkin has invited international experts to write papers that explain how managers' employment relationships have been affected by significant developments over the past two decades in each of these countries. They survey such issues as recessions; periods of inflation; the oil shocks of 1973 and 1978; the internationalism of business; changing work force demographics, such as feminization and aging; and shifting patterns of regulation and deregulation. Also discussed are the ways managers are prepared for work and advance professionally, the economics of the managerial labor market, and the role of company personnel policies in managerial employee situations.

An illuminating guide for all persons interested in the internationalism of business and the nature of indigenous managerial groups in specific industrialized countries, *Managers as Employees* will be an indispensable aid for business and human resources management students, executives, managerial trainees, managers, economists, and sociologists.

About the Author

Myron J. Roomkin is Chair of the Policy and Environment Department, and Professor of Human Resources Management at the J. L. Kellogg Graduate School of Management, Northwestern University.

MANAGERS
AS EMPLOYEES

MANAGERS AS EMPLOYEES

An International Comparison of the Changing Character of Managerial Employment

Edited by
Myron J. Roomkin

New York   Oxford
Oxford University Press
1989

93-1976

Oxford University Press

Oxford   New York   Toronto
Delhi   Bombay   Calcutta   Madras   Karachi
Petaling Jaya   Singapore   Hong Kong   Tokyo
Nairobi   Dar es Salaam   Cape Town
Melbourne   Auckland
and associated companies in
Berlin   Ibadan

Copyright © 1989 by Oxford University Press, Inc.

Published by Oxford University Press, Inc.
200 Madison Avenue, New York, New York 10016

Oxford is a registered trademark of Oxford University Press

Library of Congress Cataloging-in-Publication Data
Managers as employees: an international comparison of the changing
character of managerial employment / edited by Myron J. Roomkin.
p.   cm.
Bibliography: p.
Includes index.
ISBN 0-19-504322-7
1. Executives. 2. Executives—Salaries, etc. 3. Comparative management.
I. Roomkin, Myron.
HD38.2.M36 1989
658.4—dc19
88-738
   CIP

10 9 8 7 6 5 4 3 2 1

Printed in the United States of America
on acid-free paper

Preface

Employees who manage and direct organizations have been one of the fastest growing occupational groups in most of the western economies. Moreover, the social status and acceptability of this group have risen dramatically, especially in the 1980s, due in part to the growing dissatisfaction of voters with government's inability to solve social problems.

But those who work as managers also have faced several social and economic trends that have had an adverse impact on their education and preparation, compensation, careers, and the ways in which they perform their work. In this sense managers, like all workers, are not immune from the forces of the marketplace that shape and define the terms and conditions of employment.

While this appears to be a truism, most people tended to overlook the study of managers from this perspective. In 1981, at the beginning of a major worldwide recession, I participated in a lecture tour that took me to many of the countries discussed in this volume. I found representatives of trade unions, government, and industry greatly concerned about the labor market problems of nonsupervisory employees. Managers, it was assumed, were an elite part of the workforce and would take care of themselves. Indeed, we have tended to overlook the study of managers as employees, until their problems have become glaring. Such was the situation recently in the financial industry after the employment cutbacks following Black Monday on the world's stock exchanges.

This project was undertaken to increase our knowledge of and sensitivity to managers as employees. Its purposes are to document the terms and conditions of managers as employees and to examine how those conditions are being influenced by significant social, economic, and technological developments. The scope of the work is international and includes information on developments in nine industrialized democratic countries.

The introductory chapter is actually an overview of the volume. It contains a summary of developments in the studied countries and a comparison of findings in these essays.

Contributors wrote their chapters using a common set of research questions. Each chapter, however, can be read separately.

It was the hope of all individuals who worked on this project that it would stimulate a great deal more interest and research on managers as employees.

Credit for volumes of collected essays is generally shared by many, and this is particularly true for collections from different countries. Therefore, there are several people to thank.

The individual contributors deserve to be acknowledged first. Each participated in this study out of an appreciation for the subject. In several cases, contributors used their own money or sought special research grants to finance their work.

Financial support for organizing this project and for writing the chapters on the experiences of managers in the United States and Japan was generously provided by the Richard M. Paget Research Chair at the J. L. Kellogg Graduate School of Management of Northwestern University. Additional funding to cover the expenses of editing the volume was made available by the Kellogg Graduate School's Pepsico Research Professorship in International Business. For this generous support, I am deeply grateful to the school.

I also wish to thank the Center for Urban Affairs and Policy Research at Northwestern University for its intellectual and financial support during the initial phases of this project.

A portion of the research was undertaken while I was a visiting scholar at the Institute for International Labour Studies of the International Labour Organization in Geneva, Switzerland. The staff of the Organization encouraged my work and helped educate me in the field of comparative human resources.

Sanna Longden once again has provided indispensable editorial assistance.

Evanston, Ill.   M.J.R.
April 1988

Contents

Contributors

Greg Bamber is director of research at the University Business School at Durham University.

Karl-Olof Faxén is director of research at the Swedish Employers Federation (Svenska Arbetsgivaretoreningen).

Russell D. Lansbury holds the chair of industrial relations at the University of Sydney.

Håkan Lundgren is the director of the department of business administration of the Swedish Employers Federation in Stockholm.

Claudio Pellegrini teaches in the department of sociology at the Universita Degli Studi Di Roma "La Spapienza."

Vladimir Pucik is a professor of organizational behavior and international business at the Graduate School of Business, University of Michigan.

Annabelle Quince is a research associate at Macquarie University's Graduate School of Management in North Ryde, New South Wales, Australia.

Jacques Rojot teaches industrial relations and human resources management at the European Institute of Business Administration, popularly known as INSEAD, in Fontainebleau, France.

Myron J. Roomkin is a professor of human resources management at the J. L. Kellogg Graduate School of Management at Northwestern University in Evanston, Illinois.

David F. Smith is a senior lecturer in the department of business administration at Victoria University of Wellington in New Zealand.

Ed Snape is a lecturer in economics at Teeside Polytechnic, Middlesbrough, and research associate at Durham University Business School.

Eberhard Witte is affiliated with the Institut Für Organisation at the Universitat München.

Abbreviations

A level	Advanced Level Examination (cf. GCE)
ACOA	Administrative and Clerical Officers Association
ACTU	Australian Council of Trade Unions
ADSTE	Association of Draughting, Supervisory, and Technical Employees
AFL-CIO	American Federation of Labor-Congress of Industrial Organizations
AGIRC	General Association for Professional Complementary Retirements
AIDP	Italian Association of Personnel Managers
AMAX	American Metal Climax Corporation
AMPS	Association of Management and Professional Staffs
ANPE	National Agency for Employment
APEA	Association of Professional Engineers
APEC	Agency for the Employment of Cadres
ASAP	Employers Association of ENI Firms for the Purpose of Industrial Relations
ASTMS	Association of Scientific, Technical, and Managerial Staffs
BACM	British Association of Colliery Management
BIFU	Banking, Insurance, and Finance Union
BIM	British Institute of Management
BNT	Position Classification System
BUDACI	League of Employed Chemists and Engineers
C ENG	Chartered Engineer
CAE	Colleges of Advanced Education
CEI	Council of Engineering Institutions

CEU	Christian Democratic Union
CF	Swedish Association of Graduate Engineers
CFDT	French Democratic Confederation of Labor
CFE-CGC	French Confederation of Managers and Supervisors
CFTC	French Confederation of Christian Workers
CGC	General Confederation of Cadres
CGIL	Italian General Confederation of Labor
CGT-FO	General Confederational of Labor—Workers Force
CIDA	Italian Confederation of Firm Managers
CISL	Italian Confederation of Workers Union
CISPEL	Italian Confederation of Public Local Utilities and Transportation
Confederquadri	National Confederation of Italian Cadres
Confindustria	National Confederation of Italian Employers in Industry
CPS	Current Population Survey
CRE	Commission for Racial Equality
CSSB	Civil Service Selection Board
CSU	Christian Social Union
DACO	Employees Central Organization
DAG	German Employee Trade Union
DE	Department of Employment
DGB	German Trade Union Federation
DLA	*The Managerial Employee*
DMS	Diploma in Management Studies
EC	European Communities
ECS	Executive Compensation Service
EEF	Engineering Employers Federation
EEO	Equal employment opportunity
EESA	Electrical and Engineering Staff Association
EETPU	Electrical, Electronic, Telecommunications, and Plumbing Union
EMA	Engineers' and Managers' Association
ENEL	National Institute for Electric Energy
ENI	National Institute for Hydrocarbons
EOC	Equal Opportunities Commission
EPEA	Electrical Power Engineers' Association
ESRC	Economic and Social Research Council
FASI	Additional Coverage Fund for Medical Assistance
FCUA	Federated Clerks Unions of Australia
FDP	Free Democratic Party
Federdigenti Credito	Federation of Managerial Employees in Credit and Financial Institutions
Federdirigenti Funzione Pubblica	National Federation of Managers in Public Administration
FENDAC	National Federation of Managers in Commercial Firms

FIAT	*Fabbrica Italian Automobili Torino*
FIDIA	Italian Federation of Managers in Insurance Firms
FIPDAI	Additional Coverage Fund for Social Security of Managers in Industrial Firms
FLM	Metalworkers Union Federation
FNDA	National Federation of Managers in Agriculture
FNDAI	National Federation of Managers in Industrial Firms
GCE	General Certificate of Education
GHMA	Gas Higher Management Association
HTF	Swedish Union of Commercial Employees
ICA	Institute of Chartered Accountants
ICI	Imperial Chemical Industries
IDS	Incomes Data Services
INPDAI	National Institute for Social Security in Industrial Firms
INSEE	National Institute of Statistics and Economic Studies
Intersind	Employers' association of IRI firms for the purpose of industrial relations
IPCS	Institution of Professional Civil Services
IPM	Institute of Personnel Management
IRI	Institute for Industrial Reconstruction
ISTAT	Central Institute for Statistics
IWG	Institute for Social and Economic Policy
LO	Swedish Trade Union Confederation
MBA	Master of Business Administration
MIL	Management in Lund
MPG	Managerial Professional and Staff Liaison Group
NALGO	National and Local Government Officers Association
NUMA	National Unilever Management Association
O level	Ordinary Level Examination (cf. GCE)
OPCS	Office of Population Censuses and Surveys
PER	Professional and Executive Recruitment Agency
PTK	Swedish Federation of Salaried Employees in Industry and Services
RSA	Union representative at the firm level
SACO	Swedish Confederation of Professional Associations
SAF	Swedish Employers Confederation
SALF	Swedish Union of Foremen and Supervisors
SIF	Swedish Union of Clerical and Technical Employees in Industry
SIMA	Steel Industry Management Association
SPP	Swedish Staff Pension Society
SSCC	State Services Coordinating Committee
STAMS	Society of Technicians, Administrators, Managers and Supervisors
TCO	Central Organization of Salaried Employees

TUC	Trades Union Congress
UCC	Confederated Union of Cadres
UCI	Cadres and Engineers Union
UGICA	General Union of Engineers, Cadres, and Supervisors
UGICT	General Union of Engineers, Cadres, and Technicians
UIL	Italian Union of Labor
UKAPE	United Kingdom Association of Professional Engineers
ULA	Union of Managerial Employees
VELA	Association of Managerial Employees in Trade and Industry
VOB	Association of Senior Mining Officials e.V

I
INTRODUCTION

1

An Overview

MYRON J. ROOMKIN

Managers and management have been studied extensively from several perspectives. One stream of research has focused on the behavior of managers and their role in organizations. Another has examined the implementation of the managerial function—that is, how managers perform their tasks and responsibilities (Mintzberg 1973). Other studies have looked at managers as an interest group, class, or elite, and at least one classic inquiry (Harbison and Myers 1959) treated managers as an economic resource. A great deal of the work on managers and management has examined these perspectives across societies and cultures (Massie and Luytjes 1972; Negandhi and Prasad 1971).

Another perspective is that of manager as employee or worker. To some, the concept of managers as employees is a contradiction. They would argue that a manager is an owner of the enterprise or an agent of the owner, not an employee. Although this is sometimes true, most managers participate in an employment relationship that, in many countries, implies a specific legal status involving entitlements, duties, obligations, and responsibilities. From a practical point of view, however, managers are in fact employees because they assume the role of employees in organizations: They take orders, not just give them; they are compensated for doing specific jobs or fulfilling responsibilities; and they may be dismissed for inadequate or unsatisfactory performance. In short, managers are employees because they exchange services for pay.

This volume looks at the role of managers as employees in several industrialized noncommunist societies. This is an opportune time for such a study as more and more businesses are expanding internationally and need information on how to deal with indigenous managerial groups. While there have been a number of comparative studies and collections of country-studies documenting employment practices (Blum 1981; Doeringer 1981; Dunlop and Galenson 1978; Martin and Kassalow 1980; Smith 1981; Windmuller and Gladstone

1984), nearly all have focused on the nonmanagerial labor force or on managerial unionism.

The scope of this inquiry is broader than unionism. Unionism is only one of several ways in which workers can act to improve their interests, either at the workplace or in the political arena. A more thorough understanding of managers as workers, however, requires that we comprehend how other forces and institutions determine the terms and conditions of their employment. Among these forces are the sociology of the occupation, which indicates how managers are prepared for work and advance professionally; the economics of the managerial labor market, which include the factors that determine compensation levels and rewards; and the role of company personnel practices and philosophy toward this group of employees. Thus, the study of managers as employees is at the crossroads of several disciplines.

Included in this book are descriptions of managerial employment in nine nations: four English-speaking countries—Britain, the United States, Australia, and New Zealand; four continental European countries—Germany, Sweden, France, and Italy; and Japan. These nine are not intended scientifically to represent all countries or even all industrialized democracies. Instead, they form the basis of what Berting (1982, 12) has called "descriptive studies—discipline oriented," that is, historicosociological descriptions of pertinent issues.

The authors of the reports worked from a common outline that stressed the major defining aspects of managerial employment. Each also was free to develop themes he or she felt were important. The studies had two objectives. The first was to document the differences and similarities that exist in the employment relationships of managers in these developed countries, and to identify the forces that shape and regulate such relationships.

The second purpose was to determine how managers' employment relationship has been affected by significant environmental developments of the past two decades that have had an impact on each of these countries. Among these developments are economic recessions and periods of inflation, the oil shocks of 1973 and 1978, the internationalization of business and foreign competition, changing work-force demographics such as increased feminization and aging, business restructurings, changes in the technology of white-collar work, and shifting patterns of regulation and deregulation. The existence of such worldwide changes gives us the opportunity to test once again the validity of the well-known "convergence hypothesis," which claims that social systems will respond to common stimuli in similar ways.

DEFINING MANAGERIAL WORKERS

The precise definition of a managerial employee is an elusive concept. One might conclude, as Mansfield (1980, 10) has, that the managerial occupation includes people who legitimately give orders to subordinates; however, those who exercise such authority constitute a very diverse occupational group. Independent managers—those who are self-employed or who work in family-owned businesses—and owners of enterprises probably have more in common among themselves than they do with managers who hold positions in an organization, a group sometimes called dependent employees. First-line supervisors or foremen, even though they spend a large portion of time giving orders to subordinates and monitoring their performance, should not be bracketed with other managers because they tend to have different backgrounds, education, and interests from their superiors. Similarly, senior executives deserve a special occupational recognition because they spend more time engaged in planning and decision-making than actually supervising subordinates. Therefore, our definition of managerial workers includes employees in the middle management levels, but not those ranked above and below them.

Also within the managerial occupation are individuals who provide the decision-makers with information and analysis or other important services, and who usually lack immediate subordinates. This group is distinct from technicians or semiskilled specialists, and includes people working in staff or support capacities such as lawyers or accountants, or in business-related functions such as marketing, personnel, and manufacturing. As Bamber (1981, 260) has noted, such personnel may be very influential within the company and often career interchanges exist between these staff and line jobs. Perhaps more important is that the employment relationship of both groups tends to be governed by the same policies, practices, and procedures. In recognition of this, it is becoming more common, especially in Europe, to refer to both the managerial and professional employees of an organization as the managerial staff.

While each author was asked to clarify the definition of managers common to his or her country, the target group was called the professional and managerial staff. It was defined as those persons (a) who are employed by organizations for a salary; (b) who have achieved a higher level of education and training or recognized experience in a scientific, technical, or administrative field; (c) who perform functions of a predominantly intellectual character involving a high degree of judgment and initiative; (d) who may have been delegated by the employer with responsibility for planning, managing, controlling, and coordinating the activities of the organization or portion of the organization; and (e) who do not occupy positions as either first-line supervisors, foremen, or top-level executives. The definition covered persons employed in the public, private, and not-for-profit sectors.*

Judging from the reports, culture and tradition continue to play a strong role in identifying individuals who are considered managers. Even in continental European countries, which require a legal definition of such workers in order to administer entitlements or systems of codetermination, managerial workers are only broadly defined by statute, leaving the court system and employer practices

*This definition is similar to one developed by a tripartite meeting of the International Labour Organization (1978, 6) with the cooperation of the International Federation of Commercial, Clerical, Professional and Technical Employees, an international federation of white-collar unions better known by its French acronym, FIET (1984, 4–5).

to define the group on a case-by-case basis. This is particularly noteworthy in the chapter on France, because the term *le cadre,* which English-speaking countries have accepted as a synonym for the managerial staff, requires extensive interpretation for the French. In Japan, there is customary acceptance of the different categories of workers considered to be managers, but even these categories tend to produce wide variations among companies. Swedish organizations have the most precise and widely accepted delineation of the managerial occupations, undoubtedly because Swedish employers participate in nationwide systems of job descriptions and evaluations for managerial positions.

There also is evidence that a comprehensive definition may be getting even more difficult to fashion as the jobs of managers become more diverse. Changes in technology, especially in the production of white-collar work, the emergence of new managerial specialties and new classes of technicians, and the trend toward greater employee involvement have blurred the lines between managerial staffs and other occupational groups. Another complicating factor is the growth of contingency and temporary employees in managerial or support positions (discussed below). These workers may hold job titles as managers or professional staff but receive different treatment and have interests different from regular (noncontingent), permanent, and full-time employees.

PATTERNS OF STABILITY AND CHANGE

Considerable diversity exists in the characteristics of managerial employment among the studied countries. In some, managers work under formal, written, and individualized contracts of employment, while in others, written contracts are not commonly used. Also, there are the well-documented differences in the components and level of compensation. In a few countries, managers have unionized; in others where codetermination is practiced, managers are represented on different governing boards. There are also differences in the ways people obtain access to managerial occupations, advance professionally, and retire.

It may be even more interesting, however, to note the broad similarities among these countries. Perhaps the strongest is that despite problems of definition, managers are recognized as a distinct group of employees by either the law, collectively bargained agreements, or employer practices. Their distinctiveness is established by company policies, the growing professionalization of the occupation, changing educational requirements, and identifiable career patterns. Moreover, managers tend to have different but not necessarily more desirable terms and conditions of employment. In several countries, specialized agencies play an important role in the way managers are treated with regard to retirement benefits, unemployment insurance, salary setting, and job search.

One explanation of this distinct status is probably a product of postindustrialism, which imposes certain requirements on organizations and societies. Among these is the need for managerial and professional staffs whose functions are to facilitate and implement, rather than to control and direct. This explanation is in contrast to a Marxist interpretation that would attribute this status to the fact that managers are an elite that has acted to ensure control of wealth and position in industrial societies.

Most of the chapters in this volume suggest that the treatment of managerial and staff employees has changed in the 1970s or 1980s. The authors note the following developments.

Witte's chapter on West Germany emphasizes the trend toward declining motivation among middle managers, a condition that has perhaps been brought about by the great success of West German business and rising living standards. At the same time, however, we are told that young people entering the market today could face diminished opportunities for advancement in business, suggesting that the problem of motivation may solve itself.

In New Zealand, the dominant experience has been that of a country poorer than the others with a severe shortage of managers. Under such circumstances, little momentum for change has developed to modify personnel practices toward managers or to increase the state's role in shaping their employment conditions.

Australia, which has drained away many of New Zealand's managers, especially among younger workers, has been experiencing a greater need for managers because of growth in the economy. According to Lansbury and Quince's survey, companies have adopted more aggressive policies and practices toward this group of employees.

New personnel practices dealing with managers are also a dominant theme in the chapter on British managers. Prompted by British industries' lack of competiveness, there is a trend toward increasing the skill of managers. This has led to a greater awareness that managerial education and training are important, and an increased willingness of employers to emphasize merit and ability rather than economic class in the development of managerial human resources.

In France, managers have experienced a process of continued professionalization but declining job security. According to Rojot's report, education seems to be playing a greater role in the preparation of managers, and family background is becoming less of a barrier to a managerial career. Worsening job security and pay status relative to others has as yet not produced a broad-based social protest movement, perhaps because the conditions of employment for managers still remain quite good.

Italian managers, especially those in the middle and lower levels, have become an important interest group in Italy. Their dissatisfaction with worsening conditions of employment have made them the focus of attention from both unions and the government.

Swedish companies have begun efforts to improve the productivity of their managers or, as they have labeled it, to revitalize management. Unfortunately, the high degree of managerial unionization and the standardized conditions of employment are making it extremely difficult for companies to reward managers who have outperformed others.

The major theme in U. S. managerial relationships has been the decline of stable employment in the larger organizations and the demise of highly bureaucratic personnel practices and traditions dealing with managers. These developments are the product of several long-term and recent trends that came together in the mid-1980s but have not yet yielded a new dominant model of employment. It has, however, created a lot of career uncertainty and competition for advancement, which in turn has resulted in making management education and training much more popular.

In comparison, the changes in Japanese employment practices toward managers have been more subtle. Roomkin and Pucik argue that due to the aging of Japan's work force and the oversupply of middle-level managers, Japanese firms long ago began rewarding managerial employees on the basis of merit, thereby deviating from the so-called traditional practices of lifelong employment and seniority-based reward systems. In the 1980s, however, companies began pursuing merit much more explicitly and visibly, enlarging the gap between those who were successful and those who were not. Such explicit appraisals are culturally awkward for both employer and manager. Unfortunately, dissatisfied or plateaued managers must live with the stigma because the economy is not growing fast enough to provide them with new employment opportunities.

Analytically, the major issue is whether or not any common themes emerge in these developments. The answer appears to be yes, but the amount of change, even though it has varied among the countries, has not been strong enough to remove cultural differences in the ways managers are treated. Moreover, contrary to popular belief, these developments did not start suddenly in the 1980s but began as many as twenty years ago.

Three interrelated themes appear in these changes. First, employers have been trying to utilize managerial employees more aggressively and efficiently. Second, patterns of employment and mobility are becoming more varied. Third, most of the surveyed countries have recently passed laws against discrimination of women for managerial positions, although much progress remains to be made.

In most cases, change can be traced to shifts in the demand for managers as a result of increased product market competitiveness. French firms, for example, were compelled to reconsider their treatment of managers because of France's entry into the Common Market. Increased competitiveness both domestically and internationally were the driving forces for change in Britain, Australia, and the United States during another period. In Japan, New Zealand, and the United States, different approaches to the management of managers also could be traced to developments in the labor market. The chapter on the Swedish experience shows that companies were motivated to address the problems caused by the increase in employee participation and the loss of management authority.

New Practices

Employers are taking a much more active role in influencing the terms and conditions of managers' employment. The common logic is to control labor costs through marginalization—that is, matching the costs of hiring, training, and compensating added managers with their true contribution to the enterprise. The chapter on Britain refers to this as the drive for individualization in the employment relationship. Europeans have also called it the drive for flexibility. In Japan it has become known as the meritocracy in employment. In the United States, it has been termed white-collar and administrative productivity, staff performance, and overhead reduction.

Marginalization is a significant change in the economic and cultural logic on which the managerial employment relationship is based. Although it may not be as important a development as Taylorism was to the way employers conceptualized blue-collar employment, marginalization represents a greater concern for the utilization of managers as human resources.

This new emphasis has resulted in the growth of several practices that have achieved different degrees of popularity. In the area of compensation practices, employers have tried to increase the role of economic variables and diminish the importance of other factors. Thus, in the United States this has meant a trend toward performance-based compensation, and in Japan a decrease in the importance of tenure as a determinant of pay and promotion. Lansbury and Quince report that Australian companies have begun conducting job evaluations and market surveys, thereby rationalizing compensation systems. An interesting case in this regard is Sweden, whose national system of compensation and extensive unionization of managers have made it difficult for employers to encourage performance. The experience of the Italians represents the major counterexample: Length of service with the firm continues to have a strong influence on the compensation of managers.

Other developments have taken place in the way firms assess managerial performance. Formal systems of performance appraisal appear to be getting more popular, although they have their strongest tradition in the United States and Japan. A related trend is the growth of programs to assess managerial career potential. Several countries report that succession planning, employee appraisal programs, and human resource planning are widely practiced, at least in larger organizations.

Perhaps the simplest way to control labor costs is to reduce headcounts. Not surprisingly, therefore, reductions in the number of managers employed and increases in the rate of unemployment among managers were reported in several countries. Nevertheless, the level of managerial unemployment relative to the rate of other groups has remained low. Managers still enjoy a privileged place in the employment queue. This special treatment is particularly evident in the ways companies have released unneeded managers: Separation payments and early retirement programs are becoming more common in most of the countries surveyed.

Reliance on temporary, part-time, and project workers as managers and professional staffs is a new, but rather modest, development in Britain and the United States. However, in Japan these staffing practices have been more widely used for several years. It is difficult to say whether such arrangements will ultimately represent a substantial portion of employment in countries other than Japan. Judging from the limited experience of American companies, which probably have the greatest potential for such flexibility, these staffing arrangements do possess significant problems of design and implementation.

To students of American personnel management, the developments discussed in this overview appear rather uncontroversial and quite commonplace; however, they are comparatively novel in the other societies to which they have spread. At least one chapter identifies the role of U. S. multinational firms in taking these techniques abroad, although the demand for expertise in personnel matters has grown beyond multinational companies.

Careers and Mobility

Patterns of labor mobility and career paths are changing in many of the countries surveyed. Access to the occupation is more open in Britain and France as socioeconomic background has declined in importance and education in management is easier to obtain. A college degree in business or management is now a popular route for those wishing to enter the profession. Ironically, however, in the U. S. where enrollees in management programs have become ubiquitous, businesspeople and educators are starting to question the efficacy of this education.

Change is also apparent in the amount of interfirm mobility for managers. Managers in Britain, Australia, the United States, and New Zealand are reported to be changing employers more often. Even in Japan, where the practices of stable employment are probably most deeply entrenched, there has been an increase, albeit a small one, in the number of persons changing jobs. More significant, however, is the much larger number of managers who, when surveyed, expressed an interest in changing employers during their working life.

Clearly, one of the causes of such mobility has been the new personnel practices described above, which have increased the incidence of involuntary unemployment and made managers more concerned about employment security. At the same time, however, there is evidence of greater voluntary mobility, as managers seek out more desirable positions. In some places, the propensity toward mobility has been fueled by the development of managerial job opportunities in either small and medium-sized enterprises or in emerging sectors of the economy. Also important has been the willingness of employers to hire experienced managers rather than to develop them internally.

Some authors mentioned the growth of managerial careers through self-employment or small business ownership and a corollary interest in entrepreneurship. While there appears to have been an increase in new entrepreneurs and owner-operators, their relatively small numbers should not be a threat to the continued professionalization of the occupation. However, the more important significance of this development may be ideological, insofar as it reenforces managers' association with the values of economic growth and the business community.

Another type of mobility is the experiences managers receive in different types of jobs during their careers. American managers, especially those in emerging companies, and Japanese managers have the most experience with cross-functional job changes, although the practice of broadening their experience is becoming more popular where promotion opportunities have lessened.

Despite the continued internationalization of business, the chapters make very little reference to the mobility of managers across borders; the exception, of course, is the common labor market between Australia and New Zealand. However, apart from those senior managers and professionals who are sent abroad to work in foreign-owned subsidiaries (a common practice in Japanese firms), there is relatively little mobility of managers from one country to another in pursuit of employment. Apparently, significant economic and political barriers remain to international job search and recruitment, even in Europe where geographic distances are comparatively small.

Women Managers

The underutilization of women in management is a problem common to all the countries in this volume. Even in egalitarian Sweden, women hold a modest proportion of entry- and mid-level management positions, but virtually none in senior management. Women have made the greatest degree of progress in the United States in entry and mid-level positions, but now seem to be facing greater obstacles in reaching senior executive ranks. Moreover, much of this limited success has been in jobs traditionally held by females or in the public sector.

The responsibility for increasing women's representation in management is not acknowledged by all societies. Some have passed laws to increase access to employment and punish employers for discriminating. The Japanese anti-discrimination law, in comparison, establishes a social obligation not to discriminate but provides no punishment for those who break the law.

Looking to the future, greater representation of women at all levels of the managerial hierarchy could be a side benefit of the new mobility in managerial careers, giving women options they have not had before. Likewise, discrimination may become harder to disguise as employers introduce compensation and reward systems based on demonstrated performance. Ironically, the Japanese have been the most resistant to equal opportunity employment for women, but as the Japanese economy passes from its current labor surplus into a period of labor shortage during the next few decades, these prejudices may receive their most direct and severe testing.

THE REACTIONS OF MANAGERS

Complaints of managers involve the traditional economic concerns of salary and job security as well as a desire to participate more actively in the decisions of the organization. Economic concerns have been made more salient because of wage compression, greater uncertainty about careers and promotions, and the aggressive personnel practices previously described. The desire to participate in decision-making stems from a loss of authority that can be traced to, among other things, growth of employee involvement and increased regulation of business.

Managers' reactions to these developments have been consistent within each countries' industrial relations and political systems. In Sweden, with its long history and strong representation of managers in unions, managers channeled their reactions through the collective bargaining system. French and Italian managerial unions are concentrated in the public sector or in nationalized industries and have not achieved levels of organization greater than the national average, although French managers also have sought greater representation through works councils. German managers have almost exclusively relied on the mandated system of codetermination to address their concerns dealing both with economics and governance. American managers, in contrast, have opted to redress their economic grievances by acting individually and relying on litigation.

The prospects for the growth of unionization among managers are not strong, even though their employment problems may be growing. At a minimum, traditional obstacles to unionization remain: Managers themselves are not convinced of the legitimacy of managers' unions and may not be willing to cooperate with unionized nonmanagerial employees; at the same time, employer resistance to the concept remains strong. In addition, it is difficult to imagine unions having greater success organizing managers when union membership among traditional groups is on the decline.

With regard to political activism, several chapters report early indications of greater cohesiveness among managers to achieve legal protections already given to other employees and to compete more effectively for political spoils. However, these developments fall far short of convincing us that managers have become a so-called "third force" in society between employers and unions. Even if they are more active politically, it appears that managers are generally politically conservative and tend to support the position of business interests.

In summary, managerial employment is an evolving relationship, affected by forces in the society, the economy, and the firm. The chapters that follow describe the kinds of changes that have taken place in the past few years and those likely to occur in the near future.

REFERENCES

Bamber, G. 1981. Review of "Managerial roles in industrial relations: Towards a definitive survey of research and formulation of models," edited by M. Poole and R. Mansfield, *British Journal of Industrial Relations* 19 (July):259–61.

Berting, J. 1982. Why compare in international research? Theoretical and practical limitations of international research. In *International comparative research: Problems of theory, methodology, and organization in Eastern and Western Europe,* edited by M. Niessen and J. Peschar, 5–16. New York: Pergamon Press.

Blum, A. A. 1981. *International handbook of industrial relations.* Westport, Conn.: Greenwood Press.

Doeringer, P. B., ed. 1981. *Industrial relations in international perspective.* New York: Homes & Meier, Inc.

Dunlop, J. T., and W. Galenson, eds. 1978. *Labor in the twentieth century.* New York: Academic Press.

FIET. 1984. *Action program for professional and managerial staff.* Geneva, Switzerland: International Federation of Commercial, Clerical, and Professional and Technical Employees.

Harbison, F., and C. A. Myers. 1959. *Management in the industrial world: An international analysis.* New York: McGraw-Hill Book Company, Inc.

International Labour Organization. 1978. *Report of the Tripartite Meeting on Conditions of Work and Employment of Professional Workers,* November 22–30, 1977. Geneva, Switzerland: International Labour Office.

Mansfield, R. 1980. The management task. In *Managerial roles in industrial relations,* edited by M. Poole and R. Mansfield, 1–12. Farnborough, England: Gower Publishing Company, Ltd.

Martin, B., and E. M. Kassalow. 1980. *Labor relations in advanced industrial societies: Issues and problems.* Washington, D.C.: Carnegie Endowment for International Peace.

Massie, J., and J. Luytjes. 1972. *Management in an international contest.* New York: Harper & Row.

Mintzberg, H. 1973. *The nature of managerial work.* New York: Harper & Row.

Negandhi, A. R., and S. B. Prasad. 1971. *Comparative management.* New York: Appleton-Century-Crofts.

Smith, E. O. 1981. *Trade unions in the developed economies.* New York: St. Martin's Press.

Windmuller, J. P., and A. Gladstone. 1984. *Employers associations and industrial relations: A comparative study.* Oxford, England: Clarendon Press.

II
ENGLISH-SPEAKING COUNTRIES

2
Britain

GREG BAMBER AND ED SNAPE*

The individual employment relationship of managers and professional employees in Britain is largely determined by corporate personnel practices rather than by collective bargaining and legislation. We analyze these practices by reviewing the terms and conditions of employment for managers in Britain and commenting on some current trends.

MANAGERS AND PROFESSIONALS

We use the term managers to include all those employees above the level of first-line supervisor but below senior executive level, along with professional and technical staff of comparable job status. All these occupational groups tend to have a similar relationship with the employer. Our discussion excludes foremen, forewomen, and other first-line supervisors, who in Britain have usually been seen as a distinct occupational group from managers. The background, training, and working environment of such supervisors means that they generally have more in common with their subordinates (Child and Partridge 1982).

Some ambiguity exists about whether managers are employers or employees. Even if they do not have direct line authority, such staff often have a relatively high level of autonomy and discretion. Subordinate grades generally see managers as bosses, while directors may see managers as agents of the employer and expect them to act accordingly. A manager performs a boss's role when organizing and controlling staff (Bamber 1986). When referring to such

"This chapter draws on research funded by the Economic and Social Research Council (UK), reference F/00/23/00 98. The authors gratefully acknowledge the support of the ESRC, the assistance of the Durham University Library staff, and Chris Harper, a conscientious and patient research secretary.

17

activities, we use the term employer. However, the major focus of this chapter is on managers as employees.

In smaller private-sector organizations, contracts of employment for managers are often personal and individualized. In large private-sector organizations and in the public sector, standardized contracts are usual for all but the most senior executives. Senior executives in the private sector usually have personal contracts and, in the 1980s, there has been an increasing tendency for top executives to have fixed-term contracts, typically for three years. Longer contracts have become less common in recent years, partly because of the unfavorable publicity given to large termination-of-employment payments during the recession (Vernon-Harcourt 1983, 15).

Changing Role of Managers

After World War II, there was an increasing division of labor as line managers relied more on specialists. Employee relations in general were regulated by more legislation, so that specialists took over many of the personnel responsibilities formerly exercised by line managers.

Managerial employees were also affected by several trends in the organization of enterprises and production. For much of the post-1945 period, Britain had an increasing concentration of employment in large organizations. In many companies, there was growing bureaucratization and a decline in the traditional close personal contact between individual managers and their employers.

Since the 1970s, however, many employing organizations have reduced the size of their work forces. Managers have not been exempt from these reductions—numerous companies have specifically aimed to flatten their managerial hierarchies. Recent increases in the use of subcontracting and experiments with networking and intrapreneurship also have important implications for the future of managerial work. There is a trend toward greater flexibility in the structure of organizations and in the skills and mobility of their managers (Institute of Manpower Studies (IMS)/Manpower Ltd. 1984). The development of information technologies and other forms of technical change are currently important for many managers in relation to their own jobs and also as they implement change within their areas of responsibility and influence (Bamber and Lansbury 1989).

Family Background

What are the predominant occupational origins of British managers? Few people enter directly into management. Crockett and Elias (1984) found that only 4 percent of the managers surveyed (excluding professional and technical staffs) began their working lives as managers. Usually they started in clerical, craft, or semiskilled operative jobs with only 9 percent beginning in managerial, professional, or technical occupations. Leggatt (1972) found that 74 percent of managers in his sample first achieved managerial status after the age of 26, and 42

Table 2.1   Four studies of occupational categories of managers' fathers

Registrar general's occupational classification	Clements 1954/55	Clark 1964	Leggatt 1970	Poole et al. 1980
Professional and administrative	20%	7.8%	5.8%	25.5%
Managerial	17	34.7	20.0	32.2
Clerical and skilled manual	55	43.6	62.0	28.4
Semiskilled manual	6	11.4	6.7	8.0
Unskilled manual	2	2.4	4.5	5.9

Source: Poole, Mansfield, Blyton, and Frost 1981.

percent after 30. However, the traditional background of managers may be changing. Stewart, Prandy, and Blackburn (1980) concluded that "in the younger age ranges there are higher proportions of managers who started as management trainees, managers, and professionals, and lower proportions who started as manual workers and clerks" (p. 22).

With regard to their social backgrounds, Table 2.1 illustrates the occupations of managers' fathers. It shows that between the 1950s and 1980s there was no dramatic increase in the proportion of managers coming from the lower social classes. It also shows a significant increase in the portion from a professional or administrative background. However, since people from clerical or blue-collar families have become managers, this group cannot be seen as a closed social elite. In the steel industry, for example, two-thirds of a sample of managers described their childhood family background as working class (Bamber and Glover 1975).

Social and Professional Status

Managerial and professional employees in industry have a lower status in Britain than in such countries as West Germany and the United States. Top British university graduates tend to choose careers in the civil service, finance, academia, and higher-status professions such as law and medicine.

There has been concern in government and industry because managers in the engineering function have lower pay and fewer fringe benefits than their counterparts in other functions (Dixon 1985b, 13). This may reflect the lack of prestige of the engineering profession as there is no one generally accepted qualification signifying their professional competence, and there are many different professional institutes for the various specialties.

Against such a background the Callaghan Labour government set up a Committee of Inquiry to examine the engineering profession (Finniston 1980). The Committee recommended a thorough reorganization, a reduced role for the professional institutions, the setting up of a quasigovernmental engineering authority, and a new system of training. These recommendations, however, were not fully implemented because they were opposed by vested interests among the institutions and not supported by the subsequent Conservative government (McLoughlin 1984).

EMPLOYMENT TRENDS

As in other countries, the number of managers in Britain has increased in the twentieth century. In absolute terms, the number of managers, administrators, and higher professionals increased from 813,000 in 1911 to 3,438,000 in 1981; in relative terms, the increase was from 4.4 to 13.5 percent of the occupied population (Routh 1980, OPCS 1984). Unfortunately, these data are not sufficiently disaggregated to separate managerial and professional employees from those who are self-employed. Nevertheless, a rapid growth of managerial and professional employment has undoubtedly taken place.

This growth reflects several changes in the economy, including a move toward more sophisticated technologies that demand more technical expertise, with a consequent reduction in the need for less skilled operatives.

Differences Between Sectors

Shifts in employment between sectors have contributed to changes in occupational structure. Table 2.2 shows that 9.8 percent of employees in British industry are managers (using the occupational definitions of the *Census*, which exclude some professional groups). Declining industries such as coal mining and metal manufacture, however, are among those with a lower proportion of managers. The expanding services industries, such as banking and finance, employ a higher proportion of managers. Within the manufacturing sector, the new in-

Table 2.2 Managers as a percentage of total employment in selected industries

	All	*Men*	*Women*
Banking and finance	11.6%	24.2%	2.2%
Instrument engineering	7.4	10.0	2.4
Insurance	7.1	10.9	2.2
Chemical industry	6.9	8.5	2.9
Business services	4.9	6.6	2.7
Metal manufacture	4.8	5.2	2.3
Coal extraction and man-ufacture of solid fuels	2.8	2.7	4.2
All industries	9.8	12.6	5.6

Source: OPCS 1984 (data for Britain).
Note: Data derived from the "managerial" occupation order in the Census. This excludes certain professional groups, and so is not directly comparable with the data on the number of managers, administrators, and higher professionals mentioned earlier.

Table 2.3   Percentage of vacancies remaining
unfilled for at least 8 weeks

Occupational group	Percent of all vacancies at job centers
Managerial and professional	18.6
Clerical and related	10.7
Other nonmanual occupations	13.5
Craft and similar occupations	17.5
Laborers	3.8
Other manual occupations	9.8
Total	11.4

Source: DE 1985, 389 (data for September–November 1984).

dustries with more complex technologies, such as instrument engineering and chemicals, have more managers.

Unemployment Among Managers

One indicator of the balance between supply and demand is the length of time taken to fill vacancies. Table 2.3 indicates that managerial and professional vacancies generally remain unfilled longer than other categories, suggesting that managerial labor is relatively scarce, although it also takes longer to fill such vacancies because selection methods are more elaborate for managers than for subordinate grades.

Managerial employment has generally been regarded as secure, but the view that managers and professionals have a job for life was changing by the late 1960s. In a series of major company takeovers, publicity abounded about the consequential redundancies among managers. More recently, many other companies have reduced the number of their employees, including managers, as part of cost cutting.

Managers suffered a greater than average increase in unemployment in the early 1980s. In September 1980, managerial and professional unemployment in Britain (almost 150,000) accounted for 8.6 percent of total unemployment. Two years later, it accounted for 11.1 percent of total unemployment (or 328,500 people). A Durham University survey of large manufacturing companies found that 63 percent had reduced the number of managers between 1979 and 1984 (*The Economist,* April 6, 1985). Only 20 percent of the companies surveyed had some form of in-house resettlement unit to aid redundant managers. In some cases this involved helping them start their own businesses; in a few others, independent agencies provided counselling and resettlement assistance.

Managers often receive a full pension and a substantial cash payment on being made redundant, particularly those over 55 years old in the public sector and in the larger firms. The cost of such redundancy payments can reach £75,000 per redundant manager. Employees below managerial level rarely receive such substantial compensation.

After retiring early or becoming redundant, many managers fail to find another job of similar or higher status. Some of them become freelance consultants or start other forms of business. Often, however, this is merely a way of disguising long-term unemployment, which carries the stigma of failure, particularly among the middle classes; such new businesses have a high failure rate. But there is an increase in support arrangements for those displaced. Several business schools train and counsel individuals who set up new enterprises. Such help is financed by the tripartite Manpower Services Commission. There are also arrangements for seconding older managers from large organizations to help small businesses.

Another interesting development in the 1980s is the use of temporary employees in senior management positions. Following the earlier growth of secretarial and clerical staff agencies, temporary employment agencies have emerged, through which companies can hire specialized managerial expertise on a short-term basis. Temporary employment has been increasingly popular in the context of leaner management structures following the recession and with the need to implement new and complex technologies. The executive "temps" are hired for a month to two years on a fixed-contract basis. A typical fee would be £5,000 to £8,000 per month. One such plan, which has been operating since 1982, has about one thousand executives and specialists on its lists. Some of these have been laid off from permanent jobs, but others have specifically chosen self-employment.

DEMOGRAPHIC CHARACTERISTICS

Sex

The proportion of "economically active" women increased from 33 percent in 1959 to 49 percent in 1985 (Manley and Sawbridge 1980, 29; Department of Employment (DE) 1986, 136). While the economic activity rates for unmarried women and men have fallen, the rate for married women more than doubled between 1951 and 1981. However, more than half of employed or self-employed women work part-time.

In 1985, 9.3 percent of women employees worked in management and related professional jobs, compared to 8.5 percent in 1984. Nevertheless, these percentages were still substantially lower than 20.8 percent and 19.7 percent, respectively, for men (data calculated from DE 1986, 138 and DE 1985, 178, using major occupational groups I and V from DE 1972). In the mid-1970s among the major Western economies, Britain and Italy had the lowest percentages of women represented in managerial and professional jobs (Werneke 1983, 39).

Women managers in Britain tend to be concentrated in the service sector, particularly in catering, retailing, and office management, where the majority of their subordinates are also women (Crockett and Elias 1984). There are even fewer women in senior management than in middle management and professional positions.

The finance sector provides a poignant example of the role of women in the labor force. This sector employed over 800,000 women in the mid-1980s, constituting a majority of employees in the banks and building societies and about half the employees in insurance. The traditional career path in this sector has involved recruitment of school-leavers aged about 16, practical training and study for professional examinations, with gradual promotion into administrative and managerial positions. Particularly in the larger firms, career staff have typically spent their entire working life with a single employer. Women, however, have tended to be excluded from this career path and are concentrated in the lower-grade jobs. For instance, in 1983, 84 percent (29,665) of the National Westminster Bank's full-time female staff were in the bottom two grades, working as cashiers, clerks, typists, and machinists. Only 2 percent (714) had administrative or managerial jobs, compared with 37 percent of the men. There were only 74 women managers, compared to 4,936 men. In addition, the bank employed 4,450 part-time women, all in the lower grades. Such a pattern is typical of the finance sector (BIFU, no date).

Why are there relatively few women managers? Rothwell (1985) argues that management is regarded as requiring certain "male" characteristics such as aggression and drive that the stereotypical female is said to lack. In addition, personnel policies may discriminate against women, perhaps unintentionally, since they assume an uninterrupted and typically male career pattern. Furthermore, women are socialized into attitudes that discourage themselves and others from viewing them as ideal managers.

A common explanation for the lack of women's career progression is the finance sector, in particular, is that they are less mobile than men. This is important in an industry with extensive branch networks, so that promotion often involves moving. Many employers in finance and retailing have mobility clauses in their employment contracts for managers, which often deter women from seeking promotion. This has been controversial; the unions and the Equal Opportunities Commission have become increasingly concerned about such discriminatory implications (Thomas 1985). Women have not usually been encouraged to study for professional qualifications and, if they have children, they tend to give up work, at least temporarily.

Many women who return to work after having children enter part-time employment. Part-timers are almost exclusively in the lower status jobs. They are denied training and development opportunities, and may lack some of the legal rights and fringe benefits available to full-time staff (such as cheaper mortgages or special Saturday working payments in the finance sector). Consequently, where particular skills have been scarce, some employers have initiated structured re-entry or retainer plans so that women can accommodate their family responsibilities (see Engineering Council 1985b).

The concentration of women in lower-status jobs has made promotion easier to achieve for men. In their study of clerks in three organizations, Crompton and Jones (1984) calculated that "even if only 10 percent of all young women aged under 25 years were to achieve promotion, then *male* promotion chances would be reduced by a third" (p. 247).

Nonetheless, the proportion of women managers will probably increase. Social stereotypes are changing (albeit slowly), there is a growing proportion of women in higher education, and an increasing tendency for women graduates to enter industrial and commercial employment. Men's opposition to women managers is declining (Hunt 1975; McIntosh 1980), so the feminization of management may accelerate, once attitudes and ambitions adjust to any initial increase in the number of women managers.

Race

The proportion of nonwhite people in the labor force has greatly increased since World War II. Asians constitute the largest nonwhite ethnic group (about 2 percent of the population), and West Indians the second largest (about 1 percent). Others are African, Arab, Chinese, and mixed groups (altogether about another 2 percent). According to the broad definition used in Table 2.4, in total, 22 percent of white men are employed in the professional, employers, and managers categories. This is slightly more than for Asians, and much more than for West Indians. Among the "other" groups, a surprisingly high total of 24 percent are employed as professional employers and managers.

Whites account for the highest proportion of employers and managers, but both the Asian and "other" groups have higher proportions of professionals. A relatively high proportion of hospital doctors, for example, are recruited from the Asian group. The West Indian group is the most disadvantaged in terms of managerial and professional employment.

Public Policy
Since the 1960s, several public policies have been introduced in an attempt to prevent discrimination against women and ethnic minorities. The government established two tripartite agencies: the Equal Opportunities Commission (EOC) and the Commission for Racial Equality (CRE). In the 1980s, both commissions published codes of practice encouraging employers to promote equal opportunities and to develop their own monitoring systems. Several banks and other large employers have responded, in some cases by appointing a full-time manager to monitor recruitment and promotion. However, unlike some of their American counterparts, British employers generally have not yet begun to discriminate positively in favor of women and ethnic minorities.

Region

Proportionally more managers are in the relatively prosperous southeast of England, where they are better paid and most large organizations have their

Table 2.4 Men in employment by socioeconomic group

Socioeconomic group	Percentage of group				
	White	West Indian (including Guyanese)	Asian (Indian/ Pakistani/ Bangladeshi)	Other[a]	All ethnic groups[b]
Professional	6 } 22	2 } 6	8 } 20	10 } 24	6 } 22
Employers and managers	16	4	12	14	16
Intermediate and junior nonmanual	18	7	14	23	18
Skilled manual and own account nonprofessional	38	49	35	27	38
Unskilled and semiskilled manual and personal service	21	38	31	24	21
Armed forces and inadequately described[c]	1	1	—	2	2
All males aged 16 and over in employment (thousands)	13,325	120	243	114	13,962

Source: Barber 1985.

[a]African, Arab, Chinese, other stated, and mixed.
[b]Includes ethnic group not stated.
[c]Includes not stated.

head offices. Conversely, there are disproportionately few managers in the industrial communities of Wales, Scotland, and the north of England. These regional differences have political implications that are discussed later.

PREPARATION AND EDUCATION

A traditional British view is that leaders are born and not made. This was reflected in the relative lack of management education in Britain, at least until the 1960s.

Formal Education

For most of the postwar period, the General Certificate of Education (GCE) was the major academic qualification for able students in England and Wales. It came in two parts: GCE Ordinary (O) levels are taken at about age 16, near the end of compulsory schooling, while GCE Advanced (A) levels were taken two years later. Higher education institutions used GCE A level results when selecting candidates for places.

British managers tend to be less well qualified than managers in many other countries (Fores and Clark 1975; Poole et al. 1981; Constable and McCormick 1987; Handy 1987). In countries such as the United States, Japan, Sweden, and Germany, a higher proportion of managers are university graduates than in Britain. In particular, Britain lags behind other countries in the number of engineering and technology graduates in management (Mant 1979, 106).

Table 2.5 shows the educational qualifications of a sample of managers studied by Poole et al. (1981). This table reveals a broad range of qualifications among managers, reflecting the lack of a uniform entry requirement; public sector managers seem to be more highly qualified than those in the private sector, not least because selection procedures are usually more formal in the public sector.

Managers are better qualified than the general population; for example, 76.4 percent of existing managers had passed GCE O or A level examinations. By contrast, in the academic year 1981–82, only 55 percent of school-leavers in general obtained GCE O or A level passes. We can infer from Table 2.5 that more than 36 percent of existing managers have a degree. However, in 1981, only 9.7 percent of the general population (11.5 percent of men) had any post-18 educational, technical, or professional qualifications (OPCS, 1984).

The proportion of managers with university degrees has increased slowly in Britain, even though higher educational opportunities expanded rapidly after the mid-1960s. Perhaps the graduates produced by this expansion have yet to work their way into managerial positions.

Management is not generally seen as a profession; specific qualifications are usually required only where the job involves specialized technical work. Few managers have had much formal off-the-job training in management skills; most learn by experience. As Crockett and Elias (1984) report in their study of over 2,600 managers, "We found that the majority of firms do not train their managers for the jobs they hold, other than the usual 'Cook's Tour' of the establishment" (p.42).

Such civic universities as Birmingham and Manchester have had departments of commerce or management since before World War II. Colleges at Ashridge, Cranfield, and Henley have run courses in business administration for much of the postwar period. However, business schools were not launched in Britain until 1963, following the Robbins (1963) and Franks (1963) reports (see Manley 1986).

By 1983, more than half of Britain's universities had management departments or business schools offering Masters of Business Administration (MBA) degrees or an equivalent qualification. However, in that year, only 1,350 MBAs were awarded in Britain. To match the United States proportionately, Britain would have to produce about 15,000 business graduates per year (Griffiths and Murray 1985, 14). In comparison with their North American counterparts, MBAs have been accepted less readily by most British employers, who prefer to see managers receive training in functional specialties such as accounting and engineering. Besides the MBA, most of the business schools offer shorter man-

Table 2.5 Educational qualifications of managers

Qualifications	Percent of private sector managers (n = 731)	Percent of public sector managers (n = 320)	Percent of all mangers (n = 1058)
GCE O levels or A levels	74.5	80.9	76.4
Technical qualifications (e.g., ONC, OND, HNC, HND)*	38.4	39.7	38.8
Science degree	13.0	10.6	11.7
Technology degree	7.4	10.0	8.4
Other degree	14.5	20.3	16.1

Source: Poole et al. 1981, 48.

*Ordinary National Certificate (ONC).
 Ordinary National Diploma (OND).
 Higher National Certificate (HNC).
 Higher National Diploma (HND).

agement development courses, either on management in general or in specific fields such as finance, marketing, or industrial relations. Such courses may be open or tailor-made for particular firms. Most polytechnics and some universities also offer three- or four-year undergraduate degree courses in business studies. During a four-year course, the student would usually have a total of one year's work experience. Polytechnics also offer a part-time Diploma in Management Studies (DMS) mainly to those with management experience.

Study for professional qualifications is mainly done by part-time, day-release, evening, or distance-learning (correspondence) courses, while doing a relevant full-time job. For example, to become an Associate of the Institute of Chartered Accountants in England and Wales involves serving a three-year training period working for a practicing accountant while completing professional examinations. For such purposes, many employers provide financial assistance for fees and paid study leave.

While certain of the older professional institutes, for example, law and accountancy, effectively license people to perform a given job, this is not the case for all professions. The main professional qualification in engineering, the Chartered Engineer (C Eng) status, is not automatically recognized by all employers as the sole hallmark of competence (McLoughlin 1984).

Traditionally, most of the professions have recruited school-leavers (aged between 16 and 19), but there is a trend toward more graduate recruitment. Since 1974, the Institute of Chartered Accountants (ICA) has no longer accepted student entrants with only GCE O level passes. In that year, 50 percent of student entries had degrees, but by 1983 this had risen to 85 percent. Interestingly, of these graduate entries, only 30 percent had degrees in a relevant subject such as accountancy or business studies (DE 1985, 345).

In addition to the courses run by professional and educational institutions, there is increasing provision by chambers of commerce, employers' organizations, management consultants, and other entrepreneurs. Furthermore, some larger employers provide their own in-house management development, often using external consultants and lecturers in conjunction with their own specialists. For example, Unilever, Courtaulds, British Gas, and British Steel each have their own management colleges.

British Institute of Management (BIM)

Following a government initiative, the BIM was set up in 1947 to help promote managerial effectiveness. It publishes a journal, *Management Today,* and a newspaper, *Management News,* as well as various books and reports on management topics. The BIM also maintains a library, publishes research, and organizes courses, seminars, and conferences. The BIM does not function as a union for managers, nor does it generally seek to represent managers vis-à-vis their employers. However, it does function as an interest group by presenting members' views to the government on a wide range of issues, including pensions, fiscal policy, and employee involvement. BIM membership is open to those educated at least up to a DMS or degree level with several years' management experience. In 1985, the BIM had over 76,000 individual members and some 8,000 corporate members.

The Status of Managerial Education

In short, the British provision for management education and training is varied and ad hoc. Many British employers seem to give a lower priority to management education and training than their competitors in other countries.

The growing concern at Britain's poor record on management education, training, and development was highlighted in two major reports, by Constable and McCormick (1987) and by Handy (1987). Both recommended increased provision of management education and training, with greater flexibility to improve access, and more cooperation between employers and educational institutions. In addition, they called on employers to give greater emphasis to careful recruitment, training, and development, and asked large corporations to set a good example in these areas. Such reports have prompted several important initiatives, both in the education and corporate arenas. These seem to be heralding a substantial growth of management education and development.

There has also been concern that the supply of engineers has fallen behind that of Britain's major competitors, not least because the employers in Britain do not take enough responsibility for their training and education (IMS 1984).

LABOR MARKET PROCESSES

Entry-level Jobs of Managers

A fourfold typology of recruitment patterns developed elsewhere (Snape and Bamber 1987) describes how employing organizations interact with the external labor market.

Type A patterns restrict entry to the junior levels of the organization and promote managers to higher positions from within. Examples can be found in the finance sector, particularly among the larger banks, which have tended to recruit most of their junior staff as clerical employees and to promote them from within to managerial positions.

Because firms with strict internal promotion practices may fail to attract sufficient staff with the necessary potential for promotion, particularly to senior positions, there is an increasing use of tiered recruitment, often with a graduate entry stream providing a high proportion of future managers. This practice, *Type B,* involves external recruitment at junior managerial levels, along with some promotion from manual or clerical workers, usually via technical or first-line supervisory positions. Higher-level managerial positions are then filled mainly by internal promotion.

Type C involves external recruitment into junior managerial posts, with subsequent internal promotion to fill higher-level jobs. With this type, however, there is no significant promotion into managerial jobs from among manual or clerical workers, who rarely progress beyond first-line supervisory level. This situation often arises where managerial jobs require specific qualifications, for example, in retail pharmacies where managers are required by law to be professionally qualified.

Type D is an open recruitment policy, with external recruitment and internal promotion possible at all levels. This pattern often develops where labor markets are tight and highly competitive, or where organizations are growing so rapidly that they may be faced with staff shortages and use any means to recruit. The larger retail chains pursue such a policy, as do companies in the expanding high-technology industries.

Recruitment Practices

An Institute of Personnel Management/BIM survey of 335 British companies found that promotion from within was the most usual means of recruiting managers (IPM/BIM 1980). This is an explicit policy of many large employers; they recruit either through internal advertising or by succession planning. An organization may recruit externally if it lacks suitable internal candidates, when specialist skills are required, or when it wishes to bring in new blood. Smaller employers are less likely to employ enough people with potential for promotion.

As Table 2.6 shows, national, local, and trade press advertisements were most often used when recruiting externally. Management selection consultants and executive search consultants (headhunters) were used less often, although both were used particularly when recruiting senior managers, by larger organizations, and in London (rather than in the rest of Britain).

The British government runs a specialist Professional and Executive Recruitment Agency (PER). This produces the *Executive Post,* a job advertisement publication mailed to over 130,000 job-seekers each week. However, the IPM/BIM survey suggests that the PER service is used frequently by only 11

Table 2.6   Recruitment methods and extent of use

Method	Percentage of companies surveyed that used each method frequently
Internal advertising/promotion	49
Local press advertisements	45
National press advertisements	39
Trade journal advertisements	33
Management selection consultants	14
Government recruitment agency professional and executive recruitment/job center	11
Executive search consultants	4
Professional registers	2

Source: IPM/BIM 1980, 13.

percent of the companies surveyed. This service is generally seen as most appropriate for graduate recruitment and junior management positions.

The survey shows that other professional registers are used frequently by only 2 percent of companies. They tend to be used only for specialist fields such as accountancy and scientific or technical posts. Other sources of recruitment include personal recommendations (around 20 percent of companies in the survey claimed to use this more than occasionally) and from direct applications by candidates (over 15 percent used this more than occasionally).

Recruitment agencies advertise on behalf of client companies and advise on the appropriate media and format for advertisements. Larger employers are more likely to use such agencies (one in three companies with over 5,000 employees, compared to one in ten for companies with fewer than 1,000 employees, according to the IPM/BIM survey).

How do organizations select recruits from among the available candidates? The 1940s' War Office Selection Board procedures included a range of interviews, tests, and individual and group exercises. In 1970, following criticisms of the civil service in the Fulton Report (1968), the government revised these procedures to form the Civil Service Selection Board (CSSB) for appointing fast-stream public servants (Thody 1985). Similarly sophisticated procedures have been introduced for recruiting managers and professional employees by other large organizations.

Nevertheless, more than 90 percent of companies still rely almost exclusively on interviewing. Panel selection boards are used by over 15 percent of companies, but by a third of companies with over 5,000 employees. Other selection methods are used less often; selection tests are used by only 10 percent of companies, while group selection methods involving various exercises, tests, and interviews on a collective basis are used by less than 5 percent, and then mainly for graduate recruitment. Selection tests are sometimes seen as inappropriate at the managerial level. Most companies have a traditional approach to management recruitment and selection methods, and few significant innovations have occurred in either since the 1970s.

Transitions from Education to Work

Many employers recruit first-degree graduates by interviewing extensively at universities and colleges before inviting the more promising candidates to intensive second interviews. The process, referred to as the "milk round," is a useful way of dealing with mass applications from what initially appears as a fairly undifferentiated group.

Such employers usually have a management induction plan. Recruits may be designated as management trainees and complete off-the-job training courses and projects before taking up junior managerial positions. Such programs often involve a series of short placements in various departments and sites, extending from six weeks to two years, before a recruit is given a proper job. There have been more of these plans in Britain since the 1960s as an increasing number of organizations have aimed to recruit graduates. Nevertheless, many graduate trainees express dissatisfaction with the adequacy of their induction training (Keenan and Newton 1984).

Table 2.7 shows the first employment of those graduating in the years 1976 and 1983. There was a substantial increase in the number of graduates in this period, with industry and commerce recruiting only 12,300 university graduates in 1976, but almost 19,000 in 1983.

Since the 1960s, graduates have increasingly been employed in such areas as retailing, banking, accountancy, and insurance. In general, most of these had not previously recruited many graduates. This increase reflects the changing structure of the economy and the upgrading of jobs, in view of new technologies and the changing labor market. Also, the growth in the number of graduates has led to their being displaced into traditionally nongraduate jobs, such as sales representatives and first-line supervisors.

Many graduates are soon disillusioned with their first job since there is often a mismatch between what they and employers expect of each other. Graduate turnover from the first job approaches 50 percent after 5 years (Mabey 1984). Ambitious individuals in their twenties often move between employers in an attempt to win more experience and more rapid promotion than they would get with one employer.

Job Mobility

Using the results of five surveys conducted between 1958 and 1983, Alban-Metcalfe and Nicholson (1984) show an increasing tendency for managers to move between employers. In 1958, 34 percent of the managers surveyed had spent their whole career with one firm; by 1983, the figure was under 10 percent, showing managers changing employers on the average of 3.4 times during their careers.

Table 2.7 Employers of first-degree graduates (as a percentage of those entering home employment)

	Civil service and central government bodies	Armed forces	Local and other public authorities	Education	Total industry and commerce	Specific fields					Total entering home employment
						Industry	Accountancy	Banking, insurance, and finance	Other commerce and commercial services	All others	
Universities											
1976	4.9	1.0	24.1	5.8	53.4	34.0	8.4	3.7	7.4	10.7	23,053
1983	3.4	1.3	22.0	5.5	59.4	29.8	9.8	6.3	13.5	8.4	31,934
Polytechnics											
1976	4.0	1.0	16.0	9.8	63.3	45.8	3.4	2.5	11.6	5.9	4,842
1983	3.0	0.7	15.6	12.2	58.4	35.3	4.0	2.8	16.4	10.1	9,194
Colleges of higher education											
1983	3.6	1.0	16.4	8.1	44.6	16.0	2.2	4.7	21.8	26.3	1,611

Source: Derived from Adams and Meadows 1985, 344.

Table 2.8 Relative frequency of different types of job change

Type	Dimensions of job change*			Percent of sample with at least one such move in last 5 job changes	Last job change: no. of changes of each type	Percent
1	EMPLOYER	↑ STATUS	FUNCTION	53.6	280	25
2		↑ STATUS	FUNCTION	49.6	307	27
3	EMPLOYER	↑ STATUS		23.1	97	9
4	EMPLOYER		FUNCTION	21.5	83	7
5		↑ STATUS		21.3	95	8
6	EMPLOYER			16.2	44	4
7	EMPLOYER	↓ STATUS	FUNCTION	15.9	57	5
8				6.1	26	2
9		↓ STATUS	FUNCTION	3.0	18	2
10	EMPLOYER	↓ STATUS		2.8	8	1
11		↓ STATUS		0.2	2	0
Total					1144	100

Source: Alban-Metcalfe and Nicholson 1984.

*Empty boxes mean no change on this dimension.

↑ = increase in status.

↓ = decrease in status.

A 1983 BIM survey examined interorganizational mobility as well as job changes within an organization involving changes in level or status and function. Table 2.8 reports the finding for eleven different types of managerial mobility.

The two most important forms of job change, involving cross-functional promotions between organizations (Type 1) and within organizations (Type 2), account for the majority of moves. Changes in function are frequent and job changes within the organization are an important aspect of mobility. Younger managers and women were more likely to experience an increase in status after changing jobs than were older managers and men. This does not necessarily imply that women gain more promotion than men, merely that women make fewer nonpromotion job changes.

The respondents in the 1983 survey cited career objectives and the chance to do more challenging and fulfilling work as their main reasons for changing jobs. A significant number of managers over the age of 50 cited redundancy.

In spite of some cross-functional mobility, British managers are more likely than Americans to pursue a career within their own specialties. Many British organizations have a rigid functional structure, with little cross-fertilization at the middle management level (Peach 1985).

Promotion policies are often linked to policies on appraisal, training, and development. In a BIM survey of 240 companies (Holdsworth 1975), 94 percent claimed that past appraisals were important when making promotion decisions, although only 75 percent had formal appraisal schemes for managers. These were supplemented by interviews (90 percent), references, and discussions with superiors. Only 10 percent of companies used psychological tests and only 12 percent employed other forms of written or oral tests when making promotions. Forty-nine percent of companies had specialists responsible for management development and 56 percent claimed to have formal succession planning; in both cases, these practices were more common among larger organizations and among those with a declared policy of internal promotion. Although many companies may make such claims, we infer from our research that in practice only a small minority had a systematic approach to management development and succession planning.

A change of job can bring problems of adjustment for the manager; a change of employer may be even more difficult. However, a job change that necessitates moving can be the most difficult. A BIM survey of 218 managers (Guerrier and Philpot 1978) found that their main concerns in locational moves were the effect on their children's education; the disruption to friendships and social life; and the quality of health, educational, and social facilities within the new area. Managers were less concerned about the problems of house-moving, leaving family members, the effect on their spouse's job, and uncertainty about the new job itself. Individual managers were often reluctant to move to certain regions or cities; for example, southerners often will not move north and vice versa. London is particularly unpopular for many from the provinces, not least because of its very high cost of housing and transport.

Human Resource Planning

Since the 1973 oil crisis, many employers have found it increasingly difficult to meet the career aspirations of their managers. There have often been career blockages where organizations are retrenching or growing more slowly than previously. Blockages have been exacerbated by a lack of voluntary turnover among mid-career managers, as the number of external job opportunities has declined. Low morale and poor performance may result, as managers become bored and frustrated, especially if career aspirations remain high because of the more favorable experiences of their predecessors.

The lack of career opportunities is a problem for many organizations in the public services, in traditional manufacturing, and for the larger banks and financial institutions. There are exceptions to this, however, in expanding sectors such as retailing and electronics, and in such occupations as data processing, financial services, and marketing.

Career blockages are increasingly seen as a problem by those responsible for management development and various remedies have been proposed. A reexamination of career paths, with more lateral transfers and even downward moves toward the end of a career, could ensure a better use of managerial resources and avoid boredom and frustration. Some organizations are experimenting with job rotation and secondments; others are changing their organizational structures and moving into new intrapreneurial ventures that may provide alternative job opportunities. Such innovations may conflict with managers' career expectations, however, and thus be difficult for them to accept.

In the 1970s, many organizations encouraged managers to opt for early retirement to reduce numbers and career blockages. But this may not provide a long-term solution to the problem since it allows only a once-and-for all upward movement, unless future managers can also be retired early.

Unlike the United States, France, West Germany, and Sweden, Britain has no legislation concerning age discrimination. Many advertisements for managers specify a preferred age range (e.g., 35–45); therefore, it becomes increasingly difficult for older managers to join a new employer. Those over 45 who are laid off or retired early may never be able to reenter managerial employment.

Public-Private Sector Comparisons

The public sector in Britain is less extensive than in France and Italy, but much more extensive than in the United States and Australia. Besides national and local government, the Post Office, and education, the British public sector includes the National Health Service (the largest employing organization in Western Europe) and a series of nationalized corporations in such industries as coal mining, shipbuilding, and rail transport. There is often a different ethos of management between the public and private sectors. In general, more sophisticated selection, induction, training, and staff planning techniques have been used to a greater extent in the public sector. By contrast, the public sector is often seen as slower to change and less responsive to market forces and customer preferences than the private sector.

There has been a privatization program in the 1980s which involves selling parts or all of some public-sector corporations. Nevertheless, relatively little voluntary movement of individual managers in mid-career occurs across the public/private sector boundary.

There are at least three inhibitors of such movement. First, the pay levels and scales are often very different. Second, pension plans are usually fully transferable between public-sector organizations but less easily transferable to the private sector, or from the private into the public sector. Third, most public-sector organizations have well-developed internal labor markets that may discourage external recruitment.

However, some movement across the boundary has taken place at the most senior levels. Senior civil servants must seek formal permission before moving to the private sector on the grounds that their knowledge of "official secrets" could give their new employer a competitive advantage, for instance, when tendering for government contracts. Nonetheless, some government officials have retired early and moved to a senior position in the private sector.

Moves from the Ministry of Defence to private-sector arms suppliers have been particularly controversial. Between 1979 and 1983, more than 1,400 people left the Ministry for private-sector jobs. In 1985, a House of Commons Select Committee recommended a tightening of the rules on senior civil servants and officers in the armed forces moving to the private sector, though the government eventually decided that this was unnecessary. Nevertheless, it began publishing statistics on the movement of civil servants into the private sector and monitoring all job applications made by those in the top three civil service grades.

There have also been much publicized moves at a senior level from the private to the public sector, often on a temporary basis. Mrs. Thatcher's post-1979 Conservative Government aimed to inject private-sector expertise into the civil service by commissioning selected corporate executives to review certain activities. One of the most celebrated of these was Sir Derek Raynor of Marks and Spencer, Britain's most successful retailer. Similarly, several businessmen have been appointed to head publicly owned industries. Sir Michael Edwardes was recruited from Chloride to be Chairman of British Leyland (which later became the Rover Group). Sir Ian MacGregor, who rose to prominence with the American Metal Climax Corporation (AMAX) in the United States, was appointed to head British Steel and then British Coal. He was succeeded in both posts by Sir Robert Haslam, who was previously with Imperial Chemical Industries, (ICI), and Tate and Lyle.

Such top-level transfers between the private and public sectors are exceptional. Although they may be expedient from the viewpoint of the government or the corporations, they are often resented by the existing managers who see such transfers as blocking internal promotion prospects and as introducing an alien organizational culture. This was the view of many managers, for example, during Sir Ian MacGregor's period at British Coal, especially in the way he handled the 1984–85 miners' strike. His policies and style aroused protests even from the usually moderate managers' union, the British Association of Colliery Management.

Career Success

Relatively few managers admit to planning their careers. We asked 216 middle managers in the steel industry to look back on their own careers. Only 18 percent said that it had "more or less followed a plan," compared with 82 percent who said that it was "a case of being in the right place at the right time" (Bamber and Glover 1975).

What determines the winners in the race for managerial promotion? We can begin to answer this question by examining the characteristics of top managers. Surveys of 150 British chief executives were conducted in 1974 and 1984 (BIM 1984). In 1974, the most usual background for a chief executive was finance or sales. By 1984, the functional background was more diverse with finance being less common, but production, sales, marketing, and engineering all more important. In 1984, the chief executives surveyed had been more mobile. Companies were appointing younger and more highly qualified chief executives with broader experience from different companies and functional areas.

REMUNERATION

Salaries

During the 1970s, pay differentials between nonmanual and manual employees narrowed, with the pay of manual workers achieving 82 percent of nonmanual pay by 1979. In the early 1980s, this differential expanded again and was 73 percent by 1984 (calculated from DE 1970–84).

As seen in Table 2.9 pay differentials within management have followed a similar trend, although, by 1985 the differentials had not regained their 1971 levels. After-tax net differentials (in parentheses in Table 2.9) have increased by more than gross differentials after 1978, as there was a reduction in marginal tax rates for the higher paid.

The compression of differentials during the 1970s partly reflects the impact of incomes policies under the 1974–79 Labour Government's Social Contract.

Table 2.9 Changes in salary differential ratios—1971 to 1985*

Level	1971 base salary	Ratio of salary to level A salary								1985 base salary
		1971	1975	1978	1981	1982	1983	1984	1985	
A First-line super- visor	2,000	1.0	1.0	1.0	1.0	1.0	1.0	1.0	1.0	10,300
B	3,000	1.5 (1.41)	1.46 (1.36)	1.44 (1.37)	1.45 (1.40)	1.46 (1.40)	1.48 (1.42)	1.49 (1.43)	1.48 (1.86)	15,200
C	4,000	2.0 (1.83)	1.93 (1.70)	1.87 (1.73)	1.85 (1.78)	1.90 (1.79)	1.95 (1.84)	1.98 (1.85)	1.99 (2.49)	20,500
D	6,000	3.0 (2.63)	2.88 (2.33)	2.71 (2.26)	2.70 (2.34)	2.80 (2.42)	2.81 (2.45)	2.89 (2.48)	2.99 (3.01)	29,900
E	8,000	4.0 (3.25)	3.83 (2.78)	3.51 (2.64)	3.47 (2.82)	3.63 (2.94)	3.60 (2.94)	3.77 (3.02)	3.77 (3.46)	38,800
F Top man- agement	10,000	5.0 (3.80)	4.70 (3.12)	4.33 (2.94)	4.24 (3.29)	4.41 (3.36)	4.35 (3.37)	4.56 (3.34)	4.62 (3.85)	47,500

Source: IDS Top Pay Unit 1985c.

*Data are for July each year. Figures in parentheses are for post-tax salaries.
All other figures refer to gross salaries.
Salaries are averages for the job levels analyzed.
Tax deduction calculated on the basis of a married man with two children under 11 years old and a dependent wife.

Table 2.10   Some pay comparisons (in pounds sterling)

Northern Rock Building Society (as of 1 April 1985)	
Branch Manager:	
large city–center branch	£12,351–£16,306
Clerk: Grade 3	£4,116–£6,317
Renault Truck Industries, Ltd. (as of 1 January 1985)	
Systems and Data Processing Manager	£14,131–£21,197
Area Sales Manager	£9,332–£13,532
Production Operator	£6,361
English Clearing Banks[a] (as of 1 April 1985)	
Minimum managerial salary	£13,134[b]
Clerk: Grade 4	£6,960–£9,975
Clerk: Grade 1	£3,596–£4,940
The Boots Company[c] (as of 17 August 1984)	
Graduate Scientific Officer:	
Minimum on recruitment from university	£7,246
After 3–5 years' experience	£8,471–£12,100
Workshop craftsman (engineering)	£7,057
Labourer	£5,356
Rolls-Royce[d] (as of 1 October 1984)	
Principal Scientist	£8,581–£11,592
Draughtsman	£6,790–£9,161
Semiskilled process worker	£5,600–£6,033

Source: IDS Report (London: Incomes Data Services), various issues.
[a]Includes the larger banks.
[b]Most managers would be paid more than this, depending on their level
of responsibility, the size of branch, etc.
[c]Industrial Division.
[d]Bristol plants.

The policy often included flat-rate rather than percentage norms for pay increases, so that the relatively highly paid managers could be seen to be bearing their share of the burden of economic austerity (Saunders et al. 1977, 79). In addition, a high marginal rate of taxation with a maximum rate of 83 percent was levied on earned income, which meant that salary increases for the higher paid were tax inefficient.

In the 1980s, marginal tax rates were reduced and there were no formal incomes policies. Many companies increased pay differentials, often as a deliberate policy to raise incentives for managerial employees. Table 2.10 gives examples of differentials for five companies.

There also has been a trend away from general cost-of-living increases for all managers toward pay raises and cash bonuses based on company performance and individual merit (IDS Top Pay Unit 1985a). This reflects a perceived need by corporate policy-makers to link rewards more closely with results, especially as international competition is increasing. In addition, it reflects the lower levels of inflation in the 1980s, which reduced the necessity for general cost of living increases. Such developments have gained political and ideological support from the post-1979 Conservative Government (see Bamber and Snape 1987).

Only 30 percent of a sample of employers related senior managers' earnings to results in 1979; however, this had increased to 68 percent by 1986 (PA 1986,

17). These firms used share option, profit-sharing, or incentive bonus plans, increasingly on an individual or team basis. Such plans have become more common among smaller companies, where individual managers can perhaps affect corporate performance more directly than those in larger companies. British employers are probably the most incentive-oriented in Europe, especially in relation to the sales function (ECS 1986). By 1985, 50 percent of managers in Britain received a bonus payment worth, on average, 8 percent of their earnings (RE 1986).

In the mid-1980s, differentials were still widening. This reflected companies' attempts to reward managerial performance through merit payments and cash bonuses as company performance improved. In some sectors, employers were increasing managerial salaries to attract scarce expertise. Any fall in profitability, however, could reverse these recent moves toward wider differentials.

Fringe Benefits

For a long time, Britain has taxed pay more heavily than nonpay rewards. Consequently, there has been a proliferation of fringe benefits in addition to salary. (The gap between basic salary and the total value of remuneration is illustrated in Table 2.11).

Apart from a pension, a car tends to be the most expensive perk for most managers, proportionately more managers in Britain are given a company car than in most other countries. Some 63 percent of private-sector managers are provided with a company car (BIM 1984). A range of other benefits are often given to managers including private health insurance, loans for housing and other purposes, assistance with the costs of children's education, clothing, a telephone, lunches, financial counseling, professional association fees, and expense accounts (PA 1986).

Such fringe benefits can constitute a major part of the total cost of employing managers, especially at more senior levels. In 1984, on average, fringe benefits were worth 34 percent of base salary for top managers, 30 percent for

Table 2.11 Remuneration packages of managers: pay as a percentage of the total

Job title	Total pay (Median £)	Total remuneration package (Median £)	Pay as percent of package
Chairman/chief executive	40,750	54,447	74.8
Personnel director	23,026	31,761	72.5
Management information systems director	20,000	28,547	70.1
Chief accountant	17,600	24,591	71.6
Production manager	16,937	23,879	70.9
Regional sales manager	14,150	20,566	68.8
Training manager	13,270	16,144	82.2

Source: Huxley 1985. © Times Newspapers Ltd.

middle managers, and 20 percent for junior managers (IDS Top Pay Unit 1985b, 20). Also in 1984, the annual value to an employee of a medium-value family car (costing about £6,000) was £2,200, when no fuel for private use was paid for by the employer; a luxury car (costing about £19,000) was worth an annual £7,450 to the employee (Dixon 1985a).

After 1979, the reduction in income tax rates for the highly paid meant that cash payments became relatively more tax efficient, particularly since noncash benefits were taxed more heavily. Many managers and companies increasingly preferred cash rather than other benefits. Although there was a decline in the popularity of some fringe benefits in the early 1980s, the provision of company cars continued to increase, and share-option plans became more widespread, encouraged by tax concessions. Moreover, the 1985 Finance Act linked the level of employers' National Insurance contributions to the size of an individual's salary, thus again shifting the tax advantage toward nonsalary benefits.

Cars and certain other fringe benefits have been awarded to a growing number of junior managers since the 1970s. Thus, any increase in salary differentials within management has been offset to some extent by a harmonization of other benefits.

Retirement and Pensions

In Britain, the normal retirement age for men is 65 and for women 60, although since the early 1970s, there has been an increasing number of people retiring prematurely as a way of reducing staffing levels. There is growing pressure for an equalization of retirement ages for men and women and an expected European Community directive is likely to impose such an equalization.

To supplement the flat-rate basic state pension, an upper tier state earnings-related pension was introduced in 1978 by the Labour government. However, subsequent Conservative governments have decided to change this plan before it becomes fully effective. In relation to their managers (and often to other categories of nonmanual staff), most medium and large companies have long had their own occupational pension plans. Typically, these provide a maximum total benefit of two-thirds of final salary. The benefits may take the form of a tax free capital sum as well as a continuing taxed income. A simple pension accrual fraction is 1/60th per year of employment (with a 40/60 max.). A full pension can usually be achieved by thirty to forty years' *pensionable* service. For shorter service, benefits accrue at a lower level, though all plans allow members to top up pensions, within the permited maximum. The entry age to an occupational plan may vary between about 18 and 25 years. *Pensionable* salary is often less than full remuneration, in view of deductions related to the lower earnings levels that can be regarded as being replaced by the basic state pension. Also, remuneration such as bonuses, location allowances, and expenses may not be pensionable.

Most of those in occupational plans are contracted out of the earnings-related part of the state plan (Moffat and Ward 1986, 390–91), the occupational plan having to guarantee a minimum level of pension. However, before contracting out of the post-1978 earnings-related plan, employers have been obliged to consult the relevant unions. Some 28 percent of companies provide additional "top-hat" pensions for senior executives to supplement their normal occupational plan (PA 1986, 19).

To maximize tax relief, occupational plans have to be administered under a trust deed with appointed trustees, and the maximum benefit can not exceed two-thirds of final salary. Employees' pension contributions up to a maximum of 15 percent of salary are tax exempt and employers' contributions are tax deductible. Plans investment income is also tax exempt. Typically, an individual would have to contribute up to 8 percent of pensionable salary, with the employer contributing 5 to 20 percent, depending on the size of employee contribution and the level of benefits. In the civil service and in some private-sector companies, such a plan may ostensibly be noncontributory in that the individual may not have to contribute by deduction from salary.

Apart from salary, the pension plan tends to be the most important part of the remuneration package for most managers. The difficulty of establishing fair transfer values was for a long time a serious problem for managers seeking to change employers. Hence, many managers came to see such a plan not as a perk but a millstone that discouraged mobility. Following legal changes since 1973, there is now statutory provision for transferring the value of accrued benefits as a capital sum on changing employment.

The law now imposes a limited prohibition against discriminatory treatment of early leavers and requires the fair provision of preserved benefits for those with at least two years' service.

Public policy is aimed at reducing further the obstacles to occupational mobility and the provision of freedom of choice, thereby improving the efficiency of the labor market. The Conservative government has introduced a new law whereby, after 1988, employers may no longer compel membership in their plan and employees can opt out of either the state earnings-related or company pension plans, subject to arranging a private personal pension that may be transferred to the plans of subsequent employers.

The declining real value of pensions has been another cause for concern, particularly during the period of high inflation in the 1970s, since many occupational plans provided either no or limited protection. The 1985 Social Security Act does require a revaluation of part of the preserved benefits in line with the increase in consumer prices up to a maximum of 5 percent, rather than earnings, but this applies only to those who left employment since January 1986. The impact of legislative changes, which have overriding effect on plan rules, has caused occupational pension plans to be reviewed and in some cases entirely reshaped.

In the past, most private-sector employers saw occupational pensions as a unilaterally regulated benefit not subject to collective bargaining. Few unions regarded pensions as part of the work-reward bargain; although in one phase the negotiation of pensions provided a loophole through the 1970–74 Conservative government's incomes policy. More recently, many manual workers' unions have wanted to extend the provision of pensions to their members. This has been a policy of some employers, too, as a move toward harmonization of employment conditions of all levels of employees. However, some managers have opposed such moves which they have seen as another erosion of the differential between managers' economic rewards and those of their subordinates. Pensions are increasingly viewed as a form of deferred pay, which can make a significant difference to an individual's total remuneration package. Employee participation in the trusteeship of pension plans is increasingly widespread. In short, pensions have become an increasingly important issue for industrial relations specialists and for all employees, not just for managerial staff (APEX 1988).

Remuneration and Management Status

How do rewards vary according to job status? In 1984, the average gross salary of chief executives was 3.8 times that of junior second-line managers (the rank above foreman). As shown in Table 2.12, junior managers are the most likely to receive a cash-incentive bonus; however, from deputy head of function and above, the proportion receiving a bonus increases with job status. The average amount of bonus received increases with status; the average bonus was 15 percent of gross salary for chief executives and only 8 percent for junior managers. Share option programs are more common with higher status, up to departmental director level. The provision of company cars increases with job status. Free fuel is less prevalent, but it also is more usual at the higher levels. Similarly, the pension benefits and length of holidays tend to increase with status, but only from about 21 to about 30 days.

Employer Salary Policies

Most large-scale employers have an explicit salary policy, which may be more or less detailed. That of a large manufacturer of food, household products, and pharmaceuticals is summarized in Table 2.13. Salary policy is usually closely

Table 2.12 Pay and fringe benefits of directors and managers

	Average gross salary (£)	Percent receiving bonus	Average bonus received (£)	Percent receiving other benefits			
				Share option	Company car	Free fuel	6 weeks+ holiday
Chief executive	47,947	46	6,934	39	97	52	21
Departmental director	33,403	41	5,160	45	99	56	19
Top rank below director	26,603	40	2,498	41	95	44	17
Deputy head of function	19,167	38	1,449	39	70	26	12
Junior manager	12,505	51	1,007	37	30	9	10

Source: RE 1985.

Table 2.13 Management salary policies at a manufacturer of food, household products, and pharmaceuticals

---

"An effective salary policy will provide an opportunity, through salary management, to remunerate staff on the basis of a job's evaluation and individual effectiveness within the job." (Company salary policy guide, Personnel Dept., January 1983).

Job evaluation

The company uses the Hay-MSL job evaluation system for middle management jobs (those evaluated at between 380 and 699 Hay points) to establish the "job unit value" in terms of Hay points.

Salary value

The salary value for each job is calculated by applying a fixed formula to the job unit value. The formula is revised annually and is negotiated with the trade union. This means that there is usually an annual cost of living increase.

Salary range

The above salary value is the midpoint (100%) of the salary range, which is as follows:

a. From 85% to 95% of salary value: initial appointment within this range, and subsequent increases at the company's discretion on the basis of individual effectiveness (intended for training and development purposes).
b. From 95% to 100%: automatic progression through annual increments, unless performance is "unsatisfactory." The company may also award extra increments for merit.
c. From 100% to 115%: progression is wholly at management discretion to reward merit; 105% is recommended as the normal limit for full effectiveness.

Effectiveness assessment

There is an annual appraisal interview, one purpose of which is to assess effectiveness for salary review purposes, in terms of previously agreed objectives.

Comment

The system provides flexibility to reward individual performance, within a defined framework. The union also has an input in negotiating the annual adjustment of salary values.

Source: Company internal documents and interviews with company officials.

linked to other personnel policies, especially to job evaluation and performance appraisal.

Most large employing organizations have a formal job evaluation scheme for managers. In our study of twenty-one employers, only three did not either rank jobs or score them on the basis of items such as job difficulty, accountability, and knowledge requirement. Job rankings or points scores usually underpin the salary system. Jobs may be divided into discrete grades, or job evaluation points may be related directly to salary via a fixed formula.

Performance appraisal is widely used for managers in Britain, more so than for other categories of employee and has become widespread (Table 2.14). Only three firms out of out twenty-one did not have a performance appraisal system for managers. Appraisal is concerned with reviewing performance, assessing training and development needs, boosting motivation, and improving future performance, as well as with assisting career and staff planning. Performance appraisal may also provide the explicit basis for pay reviews, although some organizations avoid making such an explicit link, since individuals may be reluctant to be frank where the appraisal becomes dominated by pay considerations.

In many organizations, particularly in the finance sector, managers are on

Table 2.14   Performance appraisal: grades of employees reviewed

	Percent of companies		
	1973 survey (n = 267)	1977 survey (n = 236)	1985 survey (n = 250)
Senior management	90	80	90
Middle management	96	90	96
Junior management	93	91	92
First-line supervisors	67	60	78
Clerical/secretarial staff }	45	45	66
Shop-floor operatives }		2	—

Source: Gill 1977, 10 for 1973 and 1977, Long 1986 for 1985.

incremental salary scales. Automatic increments are given independently of any performance review, possibly being denied only to the unusually poor performer. Incremental salary scales usually specify a scale maximum, so that individuals who remain in a particular job for several years may become trapped at the top of their scale. Where promotion opportunities are scarce, such people may feel that their efforts go unrewarded and they may become frustrated. A survey of 72 incremental pay scales found that a majority of these salary systems were subject to such problems. For instance, 63 percent of nonindustrial civil servants and 42 percent of British Coal managers were at the top of their pay scales, and similar problems were reported at Philips Electronics, Phoenix Assurance, the larger banks, the British Broadcasting Corporation, the British Airports Authority, and the Greater London Council (Labour Research Department 1985).

Remuneration in the Public Sector

Although the above discussion of incremental scales would apply to many parts of the public sector, the earlier discussion of remuneration relates mainly to the private sector. There is a different picture in the nationalized corporations. Salaries of chairmen and board members have been constrained by successive governments for political and economic reasons. Consequently, pay differentials have been compressed at all levels. As such constraints have continued into the 1980s, there has been less widening of differentials than in the private sector. Nevertheless, in the civil service, some widening of differentials has occurred largely because the higher pay levels are influenced by independent review bodies while the lower ones have been squeezed by government cash limits.

In 1985, the Top Salaries Review Body awarded salary increases of between 12.2 percent and 17.6 percent for top civil servants, judges, and military officers. This award followed from comparisons with pay movements in private industry. The awards were controversial in the light of government attempts to contain public-sector pay increases generally within single figures: "It creates one law for the troops (constrained by the iron grip of cash limits) and one for the officers (where the test is the market)" (*The Economist,* July 27, 1985, 13).

In the mid-1980s, some parts of the civil service were having difficulty recruiting and retaining professional and technical specialists because salaries were falling behind those paid in parts of the private sector. Thus, the civil service unions were calling for substantial salary increases to offset this difficulty. In November 1985, the government offered additional pay increases to professional and technology officer grades. However, such increases were often made on an individual basis, rather than to everyone in these grades.

Pensions are rather different in the public sector, where most managers' pensions are fully transferable. Moreover, most pensions are index-linked to provide complete or partial inflation-proofing. Following privatization of some or all of a public-sector organization, managers often complain of a deterioration in their pensions provision as they lose such inflation-proofing. However, this loss may be offset by an increase in salaries and other fringe benefits, notably at the most senior levels of management.

UNIONIZATION

Unionization of managerial employees is relatively rare in the United States and Australia, but it is more common in Britain and some other European countries. Even in Europe, however, union density is usually lower among managers than among their subordinates.

Causes of Unionization

Traditionally, most managerial employees had their terms and conditions of employment determined by their employer on an individual basis. Between about 1940 and 1980, however, collective bargaining became increasingly common, particularly in the public sector and among some large private-sector organizations, so that by 1980 nearly 40 percent of managers were covered by collective agreements (Poole et al., 1983).

The postwar nationalization of key industries provided much of the impetus for the development of managers' unions in the public sector. For example, the British Association of Colliery Management (BACM) was founded in 1947 after the nationalization of coal-mining. It claimed to organize 95 percent of British Coal managers by the mid-1970s. Similarly, the Steel Industry Management Association (SIMA) had its origins in an earlier association formed in 1949 when steel was first nationalized. This nationalization was short-lived, and SIMA did not achieve a high density of membership until after steel had been renationalized in 1967.

The public-sector corporations were then legally obliged to engage in collective bargaining for all categories of employees, including managers. Some of these corporations argued, moreover, that managers' unionism had certain advantages. For example, British Steel pointed to three advantages from an employer's point of view:

> First, that middle managers were a large group of special importance, so it preferred to negotiate and consult with a representative organization on their behalf. Secondly, in the absence of any such organization, it would be difficult to maintain individual contact with all managers from remote head offices. And thirdly, a managers' union would be able to influence a wide range of policy issues to the advantage of both British Steel and managers themselves. (Bamber 1986, 50)

Unionism of managers in the private sector is generally more recent and less well established. Its growth was stimulated in the 1970s by several factors. Pay differentials between managers and other groups had narrowed. In the mid-1970s, many managers had inferred that if the contemporary proposals for industrial democracy were implemented, union membership would be a precondition for participation (cf. Bullock 1977). The statutory union recognition procedures then available could be used by unions seeking to organize managers. Also, there was a growing feeling of uncertainty and insecurity among managers in some companies as restructuring and redundancy became more widespread.

In 1975, the Council of Engineering Institutions (CEI), the central professional body for engineers, reacted to these factors by recommending that professional engineers should consider joining a union to safeguard their interests as employees (CEI 1975). One of the unions recommended, the Electrical Power Engineers' Association (EPEA), had previously organized only in the public sector. It transformed itself into the Engineers' and Managers' Association (EMA) in 1977 and began to recruit in the private sector. Some private-sector employers were reluctant to have their managers unionized, but others acquiesced with the trend, so that union organization and recognition for managers grew in the 1970s.

For a manager, in Britain, joining a union is a less traumatic decision than it would be in the United States, where union density, in general, is much lower (Bain and Price 1980). Many more British managers who have been promoted from a nonmanagerial job would have had direct experience of union membership than would their American counterparts.

We asked a sample of 508 managers in the steel industry about their reasons for having joined SIMA and classified their responses into three broad categories: group, instrumental, and external motives. Group motives were the most frequently cited (by almost 50 percent) and included a preference for collective representation over the previous custom of unilateral action by the employer, and a specific preference for a separate managers' union to avoid possible domination of the union by subordinate groups. Some managers mentioned the problems associated with working for a large bureaucratic organization, arguing that before renationalization they had less need for a union, since they had more personal contact with senior management.

Instrumental motives, including a concern with job security and pay and conditions, were given by only 22 percent as their main reason for joining SIMA. However, such instrumental concerns often underlie the group motives referred to above.

Several external motives were given, including pressure from employers, unions, and colleagues. Government influence was quoted by only 3 percent, and only 2 percent specifically declared themselves to be reluctant joiners (Bamber 1986, 83).

Extent of Unionization

The above reasons are similar to those found in a wider study by Poole et al. (1983). That study also found that about 25 percent of managers in Britain are union members. There is a marked difference in union membership between the private (9 percent) and public sectors (60 percent). This difference mainly reflects contrasting employer policies. Although public-sector employers have generally been required to recognize unions and have even encouraged their growth, private-sector employers have sometimes resisted unionization, particularly among managers. Moreover, in general, private-sector firms are smaller than public-sector organizations. Other things being equal, the smaller the concentration of employees, the less need people see for union membership. In addition, there are fewer economies of scale for unions recruiting and representing people employed in small firms than in large organizations (Bain 1970).

Among professional engineers, almost 41 percent are unionized, with the largest unions concentrated in the public sector. These are the National and Local Government Officers' Association (NALGO) with 10.7 percent of the unionized professional engineers; the Institution of Professional Civil Servants (IPCS) with 4.8 percent, and the Engineers' and Managers' Association (EMA) with 4 percent (Engineering Council 1985a).

The Unions

After the late 1960s, more unions tried to recruit managers. This reflects the increasing numbers of managers seeking collective representation. However, it also mirrors the views of some employers who, recognizing that unionism among managers was growing, wanted to preempt their recruitment into what they saw as more militant unions dominated by subordinate grades of worker.

In 1969, for example, members of the Engineers' Guild, a professional body that had not engaged in collective bargaining, established the United Kingdom Association of Professional Engineers (UKAPE) as a union for engineers. Initially, UKAPE excluded from membership those without chartered engineer status. It set out to foster a professional, moderate image, ruling out strike action, affiliation to the Trades Union Congress (TUC) or to the Labour Party (Dickens 1976). In view of tough opposition from TUC-affiliated unions, UKAPE found it very difficult to secure recognition from employers and the Engineering Employers' Federation (EEF). The latter did not see chartered engineers as an identifiable bargaining unit and refused recognition to avoid fragmenting the bargaining structure. In 1976, UKAPE compromised by admitting nonchartered staff doing work of an equivalent status, but by the late 1970s its membership was in decline and in 1980 it merged with the white-collar section of the Electrical, Electronic, Telecommunication and Plumbing Union (EETPU).

The Association of Management and Professional Staffs (AMPS) was established in 1972 by the Council of Science and Technology Institutes, a professional body (Gill, Morris, and Eaton 1977). Similarly, the aim was to develop a professional image (Gillibrand 1975). Strike action was not ruled out, but again AMPS did not affiliate to the TUC or to the Labour Party. Initially, AMPS was a little more successful than UKAPE in securing recognition from employers. It had a more flexible recruitment policy because it aimed to organize a broader band of managers rather than a narrow professional group. In 1976, AMPS won collective bargaining rights for middle managers at Imperial Chemical Industries (ICI). This was a significant breakthrough as ICI managers eventually made up about half of AMPS' total membership. By the 1980s, however, its membership was declining, partly because of retrenchment at ICI; hence, AMPS also merged with the EETPU.

UKAPE and AMPS are just two examples of unions that mainly catered to private-sector managers. There are others, such as the National Unilever Management Association (NUMA), that maintained their independent existence into the mid-1980s. Nevertheless, Poole et al. (1983) found that only 30 percent of the unionized managers in their survey belonged to exclusively managerial unions. It is likely that this percentage has declined since their study was conducted (July 1980) owing to the mergers between managerial unions and those with a much broader base, such as the EETPU and the Association of Scientific, Technical and Managerial Staffs (ASTMS).

ASTMS claimed to represent around 45,000 managers in 1984, out of a total ASTMS membership of 400,000. In the early 1980s, it launched a recruitment drive among managers and despite the recession, continued to attract new members. Many of these were recruited through mergers with smaller managers' unions and staff associations. For example, 2,500 members were gained when the Courtauld's managers' association merged with ASTMS.

Both ASTMS and the EETPU have encouraged such mergers as part of their recruitment strategy. One of the attractions for the smaller unions is that ASTMS and EETPU allow them to merge as largely autonomous sections, retaining control over negotiations and with minimum interference from the larger union. This is intended to allay fears of their being drawn into militant action by the majority of the members who are not managers. Nonetheless, the manager-members still have access to the full range of services and benefits from the larger union.

The merger terms offered by both ASTMS and the EETPU have proved attractive to small managers' unions and staff associations, which have suffered growing financial insecurity in the 1980s, with increasing overheads and a shrinking membership. Such mergers mean that they are not included in the TUC affiliation of their parent union, but this seems to have presented few problems and their members are able to opt out of contributing to the political levy that funds the Labour Party.

The EETPU has also sought recognition for managers in previously un-unionized and green-field sites, offering employers a single-union agreement with binding final-offer arbitration on any type of dispute that may arise. ASTMS has similarly tried to move into previously nonunion areas, but it has tended to concentrate on larger established companies such as Ferranti, Racal, and Gillette. Each of these unions has set up a management council as a forum for discussions between the various groups of managers within the union.

In certain sectors, notably the public services, and in financial institutions, managers tend to join the same unions or staff associations as their subordinates. Local government officers up to and including chief executives may join NALGO. Many financial institutions have in-house staff associations that recruit at all levels, except perhaps for senior executives. The Banking, Insurance and Finance Union (BIFU) recruits managers along with their subordinates. Managers are often in the same collective bargaining unit as junior white-collar staff. However, there are no cases known to us of managers being in the same bargaining unit as their manual-worker subordinates.

There were several important union mergers in the late 1980s. In the most significant for managers, ASTMS merged with the Technical and Supervisory Section (TASS) of the Amalgamated Union of Engineering Workers to form a new union: Manufacturing, Science and Finance (MSF), which has 700,000 members.

Closed shop arrangements, under which employees are obliged to join a union as a condition of employment, are rare among managers, even in the public sector. Only in the cooperative movement have such arrangements been common. Managers' unions generally do not favor closed shops, seeing a managers' freedom to choose whether or not to belong to a union as an important right.

Managers' unions are rarely militant in character; their relationship with employers and their styles of bargaining usually reflect this (Prandy 1965, Blackburn 1967). Poole et al. (1983) found that 52 percent of the unionized managers in their survey could not think of any circumstances under which they would take strike action. A moderate image is usually necessary to persuade managers to join a union, and managers have often been reluctant to join unions where there is a risk that they may be drawn into industrial action by nonmanagers. For example, in 1981 about 1,500 managers in the gas supply industry broke away from NALGO to form the Gas Higher Management Association (GHMA). This action was precipitated by a proposal to reduce the amount of autonomy granted to managers as a group within that union and by managers' concern about what they saw as the growing militancy of NALGO.

Impact of Unionization

The bureaucratization of large employing organizations has fostered the growth of managers' unions. Once established, a union may reinforce bureaucratic procedures in the employment relationship by pressing for standardization in the treatment of managers.

British unions have often opposed links between pay and a superiors' assessment of individual performance. Unions have traditionally sought to establish the standard rate for the job (Webb and Webb 1920, 281); managerial and other white-collar unions have generally echoed this goal. However, some managers' unions have been persuaded to adopt a more pragmatic view, not least because managers themselves have usually welcomed merit pay, which has sometimes been used to increase their salary differentials over other groups (IDS Top Pay Unit 1985a).

Like other unions, managers' unions may be suspicious of some employer initiatives. Nonetheless, most managers' unions have accepted performance appraisal and job evaluation. They usually want a say in the design and operation of such plans, however, so that there is provision for union involvement and monitoring, and an established appeals procedure. They sometimes seek representation on job evaluation panels. Unions do not necessarily oppose the treatment of managers on the basis of individual merit, but they do oppose arbitrary treatment and will try to establish structured procedures where possible. For instance, if an individual is accused of misconduct, they aim to ensure that the principles of natural justice apply.

The impact of managers' unionism has generally been confined to the public and cooperative sectors and some large private-sector corporations. There has been very little impact on small and medium-sized firms in the private sector. By the 1980s, the political and economic climate had moved against managers' unionism. Unions in general were on the retreat as the recession reduced their membership and their bargaining power. The Conservative government was restricting union power by legislation. Furthermore, some companies tried to reduce union influence, seeking to reverse the trends of the 1970s.

ICI sought to replace its collective bargaining agreement with AMPS by a looser consultative arrangement that the company claimed would allow it to treat managers on a more individual basis (Snape and Bamber 1985). Unilever sought to stop paying standard annual cost-of-living pay increases to all its managers, and instead to broaden the scope for merit-based awards. NUMA, which represents Unilever managers, resisted this. A few companies have withdrawn from recognition agreements, perhaps inspired by the Government's ban on trade union membership at the Government Communications Headquarters early in 1984. Apparently, some companies regarded managers' unionism as limiting their freedom and flexibility to manage their managers so that, in the climate of the 1980s, they were seeking to regain this flexibility. Also, in some cases employers justified de-recognition on the grounds of sharply declining union membership among their managers and senior staff members (Snape and Bamber 1988).

Managers' unionism, however, does retain some strongholds, particularly in the public sector and is unlikely to fade away completely. During 1987, general managers in the National Health Service were considering establishing a union, as a reaction against the insecurities created by the introduction of short-term contracts and individualized remuneration.

Managers as a Third Force in Society

In Western Europe, some managers' unions have subscribed to the notion of managers as a third force between capital and labor. Managers are thus seen as a distinct social grouping whose interests may differ from those of the owners and the other workers. This idea is reflected in debates about the new middle class (Carter 1985).

The third-force notion usually involves having separate managers' unions and a separate union federation, standing apart from the wider union and labor movement. In 1977, 16 British managers' unions and professional associations formed the Managerial Professional and Staff Liaison Group (MPG) to represent managers' interests to the government, the European Communities (EC), and other bodies. None of the 16 were then affiliated to the TUC or to the Labour Party funds, and they tend to ally with the right within the TUC. In the longer term, they might incline the TUC to be more politically pragmatic and less ideologically committed to the Labour Party.
public service unions. Furthermore, such MPG members as AMPS and UKAPE subsequently affiliated to the TUC through their mergers with larger unions.

The inclusion of managers' unions in the TUC does not mean, however, that there has been a significant ideological shift on the part of managers. They remain a moderate middle-class group, they usually opt out of contributing to Labour Party funds, and they tend to ally with the right within the TUC. In the longer term, they might incline the TUC to be more politically pragmatic and less ideologically committed to the Labour Party.

MANAGEMENT AND THE POLITY

British politics has been dominated by two main parties (Labour and Conservative) for most of the twentieth century. The Labour Party is mainly financed by the unions, has a left-of-center ideology, and draws much of its support from working-class communities in the older industrial areas. The Conservative Party receives funds from business, has a right-of-center ideology, and draws its support from nonmanual workers and the suburban and rural areas. This distinction is one reason why Britain is sometimes described as two nations in terms of its politics and predominant social classes.

The traditional view of British politics is that it reflects class polarization.

Robertson (1984, 25) claims that Britain had the highest level of class voting of any major country outside Scandinavia, at least until the 1970s. He argues that the split between manual and nonmanual workers and the degree of authority exercised at work are crucial factors influencing voting behavior. He supports his claim with estimated voting patterns during the 1979 general election: More than 50 percent of managers and professionals supported the Conservatives, but only 20 percent supported Labour. Nonagricultural manual workers tended to vote in the opposite direction. The policies of the two parties broadly reflect these voting patterns; Labour subscribes to egalitarian and socialist policies, in contrast to the individualist and laissez-faire approach of the Conservatives. Managers are seen as part of a Conservative-voting middle class.

The class nature of British politics may be changing. The proportion of the vote going to the two major parties has declined since the 1950s. Managers have tended to find Labour's socialism unattractive. The realignment of the political center in the 1980s may provide managers with a more palatable alternative to the Conservatives.

CONCLUSION

The absolute and relative size of the managerial and professional workforce has increased since 1945. In the late 1980s, there are some signs of a growing awareness of the important role played by such employees. A former BIM chairman asserted that British management was undergoing a renaissance and many employing organizations are giving a higher priority to developing their managerial resources. Several unions and other associations are trying to represent them. In addition, perhaps more politicians are paying heed to the interests of these employees (after all, they represent an increasing proportion of the electorate). Their pay differentials over their subordinates, and possibly their relative status, have improved since the 1970s, although it remains to be seen to what extent this represents a reversal of the longer-term trend for differentials to be compressed.

The traditional pattern, whereby managers had their terms and conditions of employment determined individually, was eroded by the development of bureaucratic personnel policies in large organizations, and also by the growth of collective organization among managers, particularly in the 1970s. These trends were particularly clear in the public sector and large private-sector corporations. While collective agreements were increasingly important in the 1960s and 1970s, government regulation of the employment relationship also increased in this period. Legislation on contracts of employment, redundancy payments, unfair dismissal, and discrimination have all made an impact, and several elements of government action in the 1970s encouraged the growth of managerial unionization. This was partly because managers saw that their authority to hire and fire was increasingly regulated by legislation, and by the apparent growth in union power among their subordinates.

In the political and economic context of the 1980s, however, some different trends have become apparent. Union growth has been checked and in many sectors reversed. Some employers have tried to reinstate an individual employment relationship by increasing the use of merit pay and introducing greater flexibility into personnel practices. Employers have, in general, sought to take more initiatives themselves. This has often involved decentralizing collective bargaining. In a few cases, managerial unions have lost bargaining rights.

In the public sector, the post-1979 Conservative government has attempted to increase flexibility by getting away from uniform salary scales, with moves toward increasing the importance of merit pay. The trend toward market-related criteria for determining terms and conditions of employment has been bolstered by the post-1979 Thatcher Government's privatization policies and an increased use of subcontracting.

It is not yet clear whether events in the 1980s represent a reversal of the longer-term trend toward collective organization and bureaucratization of the managerial employment relationship, or whether we are seeing merely a cyclical response to a period of economic recession and a related increase in free market ideology and practice.

One thing is clear, however; Britain's future will depend critically on her managers. The relatively low pay and status of industrial managers and engineers compared with the older professions is symptomatic of Britain's decline as an industrial power (Fores and Clark 1975). The changes of the 1980s may represent the first steps toward halting that decline.

REFERENCES

Adams, M., and P. Meadows. 1985. The changing graduate labour market. *Employment Gazette* (September):343ff.

Alban-Metcalfe, B., and N. Nicholson. 1984. *The career development of British managers*. London: British Institute of Management.

APEX. 1988. *Meeting the pensions challenge: A guide to current pension law and practice*. London: Association of Professional, Executive Clerical and Computer Staff.

Bain, G. S. 1970. *The growth of white-collar unionism*. Oxford: Clarendon Press.

Bain, G.S., and R. Price. 1980. *Profile of union growth: A comparative statistical portrait of eight countries*. Oxford: Bard Blackwell.

Bamber, G. 1986. *Militant managers: Managerial unionism and industrial relations*. Aldershot: Gowar.

Bamber, G., and I. Glover. 1975. *Study of the steel industry management association and its members*. Watford: SIMA.

Bamber, G., and R. Lansbury (eds). 1989. *New technology: International perspectives on human resources and industrial relations*. London. Unwin Hyman.

Bamber, G., and E. Snape. 1987. British industrial relations. In *International and comparative industrial relations,* edited by G. Bamber and R. Lansbury. London and Boston: Allen and Unwin.

Barber A. 1985. Ethnic origin and economic status. *Employment Gazette* (December):467ff.

BIFU. N.d. *Jobs for the girls: The impact of automation on women's jobs in the finance industry*. London: Banking Insurance and Finance Union.

BIM. 1984. *Management news*, (7), May.

Blackburn, R.M. 1967. *Union character and social class: A study of white collar unionism*. London: Batsford.

Bullock, Lord. 1977. *Report of the committee of inquiry on industrial democracy*. Cmnd. 6706. London: Her Majesty's Stationery Office.

Carter, B. 1985. *Capitalism, class conflict and the new middle class*. London: Routledge and Kegan Paul.

CEI: 1975. *Professional engineers and trade unions: report of a working party*. London: Council of Engineering Institutions.

Child, J., and B. Partridge. 1982. *Lost managers: Supervisors in industry and society*. Cambridge: Cambridge University Press.

Constable, J., and R. McCormick. 1987. *The making of British managers*. London: British Institute of Management.

Crockett, G., and P. Elias. 1984. British managers: A study of their education, training, mobility and earnings. *British Journal of Industrial Relations* 22 (1): 34–46.

Crompton, R., and G. Jones. 1984. *White collar proletariat: Deskilling and gender in clerical work*. London: Macmillan.

DE. 1972. *Classification of occupations and directory of occupational titles*. London: Department of Employment, Her Majesty's Stationery Office.

———. 1981. *Labour force survey*. London: Department of Employment, Her Majesty's Stationery Office.

———. 1970–84. *New earnings survey*. London: Department of Employment, Her Majesty's Stationery Office.

———. 1985. *Employment Gazette*, Vol. 93.

———. 1986. *Employment Gazette*, Vol. 94.

Dickens, L. 1976. Fighting for the professional engineer. *Personnel Management* 8 (5): 18–35.

Dixon, M. 1985a. What private use of company car is worth. *Financial Times*, July 12:10.

———. 1985b. Engineers poor third to finance and personnel. *Financial Times*, November 7.

ECS. 1986. *Top management remuneration*. Brussels: Executive Compensation Service.

Educating Britain's bosses. 1983. *The Economist*, Sept. 17:17–18.

Engineering Council. 1985a. *1985 survey of chartered and technician engineers*. London: Engineering Council.

———. 1985b. *Career breaks for women chartered and technician engineers*. London: Engineering Council.

Finniston, Sir M. 1980. *Engineering our future: Report of the committee of enquiry into the engineering profession*. Cmnd. 7794. London: Her Majesty's Stationery Office.

Fores, M., and D. Clark. 1975. Why Sweden manages better. *Management Today* (February):66–69.

Franks, L. 1963. *British business schools*. London: British Institute of Management.

Fulton, L. 1968. *Report of the committee on the civil service*. Cmnd. 3638. London: Her Majesty's Stationery Office.

Gill, C., R. S. Morris, and J. Eaton. 1977. APST: The rise of a professional union. *Industrial Relations Journal* 8(1):50–61.

Gill, D. 1977. *Appraising performance*. London: IPM.

Gillibrand, M. 1975. Forging a new link. *Physics Bulletin* (June):272–73.

Griffiths, B., and H. Murray. 1985. *Whose business? A radical proposal to privatise British business schools*. London: Institute of Economic Affairs.

Guerrier, Y., and N. Philpot. 1978. *The British manager: Careers and mobility*. London: British Institute of Management.

Handy, C. 1987. *The making of managers: A report on management education, training and development in the United States, West Germany, France, Japan and the U.K.* London: National Economic Development Office.

Holdsworth, R. F. 1975. *Identifying managerial potential*. London: British Institute of Management.

Hunt, A. 1975. *Management attitudes and practices towards women at work*. London: Her Majesty's Stationery Office.

Huxley, J. 1985. The executive carrot: The pay packets of today's managers. *Sunday Times*, October 20:57.

IDS Top Pay Unit. 1985a. *The merit factor: Rewarding individual performance*. London: Incomes Data Services.

———. 1985b. *Monthly review of salaries and benefits*, no. 58. London: Incomes Data Services.

———. 1985c. *Monthly review of salaries and benefits*, no. 66. London: Incomes Data Services.

IMS. 1984. *Competence and competition*. A report prepared by the Institute of Manpower Studies for the National Economic Development Office and the Manpower Services Commission. London: NEDO.

IMS/Manpower Ltd. 1984. *Flexible manning: The way ahead*. IMS Report no. 88. Brighton: Institute of Manpower Studies.

Innovative unemployment. 1985. *The Economist*, April 6:69.

IPM/BIM. 1980. *Selecting managers: How British industry recruits*. London: British Institute of Management Foundation/Institute of Personnel Management.

Keenan, A., and T. J. Newton. 1984. Graduate engineers' views on the adequacy of their training in industry. *European Journal of Engineering Education* 8:369–80.

Labour Research Department. 1985. *Bargaining report*, 38.

Lee, G. L. 1981. *Who gets to the top? A sociological study of business executives*. Aldershot: Gower.

Leggatt, T. W. 1972. *The training of British managers: A study of need and demand*. London: Her Majesty's Stationery Office.

Long, P. 1986. *Performance/Appraisal*. London: IPM.

Mabey, C. 1984. Managing graduate entry. *Journal of General Management* 10 (2):67–79.

Manley, P. 1986. Why public is preferable. *Transition* (March):24–27.

Manley, P., and D. Sawbridge. 1980. Women at work. *Lloyds Bank Review* (135) January:29–40.

Mant, A. 1979. *The rise and fall of the British manager*. London: Pan.

Marshall, J. 1984. *Women managers: Travellers in a male world*. Chichester: Wiley.

McIntosh, A. 1980. Women at work: A survey of employers. *Employment Gazette*, November:1142–49.

McLoughlin, I. 1984. Engineering their future: Development in the organisation of British professional engineers. *Industrial Relations Journal* 15 (4) Winter:64–73.

Moffat, G., and S. Ward. 1986. Occupational pensions. In *Labour Law in Britain,* edited by R. Lewis, 389–415. Oxford: Blackwell.

OPCS. 1984. *Census 1981: Economic activity, Great Britain.* London: Her Majesty's Stationery Office.

PA. 1986. *Annual fringe benefits report.* London: PA Personnel Services.

Peach, L. 1985. Flexibility: The flavour of the future. *Personnel Management,* October:5.

Poole, M., R. Mansfield, P. Blyton, and P. Frost. 1981. *Managers in focus: The British manager in the early 1980s.* Aldershot: Gower.

Poole, M., R. Mansfield, P. Blyton, and P. Frost. 1983. Why managers join unions: Evidence from Britain. *Industrial Relations* 22 (3) Fall:426–44.

Prandy, K. 1965. *Professional employees.* London: Faber and Faber.

Prime minister's payola. 1985. *The Economist,* July 27:13.

RE. 1985. *National management salary survey 1985.* London: Remuneration Economics/BIM.

———. 1986. *National management salary survey 1986.* London: Remuneration Economics/BIM.

Robbins, L. C. 1963. *Report of the committee on higher education.* Cmnd. 2154. London: Her Majesty's Stationery Office.

Robertson, D. 1984. *Class and the British electorate.* Oxford: Blackwell.

Rothwell, S. 1985. Women's management careers. *Business Graduate,* (April).

Routh, G. 1980. *Occupation and pay in Great Britain 1906–79.* London: Macmillan.

Saunders, C., S. Mukherjee, D. Marsden, and A. Donaldson. 1977. *Winners and losers: Pay patterns in the 1970s.* London: PEP.

Snape, E., and G. Bamber. 1987. Managerial and Professional Employees in Britain. *Employee Relations Monograph* (3).

Snape E., and G. Bamber. Managerial and professional employees: Conceptualising Union Structure and Strategy. *British Journal of Industrial Relations,* forthcoming.

Stewart S., K. Prandy, and B. Blackburn. 1980. Social stratification and careers into management. In *Managerial roles in industrial relations: Towards a definitive survey of research and formulation of models,* edited by M. Poole and R. Mansfield, 21–25. Farnborough: Gower.

Thody, P. 1985. How to get to the top. *Times Higher Education Supplement,* December 20.

Thomas, David. 1985. Bank's mobility clause "biased against women." *Financial Times,* September 20:11.

Vernon-Harcourt, T. 1983. U.K. executive remuneration—The impact of conservative government policies. *Benefits International,* vol. 12 (June):10–15.

Webb, S., and B. Webb. 1920. *Industrial democracy.* London: Longmans.

Werneke, D. 1983. Women: The vulnerable group—microelectronics at work in the office. *Employment Gazette* 91 (9):392–96.

3
United States

MYRON J. ROOMKIN

The terms and conditions of employment for managers are defined by corporate practices and economic conditions. Law plays a relatively limited role, and collective bargaining for managerial employees is rare. Individual employment contracts, which have received much discussion lately, are used for a few top executives and special types of employees.

Corporate policies and practices toward managerial employees are in a significant state of change. Behind these changes are the following major social and economic trends affecting many portions of the labor market: shifting composition of the labor force with regard to race, sex, and age; changes in employment opportunities with small and medium-sized firms accounting for a growing share of job prospects; increased business consolidation through mergers and acquisitions especially among the giant companies; and increased product market competition because of the deregulation of industries and foreign competition.

These forces have brought to an end, especially in larger enterprises, the tradition of stable employment through bureaucratic personnel and compensation systems. However, a new dominant model of managerial employment relationships has not yet emerged.

Popular belief holds that the traditional approach ended suddenly in the 1980s because of increased competitiveness. In some companies it did—and for that reason. However, the new model could be found before the 1980s, especially in newer companies that did not establish highly bureaucratic internal labor markets.

The transformation of managerial employment has given managers higher unemployment, greater fears of economic and job insecurity, career frustration, and increased dissatisfaction with work. So far managers have reacted individually and through established legal mechanisms. The challenge facing firms is to find ways of moving from the old to some new model, while at the same time continuing to build employee loyalty and motivation.

One of the advantages of studying U. S. managerial employment is the enormous amount of information published on managers and managerial practices—something that reflects a long-standing American fascination with those subjects. However, much of that information is biased toward the experiences of those employed in the largest organizations or in the businesses that attract notoriety. On the other hand, some information, particularly that published by governmental agencies, is so comprehensive that it masks the emergence of possible trends. Both types are required to get a balanced picture.

DEFINING THE MANAGERIAL WORK FORCE

The term "managerial and professional staff" is not widely used in the United States, and there is no precise equivalent for the collective of salaried white-collar employees above the level of first-line supervisor but below the dominant executive decision-makers in an organization.

At one time it was common to call these individuals businessmen; however, as more women entered the occupation and managers began appearing in non-business settings, the term has fallen from use. Actually, several definitions of mid- and upper-level white-collar administrative employees exist in the laws regulating employment relationships, the practices of businesses, and the agencies that collect social statistics.

Legal Definitions

The broadest legal category is that of the exempt work force in the Wages and Hours Laws. This group includes the executive, administrative, and professional employees who are not required to receive premium pay for working overtime (U. S. Department of Labor 1983). An executive is an employee who is compensated on a salary basis at a rate of not less than $250 a week (as of February 13, 1983) for managing a department or supervising at least two employees. An administrative employee works in directly related ways to service the business through management, planning, purchasing, sales, research, and control in either functional departments or staff capacities. A professional, in contrast, is an employee whose primary duty consists of the performance of work requiring knowledge of an advanced type in a field of science or learning customarily acquired by prolonged course of specialized study.

Other labor laws follow a similar pattern. The Equal Opportunity Commission defines officials and managers to include all occupations requiring administrative personnel who set and implement policies and direct phases of the firm's operation. According to the Age Discrimination Act and the Employee Retirement Income Security Act, a manager is an individual employed in a bona-fide executive or high policymaking position and is entitled to a pension of at least $27,000 per year. The National Labor Relations Board classifies as managers those employees who "formulate and effectuate management policies by expressing and making operative the decisions of the employer" [see *Bell Aerospace Co.* 219 NLRB 384 (1975)].

Nearly all statutes consider individuals working in an administrative or managerial capacity as employees of the firm. The one significant exemption is the National Labor Relations Act, which views managerial employees from the first-level of supervisors and above as agents of the employer and thus not eligible for the protected right to join a union.

Organizational Definitions

Firms require narrower and more precise categorizations of their managerial employees than simply the exempt group or the managerial group. At least in the larger firms, bureaucratic systems are used to define the managerial occupations and the relationship among them. Such systems are also used to cluster jobs, rank them hierarchically, and, as in blue-collar employment, link the job structure to the compensation system. For instance, the widely used Hay System of Compensation, which ranks jobs in terms of points given for know-how, problem solving, and accountability, associates 150 points with entry-level professional and supervisory positions and 1,000 points with senior management jobs. However, unless companies utilize the same system of job evaluation and pay grades, comparisons of job titles, point totals, or labor grades across companies are inappropriate and are seldom made. Salary comparisons are made more frequently, but often require considerable qualification.

Custom and tradition also play a role in categorizing the managerial work force of a firm. In a bank, for example, it is common to talk about the "executive staff" or the "official staff" or the "officers" to describe the corps of all line managers. A practice believed started at General Electric Corporation classified professional and managerial employees as either "individual contributors" or "managers," depending on whether the employee supervises others. Many individual contributors are actually professionals working in a staff capacity; others may be persons working in entry-level positions such as assistant marketing analysts. Some companies classify as managers certain staff specialists for selected purposes. Thus, for purposes of access to confidential information, the clerical staff of managers may be considered part of the management group.

Statistical Definitions

Beginning with the 1980 Census, the Bureau of the Census reclassified and redefined occupations in the U. S. economy. The previous codes identified nonfarm white-collar workers in managerial and administrative occupations but was so poorly designed that half of these employees were labeled as "other," and a significant quantity (perhaps as great as 10 or 12 percent) of persons identified as professional were in fact working in a managerial capacity (Green, tan Dinh,

Priebe, and Tucker 1983, 10). Although the new category, "executives, administrators, and managers," appears to be more precise, occupations are no longer divided into white- and blue-collar groupings. Also, technically speaking, occupational information for the 1980s is not totally comparable with earlier statistics, thus making it difficult to identify trends accurately.

This new definition takes us closer to the concept of a managerial staff. Excluded are first-line levels of supervision, but included are the top and middle management occupations that are concerned with achieving the overall objectives of the organization as well as those professionals, such as accountants, auditors, personnel specialists, economists, and engineers, who are working in a managerial capacity.

STATUS AND AUTHORITY OF MANAGERS

Three principal perspectives define the status and roles of managers in American society. One is social status based on the opinions of the population. The public's general view of business and business leaders is well documented and tends to show an appreciation for their accomplishments but a suspicion of their motives (Lipset and Schneider 1983). In comparison, the public's opinions about managers as workers (as opposed to managers as elite decision-makers) are not as clear and have not been thoroughly studied. However, one thing seems obvious from just general impressions: In the 1980s careers in management have enjoyed a very high degree of social status almost to the point of social admiration.

Another perspective on status is intraorganizational, that is, the nature of managerial authority within the company. In the first part of this century, managerial authority within organizations was considered absolute and unquestionable and was derived from the inherent rights of ownership, a belief in paternalism, or the need to control organizations.

Even during this period, authoritarian control was challenged by a changing industrial structure, the introduction of new technologies, and the rising educational attainment of workers. However, it was the rise of trade unionism after 1935 that produced the end of unilateral authority in American business by creating a system of constitutional authority in which the rights of managers and workers would be codified by contract.

Constitutional authority systems have given way to a variety of arrangements generally considered shared authority systems. One driving force behind this change has been rising worker expectations for involvement at the work place and participation in decision-making. Whereas the constitutional system of authority had to be won through confrontation, the popularity of participative systems is largely based on the belief that participatory decision-making is sound business practice.

Governmental regulations also have circumscribed the actions of managers and made them more accountable to the public. In some areas of regulation, like discrimination in employment, managers have been held financially liable for damages (see, for instance, Williams 1986); a doctrine of criminal culpability for managers in violations of the safety laws may soon evolve as well.

Current attempts to reemphasize entrepreneurship for managers in large organizations (Sandeman 1984) seem to hold important implications for future changes in managerial status within the company. Managers are caught between the pressures from above for results, the restrictions imposed by governmental regulations and to a lesser extent unions, and the demand from below for greater participation and involvement in decision-making.

All this may help to explain why managers' perception of their own status began falling in the late 1970s both in absolute terms and relative to other major occupational groups, even before they were adversely affected by the economic turmoil of the 1980s and while the job satisfaction of other occupational groups was improving (Cooper, Morgan, Foley, and Kaplan 1979; Cooper and Gelfond 1980).

EMPLOYMENT PATTERNS AND TRENDS

The important postwar trends in the labor market experiences of managers have been: (1) the rapid growth in the number of managers, (2) a broadening of demand across all segments of the economy, (3) the prolitarianization of the managerial occupation, (4) a dramatic increase in the number of women and minorities in the managerial occupations, (5) changes in the age distribution and work life span, and (6) declining degrees of job security for managers.

Growth in Employment

After a decade of modest increases, the number of persons employed in a managerial or administrative capacity increased significantly in the 1970s. Based on 1970 *Census* occupational definitions, the employment of managers and administrators, except farm, increased by 35.9 percent between 1972 and 1980 (Leon 1982, 19). Using the broader definition of the 1980 Census, the growth during that period was 40.4 percent. A 60 percent increase was recorded during the decade in the number of salaried managers, that is, excluding those managers who were self-employed and probably were working for smaller firms (Klein 1984).

As a share of total employment, executives, administrators, and managerial employees rose to 10.7 percent in 1982 from 8.9 percent in 1972. This penchant of American business for managers is more dramatically seen in the fact that between 1947 and 1983 the portion of all wage and salary earnings going to nonproduction and supervisory employees rose from 22 percent to 34 percent, while the portion attributed to production and nonsupervisory employees fell from 78 percent to 66 percent (as calculated in Gordon 1984b).

The increase in managerial employment was due not only to an increase in the number of new firms but was associated with an increase in the number of the managers employed in each firm. Between 1960 and 1980 the ratio of managers to establishments increased 280 percent, while the average number of production employees dropped by about 50 percent. (Data taken from *County Business Patterns* and the *Census*.) For the remainder of the decade, employment of managers and administrators is expected to continue growing but at a slower rate than in the 1970s and below the growth rate projected for all occupations (see Carey 1981).

Broad-based Growth

As the following data gathered by the Bureau of Labor Statistics (1982, 632–34) show, managerial and administrative jobs have increased in all sectors of the economy.

	Percent of industry	
Industry	*1972*	*1981*
Agriculture	0.7	2.6
Mining	6.6	9.8
Construction	9.8	13.2
Manufacturing	5.8	7.8
Transportation and public utilities	8.2	10.8
Wholesale and retail trade	18.8	19.5
Financial	19.2	19.4
Nonhousehold services	6.8	8.0
Public administration	12.3	13.8

With this proliferation has come a greater degree of occupational specialization for managers. The fastest growing managerial occupation has been hospital administrator. Employment also increased in less widely known areas of management including forest managers, cash managers, city managers, and managers of not-for-profit organizations, such as museums, orchestras, or opera companies. The growth in managerial employment was particularly noteworthy in smaller organizations, the type of organization that accounted for most new jobs created during the 1970s.

Prolitarianization

As in other industrialized societies, American managers have become more a group of wage-earners and employees of companies and less a group of self-employed entrepreneurs. In the 1960 *Census,* for instance, among nonfarm managers, officials, and executives, 35.3 percent of the men and 36.8 percent of the women were self employed. This compares with 8.4 percent of males and 5.9 percent of females classified as executives, administrators, and managers in the 1980 *Census*. One cause of this trend has been the transformation of the owner-manager in smaller firms into full-time managers.

Women and Minorities

Following a decade of no appreciable increase in the portion of women in managerial jobs, the 1970s and 1980s have been a period in which the female share of managerial employment increased dramatically. As seen in Table 3.1, such occupations as office manager, health administrator, and restaurant manager, already considered highly feminized in 1972, became even more feminized by 1982. However, women showed gains in virtually all the managerial occupations and in some occupations, such as bank manager, credit manager, and nonretail sales manager, the representation of females increased 100 percent or more.

As also indicated in this table, nonwhite representation in the managerial and related occupations increased relative to the national average. Nonwhite

Table 3.1 Female and nonwhite employed managers, 1972–82

| | *Percent of occupation* | | | |
| | *Female* | | *Nonwhite* | |
Occupation	*1972*	*1982*	*1972*	*1982*
Total	38.0	43.5	10.6	11.7
Managers and administrators, except from	17.6	28.0	4.0	5.7
Bank officials and financial mgrs.	19.0	37.1	2.6	5.1
Buyers & purchasing agents	21.2	35.7	3.6	4.6
Credit & collection managers	23.9	48.4	1.4	6.3
Health administrators	46.6	50.9	7.6	5.3
Inspectors, except construction	6.2	15.0	7.2	16.3
Managers & superintendents—building	42.6	52.5	8.8	7.7
Office managers, n.e.c.*	41.9	72.6	1.0	3.2
Officials and administrators, public administration	20.4	29.3	9.1	9.3
Officials of lodges, societies, and unions	18.8	28.6	7.5	7.9
Restaurant, cafeteria managers	32.4	40.6	8.9	11.5
Sales managers, retail	27.4	39.7	2.0	7.1
Sales managers, except retail	2.9	12.9	0.7	3.0
School administrator, college	25.3	36.2	9.6	13.1
School administrator, except college	26.2	36.2	7.7	13.0
All other managers and administrators	12.2	19.9	3.2	4.7
Selected related professions				
Accountant	39.3	45.1	7.2	9.7
Personnel specialist	31.0	49.6	9.0	11.1
Economist	21.3	28.0	5.7	7.5

Source: Current Population Survey.
*Not elsewhere classified.

managers, however, continue to show their greatest representation in occupations connected with the public sector.

Changing Age Distribution

Between 1975 and 1990, individuals 25 to 44 years of age, the so-called promotion age category, are expected to increase 54.9 percent, while the population of workers 16 to 24 will decline by 6 percent (Freeman 1979, 74). The emergence of this bulge in the population has had and will continue to have a particular significance for managerial occupations. As Table 3.2 shows, the number of mid-career managers, aged 35 to 54, has not been increasing as fast as those in the younger cohort of 24 to 34. At the same time, the number of workers over 65 years old continues to rise, reflecting a trend toward the prolongation of the work life (for all managers except nonwhites).

Declining Employment Security

Because of demographic trends and the increased representation of females and nonwhites, the 1980s were supposed to be a decade of thwarted expectations and heightened competition for advancement (Rosow 1979). However, the forecasters failed to see several major changes in the demand for managers that would make matters considerably worse.

Before the recession of 1980–83, it was generally believed that managers were treated as a fixed cost of production and protected from adverse consequences during economic downturns. According to this view, a manager had to be hoarded by the firm because of the difficulty of quickly finding a suitable replacement if business prospects improved. It was thought that managers enjoyed careers in which they were associated with a few firms and that changes in employers were generally voluntary turnover as managers sought greener pastures. To be sure, large-scale layoffs of white-collar and managerial workers have taken place historically, such as in the aerospace industry during the early 1970s or when merged firms eliminated redundant employees. However, these were seen as the exceptions that occurred only when the firm faced significant economic threats or challenges and other means of meeting them proved inadequate.

Looking back, we can now see that the attachment of managers to particular jobs was changing gradually during the 1960s and 1970s. By the 1980s, even though managers still suffered less unemployment than other classes of workers, they were not as insulated from the pressures of the marketplace.

Trends in Job Security

Table 3.3 reports the unemployment rates for managers and administrators compared to the rates of several occupational groups from 1970 to 1983. During this period, the unemployment rate of managers was considerably below the national average but rising. In 1982 and 1983, it reached its highest level of 3.5

Table 3.2 Growth in the employment of managers by race, sex, and age

| | 24–34 | | 35–54 | | 65+ | |
Year/sex/race	Total	Percent change	Total	Percent change	Total	Percent change
All						
1972	20.2		51.1		4.6	
1982	26.1	84.0	47.8	33.2	3.6	12.0
Men						
1972	21.4		51.1		4.5	
1982	25.0	45.9	49.3	16.6	3.8	6.7
Women						
1972	14.9		50.7		5.3	
1982	28.1	337.6	44.0	95.7	3.1	31.5
Whites						
1972	20.1		51.1		4.6	
1982	25.8	79.8	47.7	27.8	3.7	13.1
Nonwhites						
1972	23.1		49.8		4.8	
1982	32.3	500.0	46.7	23.1	2.4	−31.2

Source: Current Population Survey.

Table 3.3 Selected unemployment rates, 1970–86

Year	All workers	Managers and administrators	Managers as percent of total	Managers as percent of white collar	Managers as percent of blue collar
1970	4.9	1.3	27	46	21
1971	5.9	1.6	27	46	22
1972	5.6	1.8	32	53	28
1973	4.9	1.4	29	48	26
1974	5.6	1.8	32	55	27
1975	8.5	3.0	35	64	26
1976	8.7	3.1	36	67	33
1977	7.1	2.8	39	65	35
1978	6.1	2.1	34	60	30
1979	5.8	2.1	36	64	30
1980	7.1	2.4	34	65	24
1981	7.6	2.7	36	68	26
1982	9.8	3.5	36	71	25
1983*	9.8	3.5	36	—	—
1984*	7.5	2.7	36	—	—
1985*	7.2	2.6	36	—	—
1986*	7.0	2.6	37	—	—

Source: Bureau of Labor Statistics 1976; and *Current Population Survey.*
*New occupational codes redefined the occupation as including executive, administrative, and managerial workers.

percent; however, in relative terms, 1977 was the worst year for unemployment of managers.

Judging from Table 3.3, unemployment among managers does not appear to have any systematic relationship with the rate for blue-collar workers but has been increasing relative to unemployment among white-collar workers. This implies that employers would rather lay off blue-collar employees before white-collar ones, something companies continued to do in the recession of 1980–83 (Bureau of National Affairs 1982). However, it also implies that when white-collar employees must be furloughed, a growing share of the burden falls on managers.

A similar trend is evident in the job tenure of managers, that is, the length of their association with a current employer. Table 3.4 summarizes the distribution of the length of service reported by managers and administrators, as measured in periodic surveys done by the Bureau of Labor Statistics. The data on tenure are for experienced workers which, for this purpose, exclude those who entered the occupation in the prior five years. (The argument is that those individuals reporting five years or less tenure in one year either changed employers or entered the occupation for the first time during that five-year period. Subtracting an estimate of the new entrants should leave us with an estimate of the experienced job changers.) Without this adjustment, the distribution of tenure will become increasingly and misleadingly skewed in a growing occupation. Changes in tenure distribution reflect both voluntary and involuntary separations from the firm. Still, it is a valid measure of changes in the attachment of workers to organizations.

According to the table, the tenure of male managers with prior work experience declined between 1963 and 1981. The proportion with between 6 and 15 years of service remained relatively stable, but the proportion with more than 15 years declined from 33.8 percent to 24.6 percent, and the proportion of those with 5 or fewer years of tenure rose from 28.6 to 40.4 percent.

Among female managers with prior work experience, however, tenure with their current employer has been increasing. The percentage of those with five or fewer years of seniority has fallen from 44.3 to 26.4 percent, reflecting the sizable increases in job tenure for those with between 6 and 15 years of service to their current employer.

The Watershed 1980s
According to the Bureau of Labor Statistics (Flaim and Sehgal 1985, 7) 444,000 managers who had held their jobs for at least three years lost them between January 1980 and January 1984. This group constituted 8.7 percent of all such displaced workers upset by the recession.

Among the organizations that cut the size of their managerial work force during the recession were the following: Weyerhauser cut 700 management employees; GAF reduced its corporate staff by 26 percent; Kennecott Corporation eliminated 80 of 410 staff positions at its headquarters; at Texas Instruments 125 administrative staff employees were let go; the Bechtel Group re-

Table 3.4 Job tenure of experienced employed managers and administrators, except farm employees, by sex, 1963–81

| Sex/Date | Percentage with their current employer for | | | | |
	5 years or less	6–10 years	11–15 years	More than 15 years	Total*
Male					
January 1963	28.6	21.3	16.4	33.8	100.0%
January 1966	37.0	18.4	13.8	30.7	100.0
January 1973	40.0	20.4	13.8	30.7	100.0
January 1978	40.5	21.7	11.0	27.0	100.0
January 1981	40.4	21.7	13.2	24.6	100.0
Female					
January 1963	44.3	19.5	12.0	24.1	100.0%
January 1966	34.1	24.1	14.1	27.6	100.0
January 1973	37.1	24.2	14.5	22.3	100.0
January 1978	27.1	27.4	12.9	17.8	100.0
January 1981	26.4	35.9	17.1	20.5	100.0

Source: Bureau of Labor Statistics 1963; 1967; 1979; 1983.

*Based on total reported in the survey minus the net additions to the occupations over the prior five-year period.

duced its staff by 900 employees; Atari, Inc., as a consequence of shifting its operation overseas, gave layoff notices to more than 1,000 administrative, support, and marketing personnel; Montgomery Wards instituted a heavy cutback in the number of middle managers, Crocker National Bank did away with the job of branch managers; and Xerox cut 550 persons. Indeed, cutbacks in white-collar personnel had become so noticeable during the recession that there were rumors of possible layoffs even at IBM, which has had an ironclad policy of not laying off personnel for economic reasons (Hayes 1981); subsequently IBM indicated that this policy was actually a practice, implying it could be changed if necessary. Other reductions in managerial employment took place in the federal government.

Perhaps the largest reduction in managers and related white-collar employees was implemented by U. S. Steel (Kearns 1983). In 1982–83 it halved its nonunion work force, eliminating about 8,000 white-collar jobs among managers and professionals. Within that industry, managers had been relatively secure from the long-term decline in the demand for steel. The employment of white-collar workers fell only 10 percent from 115,763 in 1973 to 104,695 in 1981, while the employment of blue-collar workers fell about 25 percent. However, by the middle of 1983, white-collar employment had fallen to 74,220.

Another large and symbolically important reduction of managerial personnel during the recession took place at Eastman Kodak Company early in 1983. Unlike IBM, Kodak did not have a written policy of no layoffs, but provided both its blue- and white-collar employees steady employment and a very high degree of job security. However, in January 1983, 5,000 employees retired or

separated from the company through a program of early retirements and separation incentives, while another 1,100 production employees were placed on
layoff. In August, the company announced layoffs affecting more than 3,000
other employees (Berg 1983, 1).

Despite these and the host of other layoffs that made headlines during the
recession, we should not lose sight of the fact that the level of managerial layoffs
relative to other occupational groups remained very low. In 1982, for instance,
only 12.4 percent of the unemployed adult males and 5.7 of the unemployed
adult female managers were accounted for by layoffs. This compares to about
40 percent of unemployed male and female semiskilled operatives, excluding
those in transportation (Bednarzik 1983, 7–8).

Contributing Causes

The decline in managerial employment security did not end with economic
recovery. If anything, cutbacks in managerial positions became more prevalent
after the recession, further contributing to the decline in employment among
managers (Nielson 1985). Among the causes were the following quantitative
and qualitative changes in the demand for managers: shifting product markets,
computerization of managerial activities, and the changing structure of American business.

In industries such as data processing and business services, employment has
grown. In manufacturing, new managers were first retained to replace those
laid off during the downturn, then furloughed or laid off as the fortunes of that
industry changed again. Sizable cutbacks occurred in declining industries like
the petroleum industry and computer manufacturing.

At the level of the firm, employment needs changed as firms adopted new
directions or goals—popularly called strategic change. Employees were replaced
with persons who possessed skills, experiences, or even a management style
judged to be more appropriate to new organizational goals. Such "strategic"
layoffs took place in air transportation, trucking, communications, and banking
and finance where deregulation had created highly competitive business en-
vironments. One of the biggest incidents of job elimination involved AT&T,
which historically had provided stable employment resulting from its predictable and regulated product markets. However, in 1985 it announced that 7,200
management positions would be abolished as part of a realignment in its information systems division that would affect 24,000 jobs (Stevenson 1985).

Other postrecessionary reductions in managerial positions could be traced
to a general desire of firms, even prosperous ones, to control labor costs in the
face of foreign and domestic competition. A survey of large corporations conducted for the Harvard Business School by LdG Associates found that 50
percent of firms that had cut management positions between August 1982 and
August 1983 reported making high profits (Main 1984, 118). Ford, which
earned record profits during this period along with the rest of the automobile
industry, reduced its salaried workers in the U.S. by 21,000 employees between

1979 and 1984, and anticipated making further reductions until 1990. The need to reorganize and trim personnel was especially strong in the hospital supply industry, which experienced changes in the reimbursement rules of third-party payers and the spread of health care organizations.

Popular wisdom has it that the microcomputer also has helped to undermine the demand for lower and middle managers by making them more productive and eliminating the need for layers of bureaucracy to transmit information from the bottom to the top of the firm. While there is little question that the desktop computer has dramatically influenced recordkeeping and office work, as yet there is only anecdotal information about the impact of these machines on the demand for managers. Studies of employment displaced by mainframe computers suggest that employment levels ultimately rebound as the firm hires persons to service the new machines and as organizations recentralize decision-making (Osterman 1986; Stewart 1971). It remains to be seen whether the microcomputer is merely an extension of prior computerization or a revolutionary development with unique impacts on the demand for, and careers of, managers.

Change in the structure of organizations has been another factor decreasing managerial job security. Three types of organizational changes have taken place. First, the number of redundant managerial employees increased due to a spate of mergers and acquisitions, especially among the largest firms (*Wall Street Journal*, August 12, 1985).

Second, managerial jobs were eliminated in many companies as firms reduced the size of their corporate staffs, as Ginzberg and Vojta (1985) have noted, to reinvigorate performance in large businesses. Between 1972 and 1982, for instance, the number of companies with separate auxiliary offices performing only administrative functions grew 47 percent, and the number of persons in those offices employed in administrative duties increased 30 percent (Bureau of the Census 1975 and 1986). While a great deal has been said about the desire to create a "lean" staff structure, the fact is that firms have come to look at staff personnel costs a lot more critically in the 1980s. It will be a while, however, before it can be determined whether staff cutbacks have been genuinely reduced or, as in prior periods of decentralization, have merely shifted from central corporate offices to the operating units.

Third, by eliminating levels of hierarchy and increasing the span of managerial control, there has been a trend toward flatter organizational structures and, hence, a need for even fewer managers.

IMPACT ON CAREERS AND LABOR MOBILITY

How have these changes in the supply and demand of managers affected their careers and the policies and practices of companies vis-à-vis their managerial employees?

The Unemployed and Reemployed

The typical unemployed manager and administrator has been getting older. In the 1960s and 1970s, younger managers in entry level jobs were the most likely group to be unemployed. By the mid-1980s, about one-third of the unemployed managers were over the age of 44 (unpublished data from the *Current Population Survey* (CPS)) and by implication working at middle-level and middle career positions. Given the prevalence of early retirements, these figures probably understate the true extent to which age has become a liability for managers.

Nevertheless, the level of unemployment among older managers remains very low relative to most segments of the economy, despite the public's impression to the contrary. For example, since 1983 the rate of unemployment among executives, administrators, and managers has averaged about 2.5 percent and about 2.6 for those 45 to 54 years old, using unpublished data from the CPS.

Because nonwhite and female managers have less seniority than white male managers, and because women and nonwhites tend to be employed in support or staff functions that have been the focus of cutbacks, white-collar cuts could have fallen more heavily on women and nonwhite men (Lubin 1982). Unemployment among male managers increased 5 percent in 1980–81, but grew 17 percent among female managers. This, however, appears to have been a temporary development for female managers. The rates of unemployment for both male and female executives, administrators, and managers, according to unpublished CPS data, have been growing closer together during the recovery and by 1986 were almost equal, that is, 2.3 and 2.5 for men and women over the age of twenty, respectively. On the other hand, the unemployment rate for black managers has averaged about twice the level of whites.

A great deal of interest has centered on what happens to the managers who have been forced out of their jobs. The popular notion holds that they have either retired, become self-employed as consultants, or have taken positions in smaller firms. Although the total number of self-employed workers increased in the 1980s after declining since 1948 (Haber, Lamas, and Lichtenstein 1987, 17), the number of self-employed managers has not increased disproportionally to total managerial employment. Of course, many displaced managers could have become self-employed in related occupations such as independent sales representatives or as heads of their own business.

However, the majority of the displaced managers, it now appears, seek full-time reemployment. In 1983 and again in 1986, government researchers gathered data on the experiences of displaced workers (Bureau of Labor Statistics 1984; and 1986b or Horvath 1987), chronicling the labor market experiences of those displaced since 1981 who had a minimum of three years' tenure at their previous employer. A displaced worker was broadly defined as someone who lost his or her job due to a plant closing or move, slack work, or the abolishment of a position or shift. The reemployment experience found in the two surveys was as follows:

	1981–1984	1981–1986
Employed	75.7	72.0
Unemployed	15.6	16.9
Not in labor force	8.7	11.1
Total	100.0%	100.0%

These results imply a slight worsening in the reemployment prospects of displaced managers and a possible increase of those who leave the labor market to retire. However, it is perhaps more significant that managers, along with professionals, had the highest rates of reemployment of any occupational group. Considering the average age of the unemployed managers and their probable resistance to relocation, this is a surprisingly strong performance.

Dyer (1973, 972), in one of the few studies of reemployment among managers, done well before the recession of the 1980s, discovered that those who successfully found employment tended to work in smaller firms even within the same industries. Anecdotal evidence (Nulty 1987, 29) says that this is probably still true, especially since job opportunities generally appear to be more abundant in smaller firms.

A related issue is whether displaced managers have been forced to change occupations. Data from the survey of displaced workers just discussed (Horvath 1987, 12) show that only 43 percent of displaced managers who were employed in January 1986 were in their same occupation. While other occupations experienced approximately the same level of stability, it is evident that the labor market performance of this group in the 1980s is linked in no small way to the willingness of managers to enter new careers perhaps in sales, the clerical support occupations, or professional specialties including consulting.

It is interesting how the official statistics on the labor market experience of managers describe a picture that is far less bleak than the impression given by the media, particularly the business press. One explanation is that the media tend to focus on the plight of the most visible experiences of persons employed in high-status, high-paying jobs, primarily in larger companies. Undoubtedly, the experience of this group makes for the most sensational stories but, judging from the more comprehensive statistics, the narrower focus has tended to overstate the magnitude of the problem.

Public employment and training programs have not been an important factor in the efforts of displaced managers to find work in the 1980s. More noticeable efforts were expended by government during the 1970s in the aerospace industry, but that was in a period of greater public expenditures on labor market policies and programs. Government has not, and probably will not, act to address the special labor market problems of unemployed managers, although managers will benefit from broad social initiatives such as laws requiring the continuation of corporate health benefits for the unemployed and other laws improving the vesting rights of employees in their pensions. The latter would be especially helpful for managers in smaller firms if vesting is extended to cover profit-sharing funds that generally substitute for pension plans.

Private social welfare agencies have provided some services, but the task of finding reemployment has been pretty much a personal one. Forty Plus Clubs, organized locally in the major cities by formerly unemployed executives, have been very active in providing job seekers with support services and social support while they look for work.

Internal Labor Market Practices

Traditionally, most managers were hired directly into entry-level managerial positions in a particular functional area and then progressed to higher job levels in that function within a single firm through a process of promotions and horizontal job changes (see Kanter 1977, 1984; and Rosenbaum 1984). Others entered the ranks of managers typically by leaving their jobs in technical or professional specialties as individual contributors, that is, with no supervisory responsibilities. While time-in-grade has not usually been a prerequisite for promotions, careers have tended to be linear, with people entering at the bottom of the hierarchy and reaching their highest position prior to retirement.

For males who do not start their careers as managers, about half tend to change employers when becoming a manager. However, in the 1980s, women are more likely to obtain their first position as managers through promotion from within a current organization (derived from Bureau of Labor Statistics 1983, Table B-15, 33). This reluctance to hire experienced females with prior managerial experience could be a holdover from the days when there were not many qualified women available in the external market. It also could be seen as a discriminatory practice, as though firms are saying that they need to observe women much more closely before giving them managerial responsibility.

Not all managers, of course, were part of these dominant internal promotion patterns. Many specialists or professionals, as in the case of data processing specialists, entered and were promoted within narrow areas of responsibility and would move from company to company within that area of specialty.

The traditional bureaucratic model of a manager's career tends not to be found in newer and more rapidly growing organizations, in what are broadly called high-technology companies. Kanter's (1984) study of careers in such companies found that careers followed more complex patterns, both horizontally and vertically, and spanned several units of an organization. Five variations were the most evident: lateral cross-unit advancement, a generalist's track, the extra-hierarchial leap, the dual career ladder for professionals, and the high-level analyst pattern. Through these routes a manager could reach levels of significant importance in a relatively brief period after entering the organization at the entry level. Unlike the traditional organizations, entry could take place at any level, not just the low-level occupations.

While high-technology firms seem to emphasize merit over seniority as a basis for promotion, at this time it is not clear whether they do so because they are newer, or because they grew too fast to develop talent internally, or because there is something else unique about such firms. Also, even a growing high-technology company must face a need to rationalize personnel practices and procedures at some point and to reduce turnover, even if solely for the purpose of restricting the loss of proprietary information.

Equal Employment Opportunity

Federal, state, and in some cases, local statutes prohibit discrimination in employment for certain protected classes of employees. The major federal laws are: Title VII of the 1964 Civil Rights Act, the Equal Pay Act of 1963, and the Age Discrimination in Employment Act of 1967. The main groups protected by these statutes are women, racial minorities, and workers over the age of 40, although the laws also cover religious and political minorities, handicapped employees, veterans of the armed forces, and other groups. The Age Discrimination Act has generally been applied to employers who have denied workers a benefit or employment on the basis of age. These laws, and the voluntary efforts of companies, have had a great effect on the careers of women and members of minority groups (mainly blacks and Hispanics).

The advances made by women and nonwhites in the managerial occupations have been at the entry- and mid-level positions. As indicated, it is more common for women than men to become managers in internal promotions, possibly reflecting that employers are unwilling to take a risk until a woman has proven herself on the job.

The situation for senior management or upper-level executives has been conspicuously poor. Only 2 percent of 1,362 top executives surveyed in 1986 by Korn/Ferry, an executive search firm, were women; likewise, only 2.5 percent of AT&T's topmost level of executives were women in 1985, whereas 38.7 percent of first-level managers were women (Hymowitz and Schellhardt 1986). Women have had noticeably better success in reaching upper echelon positions in some industries like banking and the not-for-profit sector (Odendahl, Boris, and Daniels 1985, 3) but still occupy a disproportionally small number of upper management positions. Blacks have had greater success in government service than elsewhere (Chicago Urban League 1979), although the absolute number of senior black executives remains low.

If there is a bright spot in this picture, it is in the very small firms, frequently ones that have been started by women and minority group members.

To obtain equal employment objectives, large firms have established voluntary programs containing goals and timetables. (See the description of such programs in Shaeffer and Lynton 1982). However, most of these efforts have been concentrated at the entry- and middle-level managerial positions. Progress beyond these levels has been difficult for reasons that are not entirely known. Some contend that it is the values of white males who constitute the dominant coalition in most of these organizations. This explanation holds that initial resistance to females and nonwhites has been only temporarily overcome and has been followed by even stronger and more subtle forms of discrimination (Harlan and Weiss 1982). Another explanation is that the major techniques for achieving equal opportunity—job sharing, flexible scheduling, and day care— are better suited to production employees than to managers for whom a full-time commitment is usually required. Still another explanation holds that blacks and women are leaving organizations because they are unwilling to make the necessary sacrifices to advance in this competitive arena. Women, it is being suggested, are finding that the demands of a career interfere with their respon-sibilities as wives, and mothers, and blacks are said to be impatient (Irons and Moore 1985). At the moment, no way exists to determine the magnitude of voluntary departures; however, it should be remembered that it has been com-monplace in other occupations for women and nonwhites to avoid situations in which they anticipate being treated unfairly.

In several studies of the salaries of graduates from top schools of business administration (reviewed below), starting salaries of men and women tended to be about equal. Yet, in one study that examined salaries a few years after gradua-tion, women tended to earn less than men (Devanna 1984; Strober 1982). While some of this difference may be due to overt acts of pay discrimination, there is also evidence that women may tend to congregate in lower paying industries or occupational specialties. In addition, at the time of this study, women have accumulated less experience in the labor force, having left their jobs to have and raise children.

Open Internal Markets and Career Planning

As part of their equal opportunity programs, some companies have sought to expand promotion opportunities beyond traditional boundaries and, in the pro-cess, create new internal job ladders and more open internal labor markets. Managerial employees, however, are less likely than nonmanagerial employees to be part of such internal promotion programs. For example, a 1985 survey of chemical companies with internal promotion systems found that only 39 per-cent covered managerial positions (*Chicago Chemistry* 1985, 2).

An important by-product of the open internal market was the career plan-ning movement that became very popular during the 1970s. Corporate-spon-sored career planning encompasses a variety of programs and practices that represent corporate involvement in the assessment and obtainment of career objectives by individuals (Walker and Gutteridge 1979). Employee career as-sessment programs, workshops, and counseling allowed individuals to think about their career wants and opportunities. Employer-controlled career pro-grams were a management tool to help the organization identify its future human resource needs and to develop key people by coordinating job assign-ments and training programs accordingly.

Career planning during the 1970s was intended to deal with the expecta-tions of a better educated work force and the special needs of the increased number of women and nonwhites. Oddly enough, however, the concept remained popular in the 1980s despite the previously described changes in the status of middle managers. One hypothesis is that companies continued to provide career advice because they would have great difficulty attracting the best talent if prospective employees felt that an employer demonstrated little concern for their development. Another explanation is that career planning gives employees a more realistic understanding of their situation and thus permits them to deal better with uncertainty. By encouraging employees to take responsibility for their careers, the firm emphasizes a new social contract that no longer promises security or expects loyalty.

With regard to company-directed planning, the trends seem to be in two directions. For companies that have such systems, the emphasis has become more utilitarian by coordinating the assessment, performance appraisal, and development of managers with management succession activities for an elite group of junior managers (Walker 1983, 5/21). Other companies either adopted a more laissez-faire approach to the development of personnel or shifted the focus away from corporate-wide programs to the level of the operating units. They found that even an elaborate career planning program could not anticipate the types of managers they would need after significant restructuring or change in orientation.

Methodology of Controlling White-collar Employment

Even though unemployment among managers is more common in the 1980s, firms are still reluctant to use involuntary reductions in staff as the major means of trimming labor costs. During the 1980–83 recession, companies relied first on wage freezes, compensation cuts, and other ways of controlling labor costs short of actual terminations before first furloughing, then terminating employees (Bureau of National Affairs 1982, 1983a, 1983b, and 1984). Postrecessionary cutbacks have been achieved through the following techniques used separately or as part of a planned program of retrenchment: hiring freezes; time off without pay; layoffs by attrition; voluntary separation and early retirement programs that may or may not have given employees special incentives to leave (Hewitt Associates 1986); programs of job or position elimination, usually conducted in combination with efforts to increase white-collar productivity (see, for example, Bolte 1984); intrafirm transfers; and retraining efforts.

As a group, and compared with other groups that have faced abrupt dislocations, managers have been treated relatively well by their former employers. Most firms have followed policies of indemnification for some of the following reasons: (1) there is a conscious attempt to avoid legal actions by disgruntled employees; (2) such a strategy preserves the morale of surviving employees; and (3) it tells prospective employees that, even though layoffs might be necessary for economic reasons, the company will treat them generously and fairly.

Still, many managers adversely affected by decisions to curtail or reconfigure employment patterns felt that they had been treated shabbily. One complaint commonly heard was that the company failed to plan adequately for or give adequate notice of the change.

To date, we know very little about the consequences of alternative methods for reducing the number of managers. Anecdotally, however, the data suggest that experience with such programs has varied widely. For example, Owens-Illinois in 1985 made early retirement available to all employees in its corporate headquarters irrespective of the length of their service. Sears, in contrast, anticipated that 400 managerial employees might leave under its 1979 program of early retirement, instead of the four times that number who accepted it. Xerox found that it had to offer additional incentives to induce employees it did not want to lose from availing themselves of a program.

One increasingly popular technique for lowering head counts, that of hiring temporary and contingency employees, has not been widely used to reduce the number of managerial positions within companies (Bureau of National Affairs 1986a) because such positions are not easily staffed on a part-time basis and because a manager needs to develop strong identification with the employer to perform his or her duties. Some professions, such as bookkeeping, seem to be the most suitable current candidates for temporary employment. However, there is much speculation about the future growth of temporary employment and subcontracted staff services and how they might reduce the demand for managers in a wider set of jobs (Bennett 1987).

Formal severance plans are quite common in American business and industry for managerial employees and professionals (Bureau of National Affairs 1986b, 5). Of particular interest has been the lucrative severance arrangements to top executives made popular in hostile mergers and takeovers. The compensation consulting firm, Towers, Perrin, Forster & Crosby, estimates that in 1986 almost 40 percent of the 100 largest industrial companies offered key executives income protections from changes in control of the firm, so-called golden parachutes. This compares with less than 5 percent in 1981 (*Wall Street Journal,* August 14, 1987). Other sources claim that golden parachute contracts have become a widespread practice and can be found at 1,500 corporations (as cited in Davidson 1985, 1). Recognizing the unfairness of such practices, a few companies have extended such indemnifications to middle- and lower-level managers—so called silver and tin parachutes.

Employer assistance in the job search of discharged and laid-off employees (commonly called outplacement services) is becoming a common component of personnel practices for top- and middle-level managers. About one-third of the firms providing such assistance utilize outside consultants, and slightly more than half these firms limit such services to senior managers (Bureau of National Affairs 1986b, 13).

The Future for Employment Security

Despite the long-term and recent declines in managerial employment security, there are those who argue (and with some merit) that American business in the 1980s is not the "lean" organization it claims to be (Gordon 1984a). During the recession and the recovery, the ratio of supervisors to production employees, as well as the proportion of total employment in the central administrative offices of businesses, increased instead of decreased. Thus, even in this so-called new era, it appears that managers still enjoy comparatively high degrees of job security. Another way of looking at the data, however, is to say that there is much potential for further changes in employment practices.

Considering that a large number of younger workers are continuing to seek employment as managers and administrators, is it proper for us to worry about a potential oversupply or glut of managers in a few years? Of course, such predictions can never be made with certainty, but the real problem does not appear to be one of oversupply. Employment in smaller and nontraditional settings is likely to grow fast enough to avoid it. Rather, the bigger problem is meeting the expectation of younger managers for desirable or glamorous management positions or expectations for promotions. This has already created a demand for education and training as one means of securing preferred career paths.

EDUCATION, TRAINING, AND PREPARATION

While there is evidence that the largest organizations have been requiring a college degree as a precondition of employment and promotion since the 1950s (Warner and Abegglen 1955, 31) as few as 17 percent of all managers in 1960 had attended four or more years of college. By 1983, the percentage of managers with a college education reached 46 percent (Young and Hayghe 1984, 48), implying that a college education was becoming a prerequisite for a career in business or industry, especially in the large firms.

As significant has been the dramatic growth of programs of study in business, management, or what is generally called business administration at institutions of higher education (Cheit 1985). Of all bachelors' degrees awarded in 1985, slightly more than 20 percent, or 66,500, were in business or management. This represents a doubling of business program graduates in the past 20 years. Even more impressive, however, has been the ninefold increase since 1955 in the number of earned masters of business administration (MBA) degrees. A degree in business has been transformed from a helpful credential in a business career to a requirement for advancement and promotion.

By some accounts, presumably because of salary competition for college graduates with business training, companies are beginning to shift their hiring preferences to undergraduate majors in the liberal arts and humanities. Unfortunately, there are no comprehensive data on college placements and business hires to test this assertion. If liberal arts is going to replace technical training as the preferred preparation for business at entry-level positions, firms will have to accept the added costs of training new hires and higher levels of turnover among younger workers. Given these costs, some firms may favor the experienced managers now available in the market. At least one major bank, Citicorp, has made such a shift in its hiring preferences.

Following the pattern of a growth industry, business education has at-

tracted many new entrants and has become highly competitive. In 1982, for
instance, 544 institutions awarded masters' degrees in business administration
or its equivalent. Competition has motivated schools to differentiate their products and to tap new pools of potential students (see, for example, Fowler 1984).
One of the more significant developments has been the rapid spread of executive
MBA programs, which allow employed managers to obtain an MBA degree by
going to school on weekends or during the work week on a release-time basis.
The Graduate Management Admission Council has identified 85 executive
MBA programs among accredited schools of business and management. Enrollment in these programs is increasingly made up of managers who have a technical background or managers who are employed in the nonbusiness institutions
in which the number of managers has increased dramatically during the past
decade.

As the market in executive education matured, schools have emphasized
nondegree, short-term programs for employed managers. The Conference
Board, which for several years compiled data on such programs in the area of
general management, found only three in existence prior to 1950, 17 programs
operating in 1954, 32 in 1957, and 42 in 1969 (West and Sheriff 1969, 1). For
1986, *Bricker's International Directory of University Executive Programs* (Pond
1986) identifies 69 programs in the area of general management offered by
universities. Estimated enrollment in all general and functional university programs equalled 12,500 in 1984 and 14,100 in 1986 (Pond 1987, 4).

While institutions of higher learning have been willing to satisfy the market
demand for business education, the role of colleges and universities in the
preparation of managers has long been controversial. During the 1950s, business schools were criticized for offering narrow and vocationally oriented curricula that trained people for particular entry-level positions, and for neglecting the
production of new knowledge that would have helped to integrate business
school faculty into the academic community. Special reports by commissions
funded by the Carnegie Corporation and the Ford Foundation outlined programs for improving the academic content of management education (Pierson
and others 1959 and Gordon and Howell 1959, respectively).

Judging from today's critics, it would appear that universities have been too
successful in upgrading the scholastic side of business education. Widespread
criticism contends that business education is not relevant to the needs of practi-
tioners, that it is too theoretical and abstract, and that business schools—faculty
and curricula—have not kept up with the significant changes that have taken
place in the world of business (Business-Higher Education Forum 1985; Cheit
1985; La Force and Novelli 1985; and Miles 1985). However valid these
complaints, the demand for relevance and usefulness undoubtedly also reflects
the growing competition for employment among managers and the employers'
ability to capitalize on the available supply.

Business's dissatisfaction with formal degree programs may well be one
reason why the number of corporate-affiliated academic programs have grown
in large companies. Eurich's survey (1985, 85–122) of 18 corporate colleges

found that they emphasized curricula from management training to functional specialties and from engineering to financial services.

Nondegree training and educational activities within corporations for managers have also increased and have undergone significant changes in emphasis. In a survey of 218 major companies, Lusterman (1985) found that over the past five years nearly two-thirds had expanded their education and training staffs in the area of managerial training. The survey concludes that the cause of this expansion was a growing recognition that managers needed new competencies in the face of changing technologies and new business strategies. Similar to developments in university-based programs, the emerging emphasis in company training activities appears to be on relevancy and usefulness. This meets the needs of employed managers who are endeavoring to remain abreast of newer developments and competitive in their careers.

Eurich's (1985) study for the Carnegie Foundation for the Advancement of Teaching found that most major corporations sponsor in-house or short-term programs in subjects pertaining to the management of people, time. production, and operations. He argues that training in such skills is needed because college and formal schooling do not emphasize them. Larger companies, of course, have long trained workers in these skills, but newer efforts are more systematic.

More significant, however, is the trend toward increased efforts to coordinate training activities with the future human resources needs of the firm. Developments that reflect this trend include the growth of courses to bring about changes in organizational culture, necessitated by the adoption of new business strategies; wider use of personal development planning which forecasts the educational needs of managers on particular career paths; a greater emphasis on activities intended for lower- and middle-managers. Firms appear to be moving toward a model associated with IBM, in which the training received by employees at one occupational level or job builds on prior training.

Most managerial training takes place at the entry level and is conducted informally on the job. In a few noteworthy instances, formal entry-level training programs are conducted by companies. These tend to be highly selective and often constitute a credential in certain industries or specialties (for example, see *Business Week's Guide to Careers* 1985, for a list of the top 10 programs conducted by companies).

COMPENSATION

Americans are fascinated by the earnings of the relatively few people who are the senior executives in large organizations. Compensation for these executives tends to be set on an individual basis. Because managers at this level are highly mobile, boards of directors have historically been concerned with maintaining competitive salaries; however, more recently, attention has focused on using compensation to motivate corporate performance. It is commonplace for compensation arrangements to be codified in an executive's individual employment contract.

For managers below the top executives in medium and large enterprises, salaries traditionally have been set by compensation systems, broadly similar in concept to the ones used for hourly personnel. Both use systems of job evaluations and external salary validations and tend to treat workers as members of classes or grades, although variations within grades also exist. One of the more popular of these is the Hay System, which Hay Associates claims sets the salaries for the employees—managers included—in 200 of the *Fortune* 500 companies.

Smaller firms and those without a formal job evaluation system tend to set salary relationships among managers on the basis of the "whole job" or job title instead of its component parts and tend to pay the going rate for a job. Typically, such a firm might subscribe to a wage survey conducted by a trade association or local employer's group.

Salaries of managers tend to be heavily influenced by the tax code. In a straightforward way, the code sets marginal tax rates. However, tax laws, regulations, and judicial interpretations are also extremely important in defining a significant portion of the compensation package pertaining to long-term incentives and pensions.

Looking at the 1970s, two opposite trends in compensation programs developed as a result of the prevailing economic forces. Lengthy and severe periods of inflation were a great leveling influence on pay decisions, as higher earning workers were thrown into higher tax brackets and the amount of increase available for rewarding merit was overshadowed by the size of cost-of-living increases. Compensation systems sought ways to protect salary positions on an after-tax basis.

The second trend, noted by Ochsner (1984), was the shift toward the service economy. Compensation expenses tend to be a greater share of total revenue in service firms compared to asset intensive firms. This led to a search for pay-for-performance plans in industries where productivity is difficult to measure. Profit-sharing plans became more popular, especially in smaller companies, both as an alternative to a pension program and to allow new companies to limit their direct labor costs. The service economy also employs proportionately more educated workers. This led to a greater interest in more sophisticated compensation programs and efforts to customize programs for specialized groups of employees.

By the 1980s, the major factors influencing compensation practices were a desire to control the fixed costs of labor throughout business and industry, not just the service sector. Decentralization and the high number of mergers and acquisitions motivated firms to move to multidivisional pay plans, thereby customizing practices and pay levels to the needs of specific businesses (Prokesch 1985).

To control fixed costs, firms sought to slow the rate of growth in wages and were helped in this regard by the increase of redundant managers. While, as noted, some organizations used wage cuts and freezes during the recession, recovery did not bring an end to such practices. Perhaps the most visible example of such behavior took place in the securities industries where firms continued to institute wage cuts (Retkwa 1984)—and in one highly visible incident in 1984 at AT&T (Barnes 1984) where the salaries of 114,000 managerial employees were frozen.

Firms also sought to link compensation programs to performance, preferably individual performance instead of group or corporate performance. Thus by 1986, according to the American Productivity Center/American Compensation Association's survey of 1,600 companies (O'Dell 1987, 59), managers and supervisors were the most likely group to be included in a firm's program of individualized incentives. Moreover, 40 percent of the firms that increased use of individualized compensation programs in the prior five years reported a higher use with managers and supervisors; 51 percent of the firms planning to use individual incentives over the next five years will use them more for managers and supervisors, and less for other occupational groups. Only about 12 percent of the managers were covered by corporatewide bonus plans.

No one can tell if these trends will continue; compensation practices have tended to be cyclical. However, at least for the immediate future, the implication of current trends has less to do with the level of earnings for managers and more with the role of pay in the conduct of job responsibilities. Whether or not employers will find a way to monitor job performance fairly and accurately, managers will face increased scrutiny on the job. Pay systems will reinforce the higher levels of competitiveness now characteristic of managerial employment.

Components and Levels

Managerial compensation in the United States consists of a base salary, fringe benefits, and long-term incentive, such as a bonus or profit-sharing arrangement either in cash or in stock. The size of the bonus as a percentage of salary tends to be greater for top executives than it is for middle managers.

Top executives earn enormous amounts in the United States. A chief executive of a very large firm with $1 to $5 billion in revenue will earn on average about $700,000 a year. The chief executive of a company with $10 to $25 million—possibly one hundred times smaller—will have average earnings of $143,000. According to one study, salaries alone have increased almost 400 percent since the late 1960s (Bennett 1986).

In the 1960s and 1970s, the difference in pay between managers and blue-collar and other production employees eroded and were a major source of managerial dissatisfaction. Hay Associates (Sym-Smith and Riordan 1980) reported that the increase in the base salary for blue-collar workers exceeded the growth in managerial salaries by about 10 percent; inflation and taxation exacerbated this compression of the wage structure. Most observers attributed this compression to the declining power and status of managers within organizations. Another possible cause may be the declining productivity of managers relative to other groups of employees.

In the 1980s, salary compression between managers and nonmanagers was much less of a problem, probably due to the increased use of bonus and other performance-based incentives for managers.

A Bureau of Labor Statistics study of fringe benefit coverage (1986a) shows that most professional and administrative employees enjoy about the same types of fringe benefit programs as other employees, reflecting, to some extent, the practice of extending fringe benefit programs to the white-collar work force after establishing them for the production employees. The process has not been symmetrical, however, as traditionally managers have enjoyed perquisites that have not been extended to the nonmanagerial group. Recent evidence (O'Dell 1987) suggests that some managerial perquisites, such as a car, reserved parking, or a private dining room, are becoming less prevalent, not so much to control costs as to lessen the perceived status superiority of managers at the work place.

Determinants

In the wake of the publicity received by the size of top executives' earnings and the development of lucrative golden parachutes for executives, there has been a big increase in research on compensation for top managers. Most of this work is very theoretical and still controversial.

More straightforward has been the study of compensation for experienced middle managers, about whom research has documented relationships between salaries and the following aspects of supply and demand. On the demand side, the following correlates have been observed: (1) the size of the company (possibly as a proxy for complexity) (see Personick and Barsky 1982, and the discussion in Ciscel and Carroll 1980); (2) organizational profitability (an expression of ability to pay); (3) industry of the firm, representing interindustry differences in the marginal productivity of employees; and (4) whether or not the firm is unionized with unionized firms paying managers about 4 percent more (Antos 1983).

On the supply side, these studies show that salaries vary according to: (1) the age of the worker; (2) his or her tenure with the firm or experience in the labor market; and (3) as discussed in the section on equal employment opportunity, the sex of the employee with women earning less than men. What is interesting about these factors is that they are broadly similar to the supply and demand determinants of earnings for nonmanagerial jobs.

For entry-level managers, there have been a few studies of the correlates of earnings for graduating MBA candidates (see Langer 1978; Reder 1978; Strober 1982). Interestingly, they agree that while salaries in certain industries tend to be higher than in others, a student's academic performance does not influence salaries, while the market rewards students who have prior work experience. It is not known whether work experience is valued in its own right or that students are receiving a premium for being older and possibly more mature.

By rewarding experience in the occupation and length of service with a firm, compensation practices have historically played an important role in inhibiting voluntary mobility—a practice usually called the golden handcuffs. As more firms award annual increases based on merit or performance, the strength of experience and service as determinants of salary will lessen—but not end. For one thing, performance-based compensation continues to suffer from several well-known deficiencies, including the difficulty of measuring performance for jobs below the top managerial positions and the inadequacy of such plans during slack periods. But the greater pressure for keeping annual increments as a significant albeit lessened determinant of pay should come from competitive pressures in the labor market a few years from now. At that time, firms will recognize the high costs of replacing younger managers who may decide to leave after receiving transferable skills in company-sponsored training programs and new legislation is passed that vests pensions sooner and may make them portable.

REACTIONS OF MANAGERIAL EMPLOYEES

Even though most American managers have accepted discharge or the redefinition of the employment security without serious protest, some have not. Those protesting their treatment have acted as individuals, relying on various forms of self-help, and have taken such steps after adverse decisions already have been made.

Self-help

The major weapon available to displaced and aggrieved managers has been the courts. Women and members of minorities, as discussed, can challenge personnel decisions under various civil rights laws barring discrimination in employment. White males, in comparison, have relied on statutory bars against discrimination on the basis of age and the emerging legal doctrine of wrongful discharge.

Since 1978, the Age Discrimination in Employment Act of 1967 has prohibited discrimination in employment because of age for persons between 40 and 70. It now protects all workers over 40. Between fiscal year 1979 and 1983, the number of age discrimination complaints filed with the Equal Employment Opportunity Commission increased from 3,097 to 9,207 (Equal Employment Opportunity Commission 1984), and undoubtedly has continued to increase in the wake of the postrecessionary realignment of managerial employment. Unfortunately, we have no detailed records on the number of those filing complaints with the Commission who simultaneously pursued their complaints through the federal courts or the number who went directly to the court. In one study of 153 such federal court cases involving age discrimination, Schuster and Miller (1984) found that 57 percent involved alleged acts of age discrimination against white men in professional and managerial occupations. Employers, however, won in 63 percent of these cases for reasons that are not yet clear from this and other research projects.

There has been a spate of litigation by managers and others protesting breaches in their written and unwritten contracts of employment. The legal theory of these claims is that an employer that dismisses an employee without cause violates the terms of either a written or implied employment contract. Written contracts of employment are enforceable in the United States. However, they apply to only the top executives in about 50 percent of the larger companies; a few other managers whose work may be proprietary in nature such as accountants, lawyers, and professionals; and those engaged in research and sales (Muth 1984). Historically, companies have preferred a written contract because it could be used to detail performance standards in one's job, restrict the future mobility of an employee, or indemnify the company from certain types of mistakes. Given the turmoil of the past few years, some believe that displaced middle managers may be trying to guarantee through a written contract some of the benefits, treatment, and protections denied them in their prior jobs. Employers, however, are reluctant to make this a standard practice because such guarantees are not in their interest.

In the absence of written contracts, the courts and several state legislatures have accepted the notion that an implicit contract of employment may still govern such aspects as termination for cause and other conditions of employment. A growing number of suits are being filed seeking to indemnify employees for discharges executed without cause or breaches of promises made to employees either orally, in business communications and booklets, or through past behavior.

So far the concept of rights under implicit contracts has varied state to state and has produced contradictory judicial decisions. For example, federal appeals courts in New York and Washington, D.C., have taken opposite positions on whether an oral promise of lifetime employment to an executive is valid. (See *Ohanian* v. *Avis Rent A Car System, Inc.* CA 2 No. 85-7284, Nov. 25, 1985 and *Hodge* v. *Evans Financial Corp.;* CA DC, No. 84-5224, Dec. 3, 1985.) The Supreme Court has not dealt with the issue directly. Many observers believe that a national law in this area has been unlikely because its major constituency is the white, male managerial and professional employee under the age of 40, a group clearly in the minority and too well off to require protection in the labor market.

Collective Action and Unionization

Professional associations and societies for managers are very popular in various subfields of management expertise, but they are not aimed at improving the economic interests of managers by altering the terms and conditions of their employment. Some associations, like the American Society of Personnel Administrators, are interested in advancing knowledge in a particular field. Others resemble casual interest groups and even buying cooperatives. For instance, the Association of MBA Executives, Inc. offers its members price discounts on life insurance, business publications, auto rentals, and credit cards, as well as information on career developments, in exchange for an annual fee.

Within some companies, managers may belong to employee associations that may or may not include nonmanagerial employees. Most of these are extensions of their companies. However, in a few instances, employees have formed independent affinity groups. Generally, these are social groups, but employment-related issues are discussed. Associations of black managerial employees at both IBM and Xerox are examples of such organizations.

Managerial employee associations are perhaps most common in the public sector. Many of the groups labeled as associations are actually unions that bargain with their employers.

Trade unionism among managers is rare in the United States. One-fifth of the nonagricultural work force is unionized, but only about one in ten managers is a member of a union. (Gifford 1986, 67 reporting data from the CPS; alternatively, Freeman and Medoff 1979, 163, estimate that about 6 percent of all managers belong to unions.) In comparison, union membership among workers with professional specialties—engineers, doctors, and lawyers—totaled about 28 percent. Most unionized managers are employed in the public sector.

Historically, apart from the public sector (managers who generally work in positions covered by civil service and tend to be members of employee associations anyway), American managers have had a very low level of interest in collective action and unionization. In the public sector, managers joined unions to obtain wage increases during inflationary times or as a reaction to the unionization of their subordinates who challenged managerial authority at the work place. Most success in organizing has taken place among first-line supervisors in the public sector in such occupations as police sergeants and school principals. (In 1986, for example, the Salaried Employees of North America, a division of the United Steelworkers Union, organized 410 career managers in the City of Boston's police and fire departments and city hospitals.)

Attempts to organize managerial employees have traditionally faced three serious obstacles—the basic hostility of American managers to unions, restrictive public policy, and an apathetic labor movement. Managers' resistance to unionization is partly ideological and partly very practical. Ideologically, American managers have long held strong views about the role and consequences of unions in the operation of business and society. Managers, perhaps even more so than other U.S. workers, are extremely independent and attempts to organize them must overcome significant ideological obstacles.

Supervisors and their superiors do not have a protected right to organize in the private sector under the National Labor Relations Act. This means that a manager can be fired and otherwise discriminated against in his or her employment for participating in a union. Interestingly, the Act specifically excludes only supervisors. Exclusion of managerial employees has come about through a series of decisions by the National Labor Relations Board on the theory that an employer should expect undivided loyalty from those employees who develop and execute its policy [*Ford Motor Company,* 66 NLRB 1317 (1976)].

In the *Yeshiva University* decision (1980), the Supreme Court expanded the scope of the managerial exclusion by ruling that college professors functioned in a managerial capacity and thus are not protected by the Act. In another case, *North Shore University Hospital,* the U.S. Court of Appeals for the Second Circuit applied similar logic when it prohibited an association of professionals (who are protected by the Act) from serving as a bargaining agent because supervisors participated in the governance of the association (Lee and Parker 1987).

Reactions to the *Yeshiva* doctrine have argued that the Court's decision fails to recognize the reality that serious industrial relations problems can result when workers who want to organize are denied the opportunity. More important, as Begin and Lee (1987) have argued, the Court's definition of a manager incorrectly lumps together all managers in terms of generic managerial actions, even if they actually have very little responsibility and accountability, and fails to recognize the close bonds that exist between the loyalties and values of supervisors in traditional professions.

Another legal obstacle is found in the tax law. As a result of changes in the tax code in 1984 and 1986, contributions for unionized managers to health, welfare, and pension funds are not tax deductible unless there is a bona-fide, arm's-length relationship with the company. Practically speaking, this means that exclusive units of managers within a company are not very likely.

Considering the values of American managers and the obstacles posed by the law, the relative disinterest of unions in the sector is understandable. Moreover, it would make for a very awkward internal problem if a union sought to represent the same people that rank and file union members identified as the source of their problems.

The interesting question at this junction, of course, is whether or not the changes in the employment conditions of managers in the 1980s and the declining fortunes of American unions might result in increased trade unionism for managers, particularly in the private sector. Managers would make good candidates for organizing looking just at their experiences of declining job security, arbitrary treatment, especially resulting in wrongful discharge, increasing expectations of performance, loss of authority in a era of participative management, and increasing levels of job dissatisfaction. In addition, managerial unions might also appear to be an appropriate vehicle for addressing such problems as stress and other special health needs, or issues relating to gender, such as pay discrimination due to biased systems of job evaluation (a concept called comparable worth) (see Aronowitz 1984).

In an effort to judge the sentiments toward unionization of all workers, including managers, the American Federation of Labor-Congress of Industrial Organization (AFL-CIO) commissioned a public opinion survey in 1984. Distributions to responses to several questions on unionism and other forms of mutual assistance are given in Table 3.5.* As expected, of the different occupa-

---

*I am grateful to the AFL-CIO for making these data available.

Table 3.5 Opinions of nonunionized workers on the desirability of joining unions and other forms of mutual assistance by occupation

Do you think employees are more successful in getting their problems resolved with their employer when they bring these problems up as a group or as individuals?

	Managers	Clerical	Sales	Skilled	Unskilled	Service workers
As a group	34.6	40.5	49.4	50.7	62.0	49.0
As individuals	54.4	47.1	39.6	38.2	31.0	38.1
Makes no difference	6.0	6.4	3.2	4.7	3.6	7.7
Not sure	5.0	6.0	7.8	6.4	3.3	5.2
Total*	100.0%	100.0%	100.0%	100.0%	100.0%	100.0%

Do you agree or disagree with the statement that your employer is genuinely concerned about you and other employees?

	Managers	Clerical	Sales	Skilled	Unskilled	Service workers
Agree strongly	42.8	47.8	45.5	38.5	38.7	34.0
Agree somewhat	42.8	27.5	32.5	43.6	33.2	38.7
Disagree somewhat	11.6	9.4	14.3	6.8	14.6	18.6
Disagree strongly	2.8	14.1	7.8	10.5	12.4	7.7
Not sure	—	1.2	—	0.7	1.1	1.0
Total*	100.0%	100.0%	100.0%	100.0%	100.0%	100.0%

Would you prefer your present job to be union or nonunion?

	Managers	Clerical	Sales	Skilled	Unskilled	Service workers
Union	14.2	18.6	24.0	21.6	35.4	37.6
Nonunion	83.3	76.0	71.4	76.0	60.6	53.6
Not sure	2.5	5.4	2.4	2.4	4.0	8.8
Total*	100.0%	100.0%	100.0%	100.0%	100.0%	100.0%

How interested would you be in joining a local employee organization that provided lobbying for employee interests in legislative and policy decisions at the local and national levels?

	Managers	Clerical	Sales	Skilled	Unskilled	Service workers
Very interested	11.6	12.2	4.5	12.2	19.3	16.0
Fairly interested	26.7	25.9	30.5	30.1	24.1	33.5
Not too interested	30.8	26.6	39.0	23.3	34.7	24.2
Not at all interested	30.2	32.9	26.0	32.1	18.2	22.2
Not sure	0.6	2.4	—	2.4	3.6	4.1
Total*	100.0%	100.0%	100.0%	100.0%	100.0%	100.0%

How interested would you be in joining a local employee organization that provided you with medical or dental insurance, day care services, legal services at reduced rates, a discount on consumer goods?

Percent stating they were interested or very interested in

	Managers	Clerical	Sales	Skilled	Unskilled	Service workers
Medical and dental	61.9	60.2	73.4	67.2	75.9	74.2
Day care services	34.6	33.4	38.3	37.8	40.5	42.8
Legal services	57.5	50.4	66.9	54.4	62.0	64.9
Discounted con- sumer goods	54.7	50.6	63.6	54.1	60.9	60.8

Source: Louis Harris and Associates, "Market Feasibility Study 843008," mimeo; used with permission of the AFL-CIO.

*Total may not equal 100% due to rounding.

tional groups surveyed, managers showed the least desire to unionize and the most trust in their employer. However, the proportion of those who hold opposite views is not small. Moreover, there appears to be considerable support among managers for joining an organization of employees that would advance their interests and increase their economic well-being through actions taken away from the work place. In terms of their support for such actions, managers are very similar to other types of workers.

While the labor movement has not yet made the decision to target managers for membership, and such a decision is unlikely in the near future, important changes are taking place with possible implications for the unionization of managers. The first, and perhaps most significant development, is the creation of associate union memberships. An associate member joins a union as he or she would a club or association of people with similar interests. Such a member is not employed in a position currently covered by a collective bargaining contract. Associate members receive services for their dues, possibly including legal advice and representation, health and welfare benefits, and travel agency services. The expectation, for which there is not yet evidence, is that the associate members can be converted to regular members (AFL-CIO Committee on the Evolution of Work 1985). Some union leaders believe that the loose bond of the associate membership is the proper way to organize managers interested in mutual assistance groups, because of that group's traditional opposition to unionism per se and their highly independent nature. Managerial unionism also should receive some impetus from recently expanded efforts to organize white-collar workers and professionals in the financial, health, and high-technology industries. One organization that is focusing on managers is the Professional Guild, Local 525 of the Office and Professional Employees International Union. This small union is seeking to offer health, welfare, and pension benefits to managers who hold guild-like jobs. People working as plant or store managers or as managers of data processing departments, for instance, can have limited attachment to their organization and move among different employers in similar jobs. This is a group that also may find associate membership attractive. All in all, however, a big increase in managerial unionization particularly in the private sector is not likely. Judging from the values of managers discussed in the next section, large-scale collective action is also a remote prospect.

ATTITUDES, VALUES, AND IDEOLOGY

The problems facing American managers have not produced a group, class, or political response primarily because of their strong and long-held beliefs in individualism and economic rationality (Ward 1964). This is not to say that managers find no shame in unemployment. However, their ideology allows them to rationalize layoffs as economic necessities caused by events beyond their control, and not as a reflection of the quality of their own work. This is combined with a positive attitude about the future based on their abilities to succeed.

Recent polls confirm the continued strength of these beliefs. In a *New York Times* September 1986 survey of graduates of major schools of business, 81 percent stated that it is as possible now as it was when they finished school to start out poor in this country, work hard in business, and become rich. A Harris poll of mostly employed executives (as reported in Nussbaum 1986, 49) showed that 81 percent agreed with the statement "Cutting back on salaried employees can get rid of a lot of dead wood." Seventy-two percent of respondents believed that they could get an equivalent or better job if they were laid off. Of course, the attitudes of unemployed managers might be considerably different.

Employee attitudes toward loyalty also seem to have undergone a transformation. Sixty-five percent in the Harris poll felt employees were more loyal to their companies ten years ago. Support for, and commitment to, organizational goals, strategies, philosophies, and policies appear to be declining, especially among younger managers, perhaps because they have not yet achieved senior leadership positions (Heidrick and Struggles 1985, 13). Looking to the future, in unpublished results of a 1987 Business World Survey of holders of the MBA degree conducted by *The New York Times,* about half of those who had an opinion expected they would not be with the same employer ten years from now. Most felt that it would be their choice to leave in order to respond to career opportunities and not the boss's decision to terminate them. In lieu of loyalty to one's employer based on economic self-interest, managers appear to be emphasizing loyalty to one's family, friends, and career, in apparent efforts to maintain their psychological equilibrium.

It is unknown at this juncture how the motivation of managers will evolve. Managers as agents, a concept that has traditionally motivated strong identification with the employer, may be giving way to other motivations. Among these is professionalism. Both managers and organizations have been able to rationalize the changes taking place by claiming that managers are professionals. Clearly, managers are not professionals in the purest use of that term, although professionals of course can work within organizations. Unlike members of a traditional profession, managers have no creed or standards of ethical practice, do not control entry into the occupation, and do not enjoy extensive degrees of discretion in the performance of their duties. Professionalism in management probably has more to do with the current emphasis on quality and performance and a firm's desire to encourage pride in performance by making good job performance its own reward. By emphasizing professionalism, companies may be seeking to encourage a loyalty based on professional ethics that would frown on quitting in order to work for one's competitors.

Another motivation being widely discussed is entrepreneurship. Through entrepreneurship, the onus for success falls on the individual and minimizes the attachment between the firm and the individual. While firms may wish to instill greater entrepreneurship among their managers, the classic difficulty with this motive is that it pits one worker against another and encourages individuals to enhance their own short-run position to the possible long-run detriment of the organization. Attempts to overcome this limitation by making managers more conscious of long-run implications for the firm, such as by using long-term compensation incentives, can imply a promise of employment security if they are to be effective.

It is too soon to make any judgment on whether the professional or entrepreneurial values will remain strong, especially among those who have been hardest hit by the changes of the 1980s. As with other groups of workers, these values could give way to instrumentalism in which managers downgrade the importance of work in their lives and decrease their commitment to the company. A continued emphasis on careerism, in which long-run personal goals are stressed, could also become an important source of individual motivation.

NEW MODELS AND CONTRACTS

The modern conception of managerial careers first popularized by William H. Whyte, Jr., in *The Organization Man* (1956, recently reconsidered in Leinberger 1986) established a social contract giving employees in growing organizations a high degree of job security, status, and career advancement in exchange for commitment and loyalty. Among the alternative models now theoretically and empirically available to organizations are the following. Each deals with the way the firm will treat its employees when economic conditions require the shedding of labor.

First, there are still firms that maintain a commitment to employment security, despite major changes in their organizational structure and competitive threats. Employment contracts were achieved through voluntary means or shared sacrifice. Most of the companies that still pride themselves on such commitments have not been immune from staff reductions; instead they seem to do it through voluntary means.

Second, there is the craft model of relatively open organizations with a high degree of mobility among companies. Illustrated by several so-called high-tech companies, it is not clear that such a model is suitable for all employment relationships. This model requires employment growth in a region or industry and a relatively high degree of transferable skills. Moreover, it is also not clear that even these high-tech organizations can remain as open as their organizations mature and perhaps become rigidified. Given the high level of industry-specific knowledge and proprietary information in these settings, private employment contracts will become more prevalent.

Third, there is the current-accounts model. Under this approach, employees are treated well while they are employed. Their companies promise that if layoffs are necessary, they will be done according to some predetermined principle or formula that will reduce the unpredictability and arbitrariness of job loss and provide attractive financial indemnification to displaced employees.

Fourth, a core-periphery model (sometimes called the two-tier system), already common among nonmanagerial employees, will become more prevalent. Under this approach, the organization strikes separate contracts, representing different promises and contingencies, with various groups of employees. The company might select a cadre of key managers, develop its members, and protect them from economic downturns in exchange for loyalty. At the same time, selected members of the firm are offered a weaker association, with some even treated as agents or independent contractors while others may be employed on a temporary basis.

If the driving force behind the dissolution of the traditional model has been changes in labor and product markets, then in the future we might expect managerial employment to reflect the market and other conditions having an impact on the firm. If true, we may see greater diversity in the nature of employment conditions for managers—that is, pluralism in the relationships varying from industry to industry or firm to firm or even within a single firm.

Along with the expectations of treatment, employment relationships for managers have changed with respect to the standards of performance required and the assumptions of risks. Continued emphasis on improving white-collar productivity and controlling labor costs, combined with the excess supply of experienced managers, have resulted in higher performance requirements.

SUMMARY AND CONCLUSION

Even though American managers have been and remain an elite group of workers both economically and socially, there has been an erosion in the authority with which they manage other workers and the degree of attachment they have with an employer. These trends have been evident for some time, but were accelerated by the economic conditions of the 1980s and the policies companies implemented to deal with those conditions.

Central to those policies has been the concept of managers as a variable human resource, instead of a fixed cost of production. This shift has meant that managers face a growing vulnerability to unemployment, increased uncertainty in careers, changes in the methods of compensation to emphasize pay for performance, and more careful investments in company-sponsored training. It has also helped to develop new types of personnel practices for regulating the staffing of organizations.

To date, these changes have taken place without serious opposition from either managers themselves or government. The forces that have and should continue to mitigate against a collective response by managers are (1) the ideology and tradition of managers, (2) the effectiveness of personnel practices that seek fair treatment for redundant managers and give them the tools for making more enlightened career choices, (3) the availability of new jobs (even if they pay less and are in smaller companies), and (4) the availability of opportunities for education and retraining.

Because managers are well paid and tend to be white males, it is unlikely that government will step in to buffer this group from change. However, looking to the future, perhaps the most significant issue is the slow rate of career development for women and nonwhites, especially in top management positions. These are two groups with a history of litigation, social action, and governmental support.

REFERENCES

AFL-CIO Committee on the Evolution of Work. 1985. *The changing situation of workers and their unions*. American Federation of Labor/Congress on Industrial Organization.

Antos, J. R. 1983. Union effects on white-collar compensation. *Industrial and Labor Relations Review* 36 (3):461–79.

Aronowitz, S. 1984. ERW interview. *Employee Relations Weekly* 2, June 18:753.

Barnes, P. W. 1984. A.T. & T. is freezing salary of 114,000 in its management. *The New York Times*, July 11:1+.

Bednarzik, R. 1983. Layoffs and permanent job losses: Worker traits and cyclical patterns. *Monthly Labor Review* 106 (9):3–12.

Begin, J. P., and B. A. Lee. 1987. NLRA exclusion criteria and professional work. *Industrial Relations* 26 (1):82–95.

Bennett, A. 1986. Executives face change in awarding of pay, stock option. *The New York Times*, February 28, sect. 2:23.

_____. 1987. As big firms continue to trim their staffs, 2-tier setup emerges. *The Wall Street Journal*, May 14:1+.

Berg, E. N. 1983. Shrinking a staff, the Kodak way. *The New York Times*, September 4, sect. 3:1+.

Bolte, K. A. 1984. How one company profits by squeezing the white collar "marshmallow." *International Management Europe* 39 (June): 54–56.

Bureau of the Census. 1975. *1972 enterprise statistics, auxiliary establishment report*. Washington, D.C.: Government Printing Office.

_____. 1986. *1982 enterprise statistics, auxiliary establishment report*. Washington, D.C.: Government Printing Office.

Bureau of Labor Statistics. 1963. *Job tenure of American workers, January, 1963, Special Labor Force Report No. 36*. Washington, D.C.: Government Printing Office.

_____. 1967. *Job tenure of workers, January 1966, Special Labor Force Report No. 77*. Washington, D.C.: Government Printing Office.

_____. 1976. *Handbook of labor statistics, 1975 Reference Edition*. Washington, D.C.: Government Printing Office.

_____. 1979. *Job tenure declines as work force changes, Special Labor Force Report No. 235*. Washington, D.C.: Government Printing Office.

_____. 1981. *Employment and unemployment, a report on 1980, Special Labor Force Report 244*. Washington, D.C.: Department of Labor.

_____. 1982. *Labor force statistics derived from the current population survey: A databook, Vol. 1, Bulletin 2096*. Washington, D.C.: Government Printing Office.

_____. 1983. *Job tenure and occupational change, 1981, Bulletin 2162*. Washington, D.C.: Government Printing Office.

_____. 1984. *BLS reports on displaced workers* (news release). Washington, D.C.: U.S. Department of Labor.

_____. 1986a. *Employee benefits in medium and large firms, Bulletin 2262 (July)*. Washington, D.C.: Government Printing Office.

———. 1986b. *Reemployment increases among displaced workers (October 14)*. Washington, D.C.: U.S. Department of Labor.

Bureau of National Affairs. 1982. *White collar layoffs and cutbacks*. Washington, D.C.: Bureau of National Affairs.

———. 1983a. *Labor economic report, first half 1983*. Washington, D.C.: Bureau of National Affairs.

———. 1983b. *Layoffs, plant closings and concession bargaining, BNA's Summary Report for 1982*. Washington, D.C.: Bureau of National Affairs.

———. 1984. Labor economics. *Employee Relations Weekly*, March 5. Washington, D.C.: Bureau of National Affairs:227.

———. 1986a. *Flexible staffing (September 8)*. Washington, D.C.: Bureau of National Affairs:1–8.

———. 1986b. *Severance benefits and outplacement services, PPF Survey No. 143 (December)*. Washington, D.C.: Bureau of National Affairs.

Business-Higher Education Forum. 1985. *America's business schools: Priorities for change*. Washington, D.C.

Business Week's Guide to Careers. 1985. Spring-Summer.

Carey, M. L. 1981. Occupational employment through 1990. *Monthly Labor Review* 104 (8):42–55.

Cheit, E. F. 1985. Business schools and their critics. *California Management Review* 27 (3):43–62.

Chicago Chemistry. 1985. Newsletter of the Chicago offices of Velsicol Chemical Corporation, May:2.

Chicago Urban League. 1979. *Blacks in policy making positions in Chicago. A followup study*. Chicago: Chicago Urban League.

Ciscel, D. H., and T. M. Carroll. 1980. The determinants of executive salaries: An econometric survey. *Review of Economics and Statistics* 62 (1):7–13.

Cooper, M. R., and P. A. Gelfond. 1980. Early warning signals: Growing discontent among managers. *The Best of Business* 2 (2):3–6. Reprinted from *Business*, January–February, 1980.

Cooper, M. R., R. S. Morgan, P. M. Foley, and L. B. Kaplan. 1979. Changing employee values: Deepening discontent. *Harvard Business Review* 57 (1):117–25.

Crooks, L. A., and J. T. Campbell. 1974. *Career progress of MBAs: An exploratory study six years after graduation*. Princeton, N.J.: Educational Testing Service. Mimeo.

Davidson, K. M. 1985. *Megamergers*. Cambridge, Mass.: Ballinger Publishing Co.

Devanna, M. A. 1984. *Male/female careers—the first decade*. New York: Columbia University School of Business. Mimeo.

Dyer, L. D. 1973. Job search of middle-aged managers and engineers. *Industrial and Labor Relations Review* 26 (3):969–79.

Equal Employment Opportunity Commission. 1984. *Eighteenth Annual Report*. Washington, D.C.: Government Printing Office.

Eurich, N. P. 1985. *Corporate classrooms: The learning business*. Princeton, N.J.: The Carnegie Foundation for the Advancement of Teaching.

Flaim, P. O., and E. Sehgal. 1985. Displaced workers of 1979–83: How well have they fared? *Monthly Labor Review* 108 (6):3–16.

Fowler, E. M. 1984. Intensive M.B.A. programs. *The New York Times*, July 18.44.

Freeman, R. B. 1979. The work force of the future. In *Work in America: The next decade*, edited by C. Kerr and J. M. Rosow, 58–74. New York: D. Van Nostrand Company.

Freeman, R. and J. L. Medoff. 1979. New estimates of private sector unionism in the United States. *Industrial and Labor Relations Review* 32 (2):145–74.

Gifford, C. D. 1986. *Directory of U.S. Labor Organizations, 1986–87 Edition*. Washington, D.C.: Bureau of National Affairs: 67.

Ginzberg, E., and G. Vojta. 1985. *Beyond human scale: The large corporation at risk*. New York: Basic Books.

Gordon, D. M. 1984a. To get workers working. *The New York Times*, July 11:A25.

———. 1984b. Unpublished calculations provided the author.

Gordon, R. A., and J. E. Howell. 1959. *Higher education for business*. New York: Columbia University Press.

Green, P., K. tan Dinh, J. A. Priebe, and R. Tucker. 1983. Revisions in the Current Population Survey beginning in January 1983. *Employment and Earnings* 30 (2):7–15.

Haber, S. E., E. J. Lamas, and J. Lichtenstein. 1987. On their own: The self-employed and others in private business. *Monthly Labor Review* 110 (5):17–23.

Harlan, A., and C. L. Weiss. 1982. Sex differences in factors affecting managerial career advancement. In *Women in the workplace*, edited by P. A. Wallace, 59–100. Boston: Auburn House Publishing Co.

Hayes, T. C. 1981. Rumors of major shifts engulf I.B.M. *The New York Times*, October 1:D1+.

Heidrick and Struggles. 1985. "Mobile manager." Heidrick and Struggles, Chicago.

Hewitt Associates. 1986. *Plan design and experience in early retirement windows and in other voluntary separation plans*. Lincolnshire, Ill.: Hewitt Associates.

Horvath, F. W. 1987. The pulse of economic change: Displaced workers of 1981–85. *Monthly Labor Review* 110 (6):3–12.

Human Resources Management News. 1986. December 20:1.

Hymowitz, C., and T. D. Schellhardt. 1986. The glass ceiling, why women can't seem to break the invisible barrier that blocks them from the top jobs. *The Wall Street Journal*, March 24, sect. 4:1+.

Irons, E. D. and G. W. Moore. 1985. *Black managers: The case of the banking industry*. New York: Praeger.

Kanter, R. M. 1977. *Men and women of the corporation*. New York: Basic Books.

———. 1984. Variations in managerial career structures in high-technology firms: The impact of organizational characteristics on internal labor market patterns. In *Internal Labor Markets*, edited by P. Osterman, 109–32. Cambridge, Mass.: The MIT Press.

Kearney Management Consultants. N.d. *Seeking and destroying the wealth dissipators*.

Kearns, R. 1983. It was blue Monday at U.S. Steel. *Chicago Tribune*, September 26, sect. 3:1+.

Klein, D. P. 1984. Occupational employment statistics for 1972–82. *Employment and Earnings* 31 (January):13–16.

La Force, J. C., and R. Novelli. 1985. Reconciling management research and practice. *California Management Review* 27 (Spring):74–81.

Langer, S. 1978. 1978 MBA salary survey. *MBA* (October/November):4+.

Lee, B. A., and J. Parker. 1987. Supervisory participation in professional associations: Implications of *North Shore University Hospital*. *Industrial and Labor Relations Review* 40 (3):364–82.

Leinberger, P. 1986. "Organization man" revisited: Part 2, "The business world." *The New York Times*, December 7:46–47.

Leon, C. B. 1982. Occupational winners and losers: Who they were during 1972–80. *Monthly Labor Review* 105 (6):18–28.

Lipset, S. M., and W. Schneider. 1983. *The confidence gap: Business, labor and government in the public mind.* New York: Free Press.

Lubin, J. S. 1982. White-collar cutbacks are falling more heavily on women than men. *The Wall Street Journal,* November 9, sect. 2:37.

Lusterman, S. 1985. *Trends in corporate education and training.* New York: The Conference Board, Inc.

Main, J. 1984. The recovery skips middle managers. *Fortune* 109 (February 6):112–20.

Miles, R. E. 1985. The future of business education. *California Management Review* 27 (3):63–73.

Miner, J. B. 1974. *The human constraint: The coming shortage of managerial talent.* Washington, D.C.: Bureau of National Affairs.

Muth, L. W. 1984. Employment contracts. In *Handbook of Wages and Salary Administration,* edited by M. L. Rock. New York: McGraw-Hill.

The New York Times. 1987. *The New York Times Poll, MBA Survey #2* (unpublished results and tabulations).

Nielsen, J. 1985. Management layoffs won't quit. *Fortune,* October 28:46–49.

Nulty, P. 1987. Pushed out at 45—now what? *Fortune,* March 2:26–30.

Nussbaum, B. 1986. The end of corporate loyalty. *Business Week,* August 4:42–49.

Ochsner, R. C. 1984. Changing trends in total compensation programs. *Handbook of Wage and Salary Administration,* M. L. Rock, editor-in-chief. New York: McGraw-Hill.

O'Dell, C. 1987. *People, performance, and pay.* In collaboration with J. McAdams. Houston: American Productivity Center.

Odendahl, T. J., E. T. Boris, and A. K. Daniels. 1985. *Working in foundations, career patterns of women and men.* New York: The Foundation Center.

Osterman, P. 1986. The impact of computers upon the employment of clerks and managers. *Industrial and Labor Relations Review* 39 (2):175–86.

Personick, M. E., and C. B. Barsky. 1982. White-collar pay levels linked to corporate work force size. *The Monthly Labor Review* 105 (5):23–28.

Pierson, F. 1959. *The education of American businessmen: A study of university-college programs in business administration.* New York: McGraw-Hill.

Pond, S. A., ed. 1986. *Bricker's International Directory: University Executive Programs, 1987.* Princeton, N.J.: Peterson's Guides.

———. 1987. *The Bricker Bulletin: Executive education* 4 (1):4.

Prokesch, S. E. 1985. Companies turn to incentives. *The New York Times,* July 19:D1+.

Reder, M. W. 1978. An analysis of a small, closely observed labor market: Starting salaries for University of Chicago MBAs. *Journal of Business* 51 (2):263–97.

Retkwa, R. 1984. The compensation quandary. *Registered Representative* 8 (10):18–24.

Rogan, H. 1984a. Executive women find it difficult to balance demands of job, home. *The Wall Street Journal,* October 30, sect. 2:33.

———. 1984b. Women executives feel that men both aid and hinder their careers. *The Wall Street Journal,* October 29, sect. 2:35+.

———. 1984c. Young executive women advance farther, faster than predecessors. *The Wall Street Journal,* October 26, sect. 2:33+.

Reibstein, L. 1986. Many hurdles, old and new, keep black managers out of top jobs. *The Wall Street Journal,* July 10, sect. 2:23.

Rosenbaum, J. E. 1984. *Career mobility in a corporate hierachy.* Orlando, Fla.: Academic Press.

Rosow, J. M. 1979. The coming management population explosion. *S.A.M. Management Journal* 44 (4):4–16.

Rytina, N. 1982. Tenure as a factor in the male-female earnings gap. *The Monthly Labor Review* 105 (4):32–34.

Sandeman, H. 1984. Managerial evolution. *The Economist,* December 22:91.

Schuster, M., and C. S. Miller. 1984. An empirical assessment of the Age Discrimination in Employment Act. *Industrial and Labor Relations Review* 34 (1):64–86.

Schaeffer, R. G., and E. F. Lynton. 1982. Corporate experiences in improving women's job opportunities. In *Women in the Workplace,* edited by P. A. Wallace. Boston: Auburn House Publishing Co.

Shifting strategies. 1985. *The Wall Street Journal,* August 12:1+.

Stevenson, R. W. 1985. 24,000 A.T. & T. jobs to be eliminated at major division. *The New York Times,* August 22:1.

Stewart, R. 1971. *How computers affect management.* Cambridge, Mass.: MIT Press.

Strober, M. H. 1982. The MBA: Same passport to success for women and men? In *Women in the Workplace,* edited by P. A. Wallace. Boston: Auburn House Publishing Co.

Sym-Smith, C. I. and J. A. Riordan. 1980. Fourth annual Hay report of executive compensation. *Wharton Magazine* 5 (1):41–48.

Viscusi, W. K. 1980. Sex differences in worker quitting. *Review of Economics and Statistics* 62 (3):388–98.

U.S. Department of Labor. Employment Standards Administration. 1983. Defining the terms "executive," "administrator," "professional," "outside salesmen."

Walker, J. W. 1983. Training and development. In *Human resources management in the 1980s: Supplement to the ASPA Handbook of Personnel and Industrial Relations,* edited by S. J. Carroll and R. Schuler. Washington, D.C.: Bureau of National Affairs.

Walker, J. W., and T. G. Gutteridge. 1979. *Career planning practices: An AMA Survey Report.* New York: American Management Association.

Ward, H. W. 1964. The ideal of individualism and the reality of organization. In *The Business Establishment,* edited by E. F. Cheit. New York: John Wiley & Sons.

Warner, W. L., and J. C. Abegglen. 1955. *Occupational mobility in American business and industry.* Minneapolis: University of Minnesota Press.

West, J. P., and D. R. Sheriff. 1969. *Executive development programs in universities, studies in personnel policy no. 215.* New York: The National Industrial Conference Board.

Williams, R. E. 1986. *Personal liability of managers and supervisors for employment discrimination.* Washington, D.C.: National Foundation for the Study of Equal Employment Policy.

Whyte, W. H., Jr. 1956. *The organization man.* New York: Simon and Schuster.

Young, A. M., and H. Hayghe. 1984. More U.S. workers are college graduates. *Monthly Labor Review* 107 (3):46–48.

4
Australia

RUSSELL D. LANSBURY AND ANNABELLE QUINCE

While research in several countries has documented how the structure and content of the managerial and professional occupations have been affected by economic, social, and technological changes (see, for example, Gorz 1978, Hartmann 1974, Low Beer 1978, and Mallet 1963), managerial employment in Australia has not been extensively studied. This chapter seeks to fill the void by providing detailed information on the practices used in a sample of organizations to manage managerial and professional employees.

The chapter is based in part on information from a survey of senior executives in fourteen large-scale Australian organizations during 1985. The main characteristics of the studied organizations were as follows:

Two automobile manufacturers—one Japanese owned and one U.S. owned

Two banks—both Australian owned, one private sector and one public sector

Two computer companies—one U.S. owned and one British owned

Two chemical companies—one U.S. owned and one British owned

One international airline—Australian owned

One major retailer—Australian owned

One telecommunications corporation—Australian owned

One electronics manufacturer—Japanese owned

One consumer durables manufacturer—Australian owned

One detergent manufacturer—European and British owned

Three organizations were from the public sector and the remainder were from the private sector. Interviews were also conducted with consultants in executive recruitment, selection, development, and compensation to obtain information on currect trends affecting managerial and professional employees.

THE CHARACTER OF AUSTRALIAN BUSINESSES AND BUSINESS ENVIRONMENT

Australia is a highly urbanized, advanced industrial society with a population of 15.7 million. During the past ten years, major changes in the composition of the Australian labor force have occurred during severe cyclical fluctuations of the overall economy. Between 1973 and 1983, the number of people employed increased at an average annual rate of 0.9 percent to a level of 6.25 million persons. However, unemployment also increased steadily during this period from approximately 3 percent in 1973 to a record high level of 9 percent in 1983. Like most advanced industrial societies, Australia has experienced a steady growth of employment in the service industries, which now account for more than 75 percent of the paid labor force. Although agriculture, mining, and manufacturing occupy a central role in the Australian economy, they have declined steadily in recent years as a source of employment.

The Australian management environment has been significantly affected in the past few decades by the injection of overseas investment. Some industries are almost entirely foreign controlled: 91 percent of vehicle building, 75 percent of pharmaceuticals and aluminum. According to Dunphy (1981), the arrival of multinationals in Australia has decisively ended a century and a half of geographical isolation and thrust the country into the international arena of economic competition.

Apart from the large-scale, predominantly foreign-owned corporations, Australia also possesses a large number of small Australian-owned enterprises. The typical firm in Australia is family owned or owner managed and employs fewer than 100 people. The *Report of the Committee on Manufacturing Industry in Australia* (1975), known as the *Jackson Report,* noted that there were approximately 32,500 firms engaged in manufacturing, with 95 percent employing less than 100 people. Yet the *Jackson Report* also revealed that half the value added by the manufacturing industry was contributed by the largest 200 firms, half of which were at least one quarter foreign controlled. The decisions of these top 200 corporations greatly affect Australian industry because they employ about half of the total labor force engaged in manufacturing and account for 60 percent of the fixed capital expenditure. These firms also exercise considerable influence on the national economy through their pricing and investment decisions as well as in their general competitive capacity. In industrial relations matters, the large firms set the pattern for smaller ones.

Wealth and power are increasingly concentrated in a small number of large, dominant organizations. It has been argued that a higher level of monopoly and oligopoly exists in Australian industry than in many other advanced market economies (Connell 1977). In the past few decades, ownership has passed into fewer hands and economic power has become more concentrated.

According to Byrt and Masters (1978), the whole pattern of social relations in Australia is highly bureaucratic. Not surprisingly, the quality of management that has emerged under these conditions has been subject to considerable criticism. On the basis of his research during the 1970s, Denis Pym (1971, 202) argued that Australian managers were highly dependent on ideas and practices imported from abroad, were unwilling to accept the need for change, feared anyone who might threaten the established order through the introduction of radical alternatives, were dominated by sleepers rather than thrusters. The 1980s, however, have witnessed significant changes, as this chapter will demonstrate. Australian managers no longer live in a stable world in which they can remain complacent.

LABOR FORCE CHARACTERISTICS

Significant trends have taken place in both the employment and unemployment of Australian managers and professionals.

Employment Trends

According to the *Census* (Australian Bureau of Statistics 1981), professionals and managers constitute 13.6 percent and 5.3 percent, respectively, of the total labor force. The number of professionals and managers in Australia increased dramatically between 1947 and 1976: 319.4 percent for professionals and 120 percent for administrative, executive, and managerial workers. Since 1976, the number of professional workers increased at the slower rate of 25 percent. Managers, on the other hand, experienced a 12 percent reduction in their numbers.

This reduction has been due partly to the economic recession of the mid-1970s and early 1980s, and partly to the increase in company mergers, which have led inevitably to cuts in managerial ranks. During the initial recovery, many companies continued to operate with the same number of managers who have to assume a greater work load. However, managerial employment increased more rapidly in 1983–84.

The distribution of managers and professionals throughout Australian industry is uneven. According to the *Census,* the community service sector has the largest percentage of professionals, while agriculture has the lowest. The wholesale and retail sector has the highest percentage of managers, while agriculture, again, has the lowest. It is important to note that the financial sector, which is one of the newer and more dynamic industries, has the second highest percentage of managers and professionals.

In making these interindustry comparisons, it should be noted that the

Census occupational categories are frequently applied in a rather broad way to different industries. In some sectors, such as retailing, the term manager is used to describe a wide range of functions from someone in charge of a small section in a store to the person responsible for the whole store itself. Similarly, it appears that in the rapidly expanding and relatively new field of finance the term manager is applied to technical specialists who are not necessarily in charge of other staff.

Unemployment Trends

As noted previously, the level of unemployment in Australia during recent years increased markedly to a peak of 9 percent in 1983. Although it fell to approximately 7 percent in 1985, unemployment remains a major social and economic problem. The unemployment rate has varied considerably between different occupational groups. As shown in Table 4.1, managerial and professional occupations have been among the least affected by unemployment in the community as a whole. However, in the period 1983–85, the percentage growth in unemployment among managers was higher than in the labor force as a whole, although it did show some signs of abating. While it is not possible to accurately estimate the number of firms that have reduced their employment levels, the manufacturing jobs declined by more than 170,000 during 1970–84. Nine of the fourteen organizations in our study stated that they had reduced their number of managerial staff during the past five years. The rising levels of unemployment have been due not only to economic recession but also to technological and structural changes.

There is some evidence to suggest that the level of managerial unemployment is understated or disguised in other forms such as early retirement, which allows both employee and manager to avoid the stigma of unemployment.

The past years have shown the obvious effect of cyclical forces on the level of managerial employment and unemployment, but other long-term factors have had an impact as well. One such factor is the trend toward a flatter organizational structure, with fewer managerial levels and therefore fewer managers, which is apparent in several cases but not as yet documented comprehensively (see Dunphy 1981).

Another factor is the trend toward promoting managers to senior positions earlier in their career, thus necessitating early retirement among senior staff. For instance, when the National Bank took over the Commercial Bank, only top executives survived. Last, there has been an increasing number of mergers between organizations in the private sector during the past five years.

Faced with this high unemployment, the trade union movement in Australia sought to limit the discretion of employers to retrench or lay off workers by mounting a "job security" case before the Australian Conciliation and Arbitration Commission. In its decision on Termination, Change and Redundancy in December 1984, the Commission stated that an employer shall notify em-

Table 4.1 Unemployment of managers and professionals
in Australia

	Total	Managers and administrators	Profesional and related
Number unemployed			
1983	801,849	9,529	35,196
1984	791,753	11,133	37,305
1985	766,939	11,397	35,868
Percent of increase			
1983–84	−1.3	16.8	6.0
1984–85	−3.1	2.4	−3.8
Percent of total labor force unemployed			
1983	12.8	2.3	3.6
Percent of unemployed persons by occupa- tion			
1983	100.0	1.2	4.3
1984	100.0	1.4	4.7
1985	100.0	1.5	4.7

Source: Australian Department of Employment and Industrial Relations 1983–85.

ployees and their unions that may be affected by the proposed changes in production, organization, structure, or technology.

This and similar developments, however, have led some managers to feel that their employees have better job security than they themselves enjoy.

Increasing levels of managerial unemployment have encouraged the growth of consultants who for a fee help managers cope with the psychological and financial problems that often result from unemployment and assist redundant managers in regaining their positions in the work force. Only a small proportion of redundant managers, however, appear to use the services of such consultants. Many former managers, especially the older ones who spent most of their working lives with the same employer, find it difficult to obtain work at their previous level.

CHARACTERISTICS OF MANAGERS
AND MANAGERIAL EMPLOYMENT

Studies of American and British managers have depicted the emergence of a new managerial class, drawn from a broad cross-section of society whose success has been achieved through merit and qualifications rather than social background and property ownership (Nichols 1970, 42). This new class is developing less slowly in Australia.

Surveys by Beed (1967) and later by Encel (1970, 376) indicated that a high percentage of Australian managers had fathers in executive and professional positions, suggesting that inherited social and economic position plays a large role in the attainment of managerial status in Australia.

In comparison with their British colleagues (see Clements 1958), Australian managers enjoy less upward mobility into the ranks of management and tend to rely more heavily on family connections to attain their position. In addition, a higher proportion of managers in Britain hold relevant academic qualifications than their Australian counterparts and are more qualified than their predecessors, according to a study (Whitley, Thomas, and Marceau 1981) of graduates of the prestigious London and Manchester Business Graduate Schools.

Another aspect investigated by Encel (1970) concerned the degree of experience Australian managers obtained on the shop floor, or at lower levels in the work place, before attaining their current position. More than 40 percent of managers commenced their career in a white-collar or office job, while approximately one-third began work in a specialist or technical position. Less than one-quarter of the managers worked their way up from the bottom of the enterprise.

O'Loughlin (1974) has confirmed Encel's findings, but also reported that, among his sample of managers, one-quarter had completed their final year of secondary school and 12 percent had started a university course, but only 4 percent completed a degree. On the basis of these findings, O'Loughlin claimed that a career in management constituted a second choice for many who had been unable to obtain entry to tertiary-level studies or had failed to complete their course at this level. O'Loughlin also reported that those under the age of 40 were drawn from a much wider cross-section of society than their older counterparts. This suggests that management in Australia is developing a broader social base and that access to positions is becoming less dependent on family background. How this development will affect the beliefs and practices of Australian managers is yet to be seen.

Management in Australia has not acquired the prestige or status accorded to executives and businesspeople in many other advanced industrial societies. "In Australia," lament Byrt and Masters (1978), "the achievement of success through business does not appear to be a feat worthy of admiration" (p. 29). Certainly, managers are not held in high esteem by the Australian public. A national survey of occupational status and prestige by Congalton (1969, 56), for example, revealed that the manager of a large industrial enterprise was ranked only twelfth behind other less well-remunerated occupations. Yet chief executives and senior government officials in Australia command not only some of the highest salaries but exert considerable power within Australian society. For the most part, however, they maintain a low profile and avoid public attention.

A large proportion of Australian managers are found in the public sector which employs approximately one-quarter of the total labor force. Since World War II, with the rapid expansion of Commonwealth power (Encel, 1970) the number of public servants employed by the Commonwealth has increased from 150,000 to 400,000 of whom about 1,300 are in senior management positions.

A vast new managerial elite within the public service has been created and given the security of tenure and considerable powers. It also nurtures what Davies (1964) has called the Australian talent for bureaucracy—the penchant that colors social relations in Australia.

National Origins

According to the 1981 census, 21 percent of the Australian population was born outside Australia; for managers the proportion was 27 percent and for professionals the proportion was 24 percent. Moreover, 10 percent of all persons born in Australia, New Zealand, the United Kingdom, and northern European countries were in managerial and professional occupations, compared with fewer than 5 percent of persons born in Southern European and Middle Eastern countries (Australian Bureau of Statistics, 1981).

Age

As shown in Table 4.2, managers and professionals tend to be concentrated in older age groups, compared with the labor force as a whole. Almost one-third of all managers and professionals are between 35 and 44 years, and 80 percent are between 25 and 54 years.

This compares with the labor force as a whole in which 53 percent are under the age of 35 years and 63 percent are between 25 and 54 years. This suggests that people move into a managerial or professional occupation later in life and that they stay in it longer.

Table 4.2 Percentage of managerial and professional employees in the labor force, by age, 1981

Age in years	Percent of managerial and professional work force	Percent of labor force
15–24	2.9	26.0
25–34	23.5	26.5
35–44	32.8	20.8
45–54	24.4	15.8
55–64	13.5	9.2
65+	2.9	1.7
Total	100.0	100.0

Source: Australian Bureau of Statistics 1981.

Table 4.3 Percentage of managerial positions occupied by women and men
for various industries, 1981

Industry	Percent of managerial positions occupied by women	Percent of managerial positions occupied by men	Percent of women in each industry
Agriculture	8.2	91.8	28.4
Mining	3.3	96.7	8.9
Manufacturing	7.3	92.7	25.5
Electricity and gas	1.6	98.4	9.0
Construction	5.7	94.3	11.0
Wholesale	15.2	84.8	42.0
Transportation	8.4	91.6	15.3
Communication	6.0	94.0	25.4
Finance	15.4	84.6	46.1
Public administration	6.1	93.9	27.9
Community service	29.4	70.6	62.9
Recreation	22.1	77.9	54.9
Not classified	18.6	81.4	27.6
Total	13.2	86.8	37.3

Source: Australian Bureau of Statistics 1981.

Women

Women represent 38 percent of the total labor force, yet of this group only 13
percent are managers or professionals. As shown in Table 4.3, even in industries
such as community service and recreation in which more than half of the employees are women, women represent less than 30 percent of the managerial
personnel.

The four industries in which more than 15 percent of managers are women
are either of the caring or nurturing kind or are relatively newer industries such
as finance and retailing. The need for specialized staff in these latter industries
has grown so rapidly that new oppotrunities for women have been created.
Little progress has been made by women, however, into the managerial and
professional ranks of traditionally male-dominated industries such as electrical,
gas, mining, or construction.

Many of the women who have moved into managerial or professional
positions are in the personnel area, for women constitute almost one-third of all
personnel specialists in Australia. The personnel function includes many "caring" tasks and is therefore consistent with the traditional female stereotype. In
addition, women are typically found in lower level occupations, especially those
involving part-time or casual work with little or no career prospects. Although
some women do reach more senior positions, it is only in relatively small numbers and usually in newer areas that are less subject to traditional male dom-
inance.

Anti-discrimination

Although the 1970s and 1980s saw the introduction of both state and federal anti-discrimination legislation in Australia, the laws have yet to make a major impact on the ranks of management. Specific anti-discrimination legislation was first introduced in Australia in 1975 with the federal Racial Discrimination Act. Other acts were subsequently passed that outlawed discriminatory practices on various grounds including race, sex, marital status, physical and intellectual impairment, sexual preference, and religious or political beliefs.

Wilenski (1984) has identified three stages through which Australia is passing to achieve the goal of equal employment opportunity (EEO). The first is the goodwill phase that began in the 1970s and still exists in many areas today. During this phase it was felt that equal employment opportunity would be achieved through good intentions and that actions would follow. This was succeeded by the legislative phase, beginning with public employment, in which rights to equal opportunity were codified. The third phase of cultural change whereby community attitudes are transformed has yet to be realized.

In 1984, the Australian government instituted a voluntary affirmative action pilot program with twenty-eight private-sector organizations and three higher educational institutions that was to run initially for twelve months. A progress report on the pilot program concluded that "most companies [had] interpreted consultation in a minimal fashion" (Affirmative Action Resource Unit 1985). Progress has been greater in the Australian public service, where affirmative action programs have been legislated for under the 1984 Public Service Reform Act. All departments of the Australian public service are now required to prepare annual management plans indicating their progress in implementing affirmative action programs, and a number of state governments have followed suit. However, it remains to be seen whether this approach will yield significant changes in the composition of public sector management.

The federal government introduced legislation on affirmative action following the experiences of the pilot program and the recommendations of the working party it established in 1984. The Affirmative Action (Equal Opportunity for Women) Act 1986 requires all higher education institutions and all organizations with more than 100 employees to establish affirmative action programs along the lines of the pilot program. It also requires the creation of the position of the Director of Affirmative Action to advise and assist employers, issue guidelines, initiate community education, and monitor and evaluate the effectiveness of the programs.

Organizations within the jurisdiction of the Act are required to submit two reports annually to the director. One is a public report and the other a confidential one, which provides a detailed analysis of the processes undertaken by the employer. The Director has the power to request further information where deemed necessary. Failure to provide the required information without a reasonable excuse, however, simply means that an employer can be named in the Director's annual report to Parliament. Not surprisingly, the Act has been widely criticized as lacking adequate penalities for employers who fail to comply with its requirements.

It is generally accepted that some affirmative action programs have assisted women. This can be seen in the case of Esso Australia Limited. Esso has increased the percentage of women in its work force from 10.4 to 16.7 percent, or 203 to 424, over the past five years and at the managerial and professional level from 20 women in 1980 to 1,245 in 1985 (Kirk 1984). Even where organizations do genuinely and willingly adopt the Australian Government's guidelines on affirmative action, many forms of discrimination will doubtless continue to be unnoticed and unopposed.

EDUCATION AND PREPARATION

In the Australian system of education, higher degrees, such as BAs, MAs and PhDs, are usually gained at a university. Certificates are usually obtained at technical and further education colleges or institutes of advanced study known as colleges of advanced education (CAE).

In 1980, almost 42 percent of all managers and professionals had earned a tertiary qualification, that is, a diploma, certificate, or degree. However, managers and professionals under 40 years of age are more likely to hold tertiary qualifications, especially a degree, than their older colleagues. This is partly a consequence of the rapid expansion of tertiary education during the 1960s and 1970s, and partly due to the greater emphasis being given to formal qualifications for management.

One of the significant changes that has occurred in terms of education during the last ten years has been the growth of management education. A survey conducted by an Australian Government Inquiry into Management Education in 1980 (known as the *Ralph Report*) revealed that Australian universities and colleges of advanced education (CAEs) considerably increased their course offerings in business studies during the 1960s and 1970s (see *The Report of the Inquiry into Management Education.*) Table 4.4 sets out the number and level of courses offered by institutions in 1980.

The *Ralph Report* noted that the primary aim of undergraduate courses, particularly in CAEs, has been to equip graduates with skills in such functional areas as accountancy, computing, personnel administration, and marketing. The post-graduate level diploma and MBA courses have emphasized either functional specialities or broader aspects of business administration and management. Post-graduate management education in Australia is a relatively new phenomenon with almost all courses having begun after 1970.

Although much growth at both universities and CAEs has occurred in recent years, the greatest area of expansion of business studies has been in the CAEs. Enrollment in both undergraduate and post-graduate diploma courses

Table 4.4 Estimated number of students enrolled in management courses by level of course and type of institution, 1980

Level of course	Universities		Colleges of advanced education	
	Number	*EFTS* *	*Number*	*EFTS* *
Undergraduate				
Associate diploma	—	—	1320	780
Diploma	—	—	60	35
Degree	3400	2970	4205	2870
Postgraduate				
Diploma	285	155	1690	865
Master's degree by course work	1485	890	150	80
Master's degree by thesis	105	60	5	5
Doctorate	110	80	—	—
Total	5385	4155	7430	4635

Source: Report of the Inquiry into Management Education 1983.
*EFTS = Equivalent full-time students.

increased by 50 percent between 1976 and 1980. According to the *Ralph Report,* during the 1970s management education at the tertiary level became an important key to success in a managerial career. However, the report criticized the way in which management education was organized and taught in many Australian institutions and argued that many courses needed to be restructured and upgraded.

Significant changes in the environment of business appear to be behind this expansion. Among those noted by the Report were Australia's greater exposure to international competition at home and abroad; a move away from European markets and a greater focus on the Asian region; a demand for managers to be sensitive in interaction with the public, other businesses, and government; and the introduction of new technology.

The rationale and recommendations of the *Ralph Report* follow closely the *Franks Report* in England and the subsequent establishment of the London Graduate School of Business Studies and the Manchester Business School. Furthermore, the inclusion of Schools of Management within existing Australian academic institutions contrasts with privately established institutions in some parts of Europe and the United States and follows the pattern of management education in the United Kingdom (see Whitley, Thomas, and Marceau (1981).

Even though management education in Australia appears to be gaining acceptance, our survey of Australian firms done in connection with this chapter indicates that formal education credentials such as an MBA were not a guarantee of success. Although several organizations reported, other things being equal, that, when recruiting, they would give preference to a managerial candidate with an MBA, others said they would not. (See also Critchley 1984, 62–63; Short 1984, 29, 36).

LABOR MARKET PROCESSES

How and at what level an organization recruits its managers and professionals is largely dependent on its internal labor market. Following the internal labor market framework developed by Snape and Bamber (1985), we found the following recruitment and promotion practices in the studied firms.

Only one of the fourteen organizations could be classified as a type A organization—that is, external recruitment was limited to levels well below the ranks of management, and managerial and professional vacancies were filled from within.

Seven organizations were classified as type B. External recruitment at the lower levels of management, as well as promotion into this category, tended to come from manual or clerical workers, usually via technical or first-line supervisory positions. Type B companies seemed to distinguish between the internally and externally acquired managers, the latter going into a narrower range of jobs with limited promotion opportunities, the former being designated as "high-flier" or some equivalent.

Six companies were classified as being type C in which managerial and professional vacancies were rarely filled internally.

None of the studied companies had a policy of open recruitment at all levels of the organization—a practice Snape and Bamber labeled as type D.

Almost all the organizations classified as type B were moving toward recruitment practices closer to type C. In general, organizations were placing greater emphasis on graduate recruitment, closing off promotion from below, and developing fast-track schemes. In our survey, this was particularly apparent in a large private bank that segmented its recruiting practices into three groups: an operational group containing part-timers and others with limited promotion opportunities; a management trainee group in which each person had a high school certificate; and a graduate group whose members were earmarked for future managerial positions.

Snape and Bamber (1985) found that type D internal labor markets typically emerged in areas "with tight, highly competitive labor markets and/or where the corporation is growing rapidly" (p. 2). We found, however, that highly competitive industries such as finance and banking developed labor markets much closer to type C than type D. The development of internal labor markets may be explained by the fact that they facilitate reproduction of the specific skills required by organizations. Furthermore, employers secure the commitment of managers and professionals by offering promotion to those individuals who are cooperative and stay with the organization for a long period of time. The internal labor market and career structure within an organization, therefore, can be seen as a mechanism that enables organizations to more effectively maintain and control their managerial and professional staff.

Recruitment Methods

The methods used by organizations to recruit managerial and professional staff depend on whether they are recruiting people for senior or junior positions. At the junior level, organizations typically recruit directly from university or other tertiary level institutions via the campus interview. Thirteen of the organizations in our study held annual campus interviews.

From these interviews, the organization draws up a short list of candidates who attend a second interview, usually a group or panel interview. Six organizations also used some form of psychological or aptitude test when assessing the applicants. Considerable emphasis was placed by all the organizations on academic results. Personnel staff clearly play an important role in campus interviews; however, in three organizations, the final decision was made by a line manager. In only six of the organizations were managers recruited through newspaper advertisements. Two of these companies placed advertisements through a consultant so that their names were not identified. Organizations typically expend more money and effort when recruiting people into senior managerial positions.

One method of recruitment for management positions that has increased dramatically in the past ten years in both the private and public sectors is executive search or headhunting. Most executive search activities are confined to senior management positions. The growth and acceptance of executive search agencies undoubtedly has been related to the increasing need of organizations to recruit senior managerial and professional staff externally. A decade ago executive search was seen as something of an undercover operation in Australia, whereas today it is accepted as a legitimate method of recruitment. Although only three of the studied organizations regularly used the services of an executive search consultant, most saw it as an important and desirable method. The main reason given by organizations for not using executive search was the high cost of such services. However, it is difficult, if not impossible, to ascertain the proportion of senior positions filled by executive search methods.

Interfirm Mobility

Traditionally, interfirm mobility has been limited as managers and professionals have followed a career path within one organization. All but one of the organizations we interviewed offered their managers and professionals careers and regarded internal promotion as the most important method of filling vacancies. However, the past five to ten years have seen the emergence of a new variety of worker, a highly specialized group of managers and professionals who do not view their careers in terms of one organization. This development is related to the needs of Australian organizations in response to the rapidly changing economic environment that has included the oil crises, recessions, and the internationalization of Australian business. As one respondent observed, "Companies found themselves without managers competent to deal with some of the unforeseen and unpredictable events which they were facing. There wasn't time to train. . . . They [companies] didn't have those skills so they had to go out and buy them."

The demand for highly trained professional and managerial staff created highly competitive employment markets, thus encouraging interfirm mobility for particular types of managers and professionals. Many organizations, especially those in dynamic industries such as finance, now have two types of managers: careerists and specialists. Careerists continued to seek advancement within one organization; specialists move upward between a variety of organizations, sometimes on short-term contracts and sometimes seeking promotion elsewhere after a relatively brief period of employment.

Another factor encouraging interfirm mobility has been the growing importance of skills that are not specific to one organization, such as the personnel function.

The growing acceptance of interfirm mobility is indicated by the increasing and once unheard of willingness of organizations to reemploy managers after they have spent some years with another organization. All but one of the organizations in our study indicated that they would rehire managers and professionals if it was advantageous to their company.

One development associated with the increase in mobility in Australia is the proliferation of business magazines that regularly publish information about salaries and opportunities for managers and professionals in different industries. However, while this development has no doubt encouraged mobility, particularly among younger managers and professionals, it should not be seen as the primary cause.

Intrafirm Mobility

Career advancement within the organizations in our study was increasingly based on merit or performance on the job and less related to seniority. Many respondents identified three years as the typical length of service a manager could expect to spend in one position before receiving promotion, although this varied between organizations and industries. There was also a tendency, as one might expect, for junior managers and professionals to move more quickly than their senior colleages. People identified as high fliers were promoted more rapidly and received extra training as an attempt to give them a wider range of experiences.

Movement between functions or specialties within organizations was not common, except between related areas such as sales and marketing. Personnel managers also tended to be given experience in at least one other functional area. However, half the organizations in our sample indicated that movement across functions was desirable and was being encouraged. There also appeared to be a desire among organizations to turn away from specialization toward generalized skills.

The study also showed a tendency to reposition people either during training or while they were still at a junior management level. Once people reach the more senior levels, organizations tend to be reluctant to move them across functions. This reflects, in part, a lack of sophistication among most Australian employers in regard to career planning and development.

Overseas experience within a firm also appears to be increasingly important, and is undoubtedly related to the internationalization of Australian business. Nine of the fourteen organizations in our study stated that overseas experience was increasingly being used as a means of career development and four said it had become essential for anyone seeking a senior management position. It was felt that Australian managers and professionals would have to be given greater international training and experience as their organizations moved into world markets and international organizations moved into Australia. Banks in particular have become convinced that their managers need foreign experience.

Salary Systems

One of the most important changes in the past decade has been the development of uniform salary schemes, that is, a system where all salary levels for managerial and professional staff are arrived at by predetermined criteria rather than on an ad hoc basis in response to market forces or personal whim. Thirteen of the fourteen organizations interviewed had formal salary systems. Recent surveys done by several personnel/remuneration consultants also indicate that formal systems are now a normal part of life.

The criteria commonly used to determine salary levels are job sizing and market comparisons. Increasingly, however, salaries are determined by the size of a position rather than the worth of the individual to the organization. Twelve of the fourteen organizations in our study either had some form of job evaluation in place or were in the process of using consultants to establish such a system. A 1984 national survey by the consulting firm Noble Lowndes-CED found that 55 percent of organizations in Australia had formal job evaluation programs at the managerial level. No figures were available to compare this with nonmanagerial jobs.

Another important element in this structured approach is the continuous review of salaries in terms of market comparisons. Organizations are placing greater emphasis on establishing and maintaining salary levels that are comparable with market rates. This process has been assisted and stimulated by the growth in job evaluation, as it enables more meaningful comparisons to be made between organizations. All the companies in the Noble Lowndes-CED survey and all the organizations we studied had at least one salary review every two years, and 81 percent conducted an annual salary review.

Market comparisons are conducted mainly by using independent salary surveys or information from events such as the Canberra Salaries Conference, a privately sponsored conference of private and public sector organizations conducted each year to ascertain market rates for managerial salaries. In the 1984 Noble Lowndes-CED survey, 53 percent of companies said that independent salary surveys were the key factor in establishing salary levels and another 34 percent said they were the secondary factor. All the organizations in our study used at least one of the several salary surveys and many also attended the Canberra Salaries Conference.

The introduction of structured salary systems has substantially changed the traditionally individual relationship enjoyed by managers and professionals with their employers. When organizations argue that salaries are controlled and regulated by market forces this makes it extremely difficult for individuals to question their salary in relation to their personal worth to the organization. This trend in salary administration has enabled organizations to distance themselves from direct responsibility for setting individual salary levels.

Succession Planning and Career Planning

In order to control and utilize their managerial and professional staffs more effectively, Australian organizations have adopted the practices of succession planning, career planning, performance appraisal, and managerial traineeships. Twelve of the fourteen organizations in the study had some kind of succession plan, although several stated that they did not function as well as they would have liked. Furthermore, in several cases, it was apparent that the succession planning was a secretive process and the results known only to senior management. Seven companies in our study had a formal system of career planning and the others all stated that individual managers took responsibility for their staff career planning. Eleven companies had a formal appraisal system, but only six were linked to the salary system. Several organizations with appraisal plans admitted that the plans were not always strictly adhered to. Several companies had managerial traineeships but there appeared to be no direct connection between propensity to recruit managers externally and the presence of a managerial traineeship program.

There are two advantages to the development of such systematic personnel policies and practices. On one hand, they allow companies to organize their managerial and professional staff in a more efficient and effective manner. On the other hand, senior management gains greater control over its employees and their future careers within the organization. Many managers and professionals become locked into the company system, which then determines where and how their career should progress.

The value of employees as a strategic resource has come into sharp focus during the last ten years. Once managers are perceived as a strategic resource it becomes obvious that they must be trained, nurtured, and motivated to achieve their full potential. The roles and functions of personnel managers and management consultants have expanded to fill this need.

Additionally, personnel managers in most large organizations are becoming increasingly highly qualified individuals who act as internal consultants to senior management, but this has been a slow and uneven process. Their sphere of influence is beginning to encompass a wider array of issues and policies including: strategic planning, policy formation, training and development, career path and succession planning, and performance appraisal. However, these aspects are still underdeveloped in many Australian organizations.

The economic recession has caused organizations to focus more directly on maximizing the efficiency of their staff. Our study indicates that most large organizations have reduced the numbers of their managers during the last five years. The result is that the remaining staff is expected to work harder and perform more effectively. As a direct consequence of this quest for efficiency, there has been a growing emphasis on the need for performance appraisal. However, while an increasing number of companies indicate that they are introducing formal systems of performance appraisal, there is evidence of a high attrition rate among appraisal plans due to problems of design and implementation (Lansbury 1980).

Training and Development

Training and development appear to play an increasingly important role in human resource management in most large Australian organizations. Our study found that although on-the-job experience was still perceived as important, most organizations supplemented experience with some kind of organized training program within the enterprise. All the organizations in our study had a training and development program for their managers, which usually included a combination of external and internal courses. Internal courses tended to be for lower level managers and professionals while external ones were used mainly for senior managers. Internal courses typically involved job-related skills, while external courses were used to provide broader, general management skills.

Most of the organizations in our study provided a fairly intense period of training for graduate recruits and other individuals whom they perceived as capable of reaching senior management levels. More than half the organizations in the sample had some form of graduate training.

Four organizations also had specialized plans for people they identified as having high potential to reach senior management, sometimes called high flier schemes. These schemes provided a wide range of experiences enabling individuals to be promoted at a faster rate. Despite warnings that such plans may be based on false assumptions and not produce the results they are supposed to produce (e.g., Hirsh's 1985 study of British employers), Australian firms perceive high flier schemes as an increasingly important part of their human resources strategy.

Training or access to training is also used as a form of reward and to motivate potential senior managers. One bank, for example, motivates its junior managers by offering to pay tuition and living expenses for them and their families while they obtain an MBA degree in Switzerland.

Although organizations spend a considerable amount of time and money training certain groups for promotion and success, other sections of the work force are given substantially less training and as a consequence have fewer chances for gaining promotion. This relates to our earlier observation about the emergence of a two-tiered managerial work force, in which promotion and training opportunities are often denied to those outside the selected managerial and professional groups.

Career Success

In a recent Australian study of 420 chief executives within both private and public organizations, Mukhi (1982) developed a profile of the personal characteristics his respondents perceived as required for the achievement of managerial success. The four characteristics ranked as most important by both private and public sector executives were having a need to achieve results, the ability to work with a wide variety of people, being able to influence people, and negotiating skills. Public and private sector executives, however, differed in terms of how they ranked other characteristics. Executives in the private sector, for example, rated as very important the desire to seek new opportunities, leadership experience at an early stage in their career, and strong family support, while public sector executives gave higher ratings to having more ideas than other colleagues, possessing sound technical training and having a manager as a model early in one's career.

Mukhi concludes that "private sector managers reach top positions through achieving results via their own initiative, whereas public sector managers reach high positions not basically through results (although this does not mean to say that achieving results is not important) but through generating ideas" (p. 26). The profile of the successful private sector manager that emerges from Mukhi's study is of one "who has been thrown in the deep end to gain leadership experience" early in his or her career, has worked long hours, has attended an elite school, taken a university degree (preferably in finance or accountancy), worked for more than three organizations, and held more than eight jobs. Having done all this, the individual should have reached a senior management position by the age of 33 and be in the top job by age 40!

Our study found that younger senior managers typically had a wide range of experience. Approximately half our respondents indicated that their organizations had turned away from the idea of the specialist manager and were encouraging a more generalist approach. This reflects the changing nature of Australian organizations, the move toward decentralized organizational structures, and also increasing diversification. Several respondents spoke of the need for managers to be able to understand a range of different functions and to have had experience in both line and staff areas.

Based on responses from organizations in our study, intrafirm mobility especially early in a person's career appears to be important for managerial success. It is becoming increasingly apparent that people who remain too long in a highly specialized area will find it difficult to transfer into managerial ranks later in their career.

Successful managers need knowledge and experience of a wide variety of functional areas and industries. Those who possess these characteristics can command very high salaries. Such individuals tend to be highly mobile and are found in expanding industries such as finance and banking. This trend toward a high degree of mobility among managers is likely to continue as more organizations open up their senior positions to external recruitment.

The public sector is generally seen as providing only limited managerial opportunities. This is due in large part to lower salaries for senior managers as well as restrictive government policies. Respondents in the three public sector organizations in our study all commented that managerial and professional employees were increasingly discontented and that many were leaving to take better-paid positions in the private sector. If career success is measured in terms of remuneration, managers and professionals in the public sector have been falling further behind their private sector counterparts. Yet, the public sector still has much to offer in terms of experience and intrinsic job satisfaction.

Women in Managerial and Professional Work

As noted previously, even though women have made some inroads into the personnel and specialist areas, their numbers are still relatively small. The growing demand for highly trained specialists, expecially in the finance industry, has undoubtedly widened opportunities for women. In the words of one senior bank executive:

> Among our 3,400 managers there would probably be only about 30 women, but we would have another 150 who are not classified as managers but are being paid managerial salaries for market-related reasons. In other words, they have been hired for a special skill in a particular area and we are paying them equivalent to our lower levels of management.

Women's advances in management have been most noteworthy in the public service (Bell 1984). Both the state and commonwealth governments are under pressure from a variety of women's groups and have therefore created a number of specialized departments for women's needs. These departments have given female public servants the opportunity to progress into managerial positions at a much faster rate than if they had moved up through the normal career channels. The problem these women now face is whether their experience and seniority will be recognized if they move into other areas of the public or private sectors.

The proportion of women in managerial and professional positions in the fourteen organizations we interviewed averaged only 1 to 2 percent and appears to have remained unchanged for the past five to ten years. However, all the organizations claimed that women were now being recruited in larger numbers and beginning to move up the managerial and professional hierarchies. All forecast a substantial increase of women in the managerial ranks during the next five years.

A recent study of the perceptions of women managers by Still and Jones (1984) found a number of stereotypical attitudes toward women in managerial positions. Women are too emotional and therefore react badly under stress; women are not career-oriented; women tend to become pregnant; they lack initiative and motivation; they tend to be away from work all the time because of family problems; and women have an alternative role as wives and mothers. Still and Jones conclude, "The Australian community still has a long way to go before women will be generally accepted in positions of power and influence" (p. 284).

Most of the organizations in our study had formal policies that encouraged women to move into managerial and professional positions. The statistical evidence suggests, however, that in reality very little is done to achieve this. It would appear that the programs sponsored by the Australian government, described earlier, and the threat of U.S.-style affirmative action legislation has made some impact on both private and government organizations, at least in terms of their "formal policies," but progress remains very slow.

Women face many hidden barriers to remaining in the work force and moving into managerial and professional areas in the absence of child-care services. Unless such services are made more available, career opportunities now opening up to women may be out of the reach of many who want careers in management.

COMPENSATION

The remuneration of managers and professionals in Australia, especially at the most senior levels, is relatively low compared with most other western countries. In 1982, for instance, chief executive salaries in Australia were the lowest compared to salaries for comparable jobs in the major developed and developing economies (TPF & C 1982).

Most organizations use three distinct processes for setting compensation levels for managerial and professional staff. One process uses formalized salary systems involving job grading and is based totally on market comparisons. The second is a system of industrial awards (i.e., decrees in pay disputes) applying to professional groups such as engineers and scientists in the public sector. In the third, salaries are set through negotiation, which is used mainly for determining the level of compensation for highly specialized managers and professionals.

Compensation systems have experienced significant changes in recent years including the proliferation of fringe benefits, growth in the use of consultants, greater emphasis on market orientation, and emergence of the concept of pay for performance. The extent to which these changes have penetrated different industries has varied, but no industry has entirely escaped their effects. However, in the more dynamic and expanding industries, such as finance, banking and retailing, the effects of these changes are most pronounced. The reasons underlying these changes include increasing incidence of corporate mergers, taxation, the growing emphasis on diversification, and the impact of international markets on Australia.

As the need for more sophisticated compensation systems has emerged, the number of remuneration consultants has expanded to meet the demand. Many of these consultants have encouraged organizations toward a more structured approach to remuneration, supplying support services and market data for the new systems. Several major remuneration consultants, who came to Australia originally to service multinational enterprises, have made a considerable impact on Australian business.

The Components of Compensation

Although consultants have encouraged and stimulated changes in the area of remuneration, they have not been the primary cause of these developments. Rather, these changes have come from the changing needs of large commercial organizations to develop systems of remuneration that will satisfy their managerial and professional employees. The most noticeable change in the last five to ten years has been the proliferation and diversification of fringe benefits.

All the organizations in our study acknowledged that a certain percentage of their managers and professionals' remuneration came in the form of benefits. These were either benefits individually tailored to suit particular employees or schemes that applied to all their employees. According to Table 4.5, almost one-quarter of the employed work force in 1984 received some sort of nontaxable benefit and this development appears to be increasing. Table 4.5 also indicates that employees on higher incomes are generally more likely to receive fringe benefits than those on lower incomes.

Some of the most popular benefits (according to Noble Lowndes-CED 1984) are:

Representation/hospitality allowance
Motor vehicle or motor vehicle allowance
Employer superannuation contributions
Telephone payments
Bonus/incentive payments
Low-cost home financing
Club and professional association subscriptions
Overseas travel
Expense reimbursement
Local travel
Spouse allowance
Health insurance or expenses

Not all organizations offer this range of benefits and many only provide a few. The extent and variety of benefits tend to vary from industry to industry.

The 1984 salary survey by remuneration consultants Noble Lowndes-CED indicates that 70 percent of a manager's remuneration package is generally paid as salary and 30 percent as fringe benefits. In some industries such as merchant banking, however, the percentage of total remuneration paid as benefits is much

Table 4.5 Coverage of fringe benefits

Type of benefit	Number receiving (in thousands)	Percent of employees receiving fringe benefits	Percent increase 1983–84	Percent receiving by income level			
				Under A$200	A$200 A$360	A$360 A$520	Over A$520
Goods and services	1147	21.4	25.5	22.2	22.5	19.3	18.2
Telephone	496	9.3	11.8	5.4	6.1	14.4	25.1
Transport	469	8.7	7.3	4.0	7.0	13.6	19.7
Entertainment allowance	272	5.1	18.1	1.6	2.9	9.3	16.4
Housing	221	4.1	7.7	3.4	3.2	4.9	9.5
Holiday expenses	208	3.9	14.5	1.3	3.8	5.5	8.0
Medical	192	3.6	11.1	2.0	2.9	4.6	8.9
Low-interest finance	148	2.8	10.5	0.2	2.4	4.2	7.1
Union dues	135	2.5	25.9	1.1	1.9	3.6	7.1
Electricity	131	2.4	5.5	2.9	2.0	2.4	4.1
Club fees	97	1.8	14.9	0.5	1.0	2.8	6.7
Shares	87	1.6	4.8	0.4	1.2	2.6	4.2

Source: Australian Bureau of Labor Statistics 1984.

higher (38.2 percent). Table 4.6 indicates that only three of fourteen organizations in our study offered 30 percent or more of their remuneration package in the form of benefits and this was offered only at the more senior levels. According to one of our respondents from the banking sector, "I read in the paper yesterday that 70 percent was salary and 30 percent benefits; I guess that's not too far out at our senior levels. But it would not be as high as that when you get down to middle management and below."

It was also apparent that organizations providing a high percentage of benefits tended to make them discretionary so that managers could choose which benefits they wanted within their total package.

Over the past decade or so, managerial salary levels have not increased as rapidly as those of the average wage earner. (Blandy 1982). Table 4.7 shows that the ratio of salaries received by chief executives to average weekly earnings became progressively compressed between 1970–86. However, if the chief executives' total remuneration is taken into account, including the cash equivalents of fringe benefits, the ratio grew. Because fringe benefits are not taxed, the real differences in earnings between wage earners and managers grew even more.

The Impact of Taxation

Until mid-1984, employees were required to pay 60 cents tax on each dollar earned over A$35,001; therefore, managers preferred to receive packages of direct compensation and fringe benefits that minimized their tax liability. For this reason compensation consultants have advocated the total remuneration concept which takes firms away from competing for employees on the basis of

Table 4.6 Use of fringe benefits and external recruitment for fourteen organizations, 1985

Organization	1	2	3	4	5	6	7	8	9	10	11	12	13	14
Percentage of total remuneration taken as fringe benefits	5	33	33	20	5	15	5	5	15	20	10	25	25	30
Incidence of discretionary benefits		*	*									*		*
Incidence of discretionary and other benefits	*				*	*			*		*		*	
Incidence of company benefits only				*			*	*	*					
Extensive use of external recruitment of managers		*	*			*						*	*	*

Source: Authors' survey of major employers, 1985.

straight salaries and equalizes the net after-tax attractiveness of a compensation package.

In the past years, however, the relationship of the tax laws to fringe benefits has come under close scrutiny and changes have been instituted. *A White Paper on Tax Reform* in 1985 recommended imposing a separate tax on all employers, irrespective of their income tax status. This recommendation has been accepted by the government in principle and when implemented in 1986–87 will make fringe benefits considerably less attractive to employers. Many employees have stated that they would seriously consider doing away with benefits and moving

Table 4.7 Average remuneration of chief executives in Australian companies, 1970–86

March	Average base salary (ABS)[a]	Average total cash remuneration (TRC)[a]	Average male weekly earnings (annualized) (AWE)[a]	Ratio ABS AWE	Ratio TCR AWE
1970	18,767	20,385	3,780	4.96	5.39
1974	24,470	26,680	5,892	4.15	4.53
1978	34,945	48,973[b]	10,665	3.28	4.59
1982	54,090	69,650	17,748	3.05	3.92
1986	68,290	90,480	22,651[c]	3.02	4.00

Source: Figures from 1970–81 from Blandy, R. 1982; figures for 1982–86 are from the PA Australian Salary Survey published by the PA Consulting Group and Australian Bureau of Statistics, *Average Weekly Earnings,* Catalogue No. 63020, various years.
[a]In Australian dollars per annum.
[b]From 1978 total cash remuneration = total salary plus benefit value of company car, entertainment allowance, noncontributory superannuation, etc.
[c]Estimated.

back to 100 percent salary when the new tax is introduced. Indeed, similar behavior took place in the United Kingdom after tax reforms were introduced by the Thatcher government (Dixon 1985).

Still, a number of remuneration consultants argue (Carter 1985) that fringe benefits have more significance than simply providing tax-effective methods of remuneration. Fringe benefits, they say, are important as managerial and professional status symbols and will not disappear just because they are subject to taxation.

Compensation and Recruitment Issues

While the proliferation of benefits has been closely related to the desire of employers to use tax-effective forms of remuneration, it has also been a product of the recruitment policies of employers seeking to attract managers and professionals away from rival organizations. In our study, it was apparent that firms open to external recruitment at senior levels were more likely to offer an extensive array of discretionary nontaxable benefits than those organizations not open to such recruitment (see Table 4.6). Organizations in competitive industries where external recruitment was the norm were forced into providing packages and benefits to attract and retain staff.

Remuneration packages may also provide salaries and benefits well above those paid through more traditional compensation systems. Hence, organizations can find themselves with managers and professionals who are remunerated according to two or more different systems. A general manager who has climbed the traditional career ladder, for example, may receive a remuneration package greatly inferior to that offered to a new manager at the same level who has been recruited externally by a consultant or headhunter.

Such dual systems create strains within organizations between careerists and new recruits who enjoy superior terms and conditions of employment. Any organization with a high level of external recruitment will have to deal with the issue of motivating and retaining those people who have come up through a career structure and now feel that they are relatively deprived, in comparison with the more recent arrivals. Yet the careerists often lack the broad experience that would make them attractive to another employer.

Performance Appraisal and Compensation

All the organizations in our study had some form of annual increment for professional and managerial staff, but this was not always distributed equally; the amount an individual manager or professional received was often linked to his or her performance. Only scientists and engineers on award-related salaries received standard increments.

A number of organizations stressed the need to raise the level of performance among their managerial staff. The emphasis on greater efficiency has become more important with the changing business environment, economic competition, and increasing numbers of company takeovers and amalgamations. Many threatened organizations have been forced to reassess their reward systems for managerial staff, deemphasizing seniority or years of service and giving greater weight to performance.

Numerous personnel and remuneration consultants have noted the reluctance of Australian organizations to link performance with salary. Kavanagh (1984) claims, however, that this kind of thinking has changed in many larger organizations and U.S. subsidiaries that have adopted performance-related remuneration plans. A recent survey by Noble Lowndes-CED (1984) indicated that Australian organizations have been increasingly using incentive and bonus type schemes during the past five years, going from 13 percent of Australian owned firms in 1979 to 40 percent in 1984. Interestingly, proportionately more foreign owned firms have had such plans in both 1979 and 1984, 48 and 60 percent, respectively.

Eleven of the organizations in our study used some form of performance appraisal, but only six linked it to their salary system. All three public sector organizations claimed they would like to link salary with performance, but were prevented from doing so by legislative restraints.

Compensation and Public Sector Managers

Although most respondents from private sector organizations in our study complained that managerial salaries had not kept pace with general wage increases during the past five years, the public sector managers claimed that their relative position had declined dramatically. One of the major difficulties facing public sector organizations is that the Federal Remuneration Tribunal sets the salary levels of their chief executives. These salaries, which are not related to the market position for managers and professionals, are therefore considerably lower than their counterparts in the private sector and provide a ceiling for all other salaries in the public sector.

Another major restraint on public organizations is government policy, such as adherence to the current Prices and Incomes Accord between the federal government and the trade union movement. As long as public sector organizations are unable to pay the market rates for managers and professionals they will continue to lose staff to the private sector. Indeed, they are finding it increasingly difficult to motivate staff who realize they could be earning considerably more outside, and public disclosure of the salaries of department heads further tends to remind subordinates of the inadequacy of their pay.

UNIONIZATION

In Australia, the laws governing industrial relations have been favorable to the growth of unions. Under the Australian Conciliation and Arbitration Act of 1904, the federal tribunal was charged with the responsibility of preventing and settling industrial disputes that extended beyond the boundaries of a single state. Other tribunals with similar responsiblities were also established at the state level. The Australian conciliation and arbitration system encouraged the formation and growth of trade unions, and by the early 1920s almost half the total work force was unionized. The level of unionization has remained at around 55 percent ever since, although only in recent years has there been increasing growth of white-collar or nonmanual unions (Lansbury 1979–80).

With the exception of the public service, however, a relatively small percentage of managerial and professional employees have joined unions. This is partly because of the arbitration tribunals, attitudes to the concept of managerial prerogatives which, among other things, has been used by employers to exclude managerial employees from industrial awards and union coverage.

As in other industrialized nations (Evans 1982), especially England (*Royal Commission on Trade Unions and Employers Associations 1968*), middle managers are attracted to unions for some of the following reasons: the crisis of identity among managers, the decline in status and salary differentials, and the erosion in managerial prerogatives.

Australian employers find it difficult to accept the concept of managerial unions, especially in the private sector. The main reason identified by respondents in our survey was a concern that managers could not maintain a dual loyalty to both their employer and their union. While none of the studied private companies had official policies against the right of their managerial or professional employees to join a union, at least one employer stated that his firm would "discourage it." However, in another company, senior managers who had moved up through the corporation had retained their union membership.

In contrast, all public sector organizations studied by the authors acknowledged having unions representing employees in the managerial ranks. Respondents in these organizations tended to explain the existence of managerial unions by the federal Labour government's policy of encouraging unionism at all levels.

Managerial and Professional Unions

A number of unions, especially those covering white-collar and professional workers, include managers among their members. However, with some minor exceptions, few unions cover managers exclusively. Many existing unions are interested in extending their coverage of managerial employees and strongly challenge the formation of new managerial unions. An example is provided by a small Institute of Middle Management that formed in 1983 with the aim of recruiting private sector managers. So far, however, it has failed to obtain registration under the Australian Conciliation and Arbitration Act due to opposition from other unions and hence has been unsuccessful in attracting many members.

White-collar unions display considerable diversity in their size and coverage. The 97,000-strong Federated Clerks Unions of Australia (FCUA), for example, includes a range of occupational groups from typists to computer programmers who have little in common except that they fall within the historical jurisdiction of the Clerks' Union. Although the FCUA covers some supervisory and lower-level managerial employees, its membership comprises mainly clerical and other office staff, although this might change in the future. It may follow the example of Britain's Administrative, Professional, Executive and Computer Staffs (APEX) which, with considerable success, changed its name to appeal to more supervisors and middle managers.

One white-collar union in Australia that has penetrated deeply into the ranks of middle management in the public sector is the Administrative and Clerical Officers Association (ACOA). With approximately 53,000 members of middle management and technical and administrative positions in Australian public service, ACOA is the biggest union in the service. It owes its success to the expansion of the public service and aggressive recruiting. ACOA also plays a significant role in the Australian Council of Trade Unions (ACTU). In recent years, ACOA has been increasingly outspoken on issues concerning the management of the public sector, a militancy that reflects the changing attitude among middle-management levels of the public service toward unionism and industrial action.

The Association of Professional Engineers, Australia (APEA) provides an interesting example of a hybrid professional-managerial union with coverage in both the private and public sectors of industry. APEA is organized horizontally like a craft union, and the possession of engineering qualifications is a prerequisite for membership. Unlike some general white-collar unions, which have sought to expand their membership by organizing employees across occupational boundaries, APEA has concentrated on protecting and enhancing the position of the professional engineer. As a result of managerial career patterns followed by many engineers, however, APEA includes a high proportion of supervisory and managerial-level engineers within its ranks.

APEA also stimulated the unionization of other professional and managerial employees, especially in technical and scientific fields, following the success of the professional engineers case of 1961, when the application of the concept of "work value" by the Australian Conciliation and Arbitration Commission resulted in widening of the pay differential between managers and manual workers (O'Dea 1964). The work value concept was subsequently pursued by other professional groups, such as the Association of Professional Scientists, with some success. In recent years, however, the differentials between professional/managerial salaries and the wage levels of some of the more militant blue-and white-collar unions have declined. These factors have nevertheless stimulated the trend toward unionization and the adoption of more militant tactics among certain professional and managerial groups.

One of the most interesting examples of unionization among first-line managers or foremen/supervisors is provided by the changing pattern of membership within the Association of Draughting, Supervisory and Technical Employees (ADSTE). During the early 1970s, this union increased its membership by more than one-third, reflecting the growth of technicians in the labor force as well as successful efforts by ADSTE officials to unionize supervisors and foremen. Although the absolute membership of ADSTE has stagnated in recent years, mainly because of less demand for technicians during the economic recession, the proportion of first-line managers and supervisors within the total membership has increased from approximately 10 to 30 percent. The success of ADSTE in this area was made possible by the Conciliation and Arbitration Commission which ruled that the union had the right to organize supervisors in the vehicle-building and metal industries. These decisions underlined the changing attitudes of the Arbitration Commission toward the question of managerial prerogatives.

The most significant feature of managerial and professional unionization in Australia is that it is strongest in the government sector. A recent survey by the Australian Bureau of Statistics (ABS, *Trade Union Membership,* August 1986) found that 22.5 percent of managerial and administrative employees in Australia belong to a union. However, 66.4 percent of government sector managers and administrators are unionized, compared with only 12.5 percent of private sector managerial employees. A similar pattern emerges with professionals where 37.9 percent are union members; however, only 8.6 percent of professionals are in the private sector, compared with 55.4 percent of government-employed professionals.

Management Prerogatives

Managerial rights or prerogatives have been central to the operation of the conciliation and arbitration system in Australia and have strongly influenced management behavior in the industrial relations arena. In the past few years, however, there are signs that the scope of prerogatives may be changing and becoming less restrictive, thereby making the notion of managerial unionism less onerous and, at the same time, increasing the recognition that managers may need some form of collective action to secure their rights.

Among the developments that should be noted and watched carefully are the following. First, the Federal Arbitration Commission appears willing to depart from its traditional approach to management rights. In one dispute dealing with the redundancy of clerks resulting from the installation of computers in oil companies, the Commission suggested that in all future cases of expected redundancy, employees, "both individually and through their unions" should be brought in at the planning stage "to find a reasonable solution to the problem" (p. 41). The Commission advised the employers that if its attention was drawn "to instances in which the future welfare of employees has not, in its view, been properly dealt with in company planning, the Commission may find it necessary to intervene in the interest of industrial justice" (Isaac 1980, 41).

Similarly, the award governing the commercial clerks requires extensive consultation between employers and employees before the introduction of technological change in the work place. The employer is obliged to consult about both the proposed change and alternative proposals, and to specify management objectives.

Another noteworthy event was the decision given by the Federal Arbitration Commission in 1984 in a test case launched by the ACTU on the issue of job protection. Under the *Termination, Change and Redundancy Decision of 1984,* employers are required to consult with workers and their representatives concerning changes to the organization of work that are likely to affect employees and on matters relating to redundancy. Within the metal industry, this decision is now being incorporated into a number of federal and state awards.

One of the most significant developments bearing on managerial prerogatives has been the spread of different forms of employee participation or industrial democracy within both the private and public sectors. For the most part, these developments in industrial democracy in Australia have been at the shop-floor or work-place level within organizations and have included the establishment of joint consultative committees or councils as well as the introduction of semiautonomous work groups that give employees more direct control over the organization of their immediate tasks.

So far the manifestations of industrial democracy have not presented any major challenge to the power of management. Still, the Australian Council of Trade Unions and several individual unions have adopted policies that favor legislation to extend the role of employees, through their unions, in the decision-making process as a way to equalize power within the work place and move away from the traditional definition of managerial prerogatives that has dominated decisions of arbitral tribunals (Lansbury and Prideaux 1984).

Employers have generally rejected the term industrial democracy in favor of employee participation on the grounds that the latter implies the union is the sole channel for worker participation. Nonetheless, employers tend to be attracted to the forms of employee participation that encourage greater productivity and improved organizational effectiveness as well as the prospects of bettering the industrial relations climate. But many managers, especially those at the middle and lower levels, fear that both employee participation and industrial democracy may undermine their authority in the work place.

The Future of Managerial Unions

It is difficult to predict future trends in unionization among managers and professionals. There is often hesitation on the part of managers about joining a union that includes other levels of employees. This may be due not only to a fear of losing status by becoming a union member, but also because of concern about a conflict of interest between representing the employer and having an allegiance to a union.

Yet managers are increasingly aware that without the collective strength offered by a union they have little bargaining power with their employers.

During periods of recession, it also becomes apparent that managers, like shop-floor employees, are likely to suffer a reduction in their conditions of employment as well as the loss of their jobs.

Also as noted, issues of managerial pay and working conditions are now much more openly discussed than in the past and many managers increasingly express their dissatisfaction with their situation, especially at lower levels in the hierarchy. Hence, at the most basic level, managers are beginning to look for ways in which they might defend or enhance their position through collective action.

The increasing size of organizations is another factor that has influenced managers to consider unionization. In a large bureaucratic structure, many managers, especially at the lower and middle levels, feel remote from the source of decision-making.

A union may be seen as a forum in which managers' interests can be discussed and provide a channel for communication to higher level management. A union may also act as a pressure group to gain concessions for managers, especially when unions representing other groups of employees are seen to exercise considerable influence. The fact that managers have become more unionized in the public sector may be the result of experiencing a greater feeling of powerlessness in large government bureaucracies.

In the private sector, a closer sense of identity may still exist between managers and their companies but may also be more difficult to sustain as organizations become increasingly large and diffuse. Yet many private sector organizations do appear to be more flexible and generous in the reward systems and contracts of employment they offer to their managerial employees. Security of tenure for private sector managers is rapidly disappearing and the level of performance required of senior executives has increased. Thus, private sector managers and professionals may yet follow the example of their public sector colleagues and become more highly unionized.

CONCLUSIONS AND FUTURE DEVELOPMENTS

This chapter has traced the growth and development of managerial and professional employees in Australia. Not only is the old-style manager being replaced by the younger, more highly educated professional, but the nature of the managerial function is also changing. A diverse array of specialists now shares many of the technical aspects of what was formerly the manager's exclusive role. The fragmentation of managerial activity has also affected first-line and middle-level managers. Industrial relations and human resources specialists, for example, have taken over many of the responsibilities for recruitment, training, and even termination of staff that previously were the prerogatives of line management. The growing power of unions, not only at the shop-floor level but also within the ranks of clerical and administrative employees, has also restricted the freedom of managers to organize and distribute work at their own discretion. Pressures for greater employee involvement in decision-making and other forms of industrial democracy have caused many managers to reassess their role in the enterprise and to consider becoming unionized as a defensive measure.

One of the most significant areas of change examined in this chapter has been in the labor market processes involving managerial and professional employees. As a result of extensive changes in the Australian economic environment in recent years, including the internationalization of business and stronger competition in the marketplace, there has been much greater mobility among managers and professionals between organizations. This has eroded traditional single organization, where most senior management positions were filled by internal recruitment.

Two distinct managerial and professional groups are emerging in Australia: those who have been promoted from lower levels within one organization who tend to be older and have less formal qualifications, and those recruited into middle or senior positions externally who tend to be younger high fliers with wider experience and greater formal qualifications. Often the external managers and professionals enjoy a higher level of remuneration and perquisites than their internal counterparts since they are recruited on the basis of a special package of salary and conditions. This development has been assisted by the growth of executive search consultants or headhunters who specialize in procuring the services of senior managers from other organizations.

In the area of compensation systems, a great deal of attention has been paid to devising new tax-effective compensation systems that will attract and retain managers and professionals whose skills are in high demand. Such systems are now facing changes in the tax law that are designed to minimize the opportunities for tax avoidance. Compensation systems for managers and professionals are therefore likely to remain a dynamic area of change in the future.

It is possible that Australia will follow the trend established in other advanced industrial societies toward greater differentiation within management between a small but powerful group at the top and a middle- to lower-level group that feels powerless and demoralized. Our survey of selected companies found preliminary evidence of this trend, especially with the emergence of high fliers, a cadre recruited from the outside as needed and given special nurturing and developmental opportunities. This division is likely to deepen in the public sector where organizations are often larger and more bureaucratic and the distance between the top decision-makers and middle managers often appears to be greater. However, private sector managers are also increasingly vulnerable to retrenchment and dismissal as the result of the increasing number of takeovers and mergers. The concept of lifetime employment, particularly for managers, is no longer as tenable in either the public or private sectors.

In response to such changes, unionization may increase especially within the lower and middle levels of management. This may be achieved either by the expansion of existing white-collar and professional unions or through the establishment of new managerial unions—in the Australian context, the former is more likely. Whatever the outcome, the role of management will change in the years to come.

REFERENCES

Affirmative Action Resource Unit. 1985. *Affirmative action for women: A progress report on the pilot program*. Canberra: Prime Minister and Cabinet.

Australian Bureau of Labor Statistics. 1970–86. *Average weekly earnings*. Catalog No. 63020. Canberra: Australian Government Publishing Service.

————. 1984. *Employment benefits, Australia*. Canberra: Australian Government Publishing Service.

Australian Bureau of Statistics. 1981. *Census*. Canberra: Australian Government Publishing Service.

————. 1986. *Trade union membership*, August 1986. Canberra: Australian Government Publishing Service.

Australian Department of Employment and Industrial Relations. 1983–85. *Labor statistics*. Canberra: Australian Government Publishing Service.

Beed, C. S. 1967. *Career structures of Australian company directors*. Master of Commerce thesis, University of Melbourne, Melbourne.

Bell, G. 1984. Equal rights among the fat cats. *The Bulletin* (April 3):38–43.

Blandy, R. 1982. The senior executive. In *How labour markets work*, edited by R. Blandy and S. Richardson, 161–200. Melbourne: Langman Cheshire.

Byrt, W. J., and R. R. Masters. 1978. *The Australian manager*. Ringwood: Penguin.

Carter, D. 1985. Executive remuneration after tax reform. Paper read at conference, Issues for the '80s, July. Towers, Perrin, Forster and Crosby, Inc., Sydney.

Clements, R. V. 1958. *Managers: A study of their careers in industry*. London: George Allen and Unwin.

Congalton, A. A. 1969. *Status and prestige in Australia*. Melbourne: Cheshire.

Connell, R. W. 1977. *Ruling class, ruling culture*. Melbourne: University Press.

Critchley, B. 1984. Wanted: MBA's who have had a baptism of fire. *Rydges* (March):62–63.

Davies, A. F. 1964. *Australian democracy*. Melbourne: Cheshire.

Dixon, M. 1985. Money: It's also the root of all motivation. *The Australian Financial Review*, August 6.

Dunphy, D. C. 1981. *Organizational change by choice*. Sydney: McGraw-Hill.

Encel, S. 1970. *Equality and authority*. Melbourne: Cheshire.

Evans, J. 1982. *The unionisation of professionals and managerial staff in Europe*. Brussels: European Trade Union Institute.

Gorz, A., ed. 1978. *The division of labour: The labour process and class struggle in modern capitalism*. London: Harvester Press.

Hartmann, H. 1974. Managerial employees: New participants in industrial relations. *British Journal of Industrial Relations* 12 (2):268–81.

Hill, J. D., W. A. Howard, and R. D. Lansbury. 1983. *Industrial relations: An Australian introduction*. Melbourne: Longman Cheshire.

Hirsch, W. 1985. Flying too high for comfort. *Manpower Policy and Practice* 1 (Summer):14.

Isaac, J. E. 1980. Industrial democracy in the context of conciliation and arbitration. *Democracy in the work place,* edited by R. D. Lansbury, 34–53. Melbourne: Longman Cheshire.

Kavanagh, J. 1984. More money for executives (but you're gonna work for it) *Rydges,* 58 (February):17–18.

Kirk, J. F. 1984. A case study of affirmative action. *Australian Bulletin of Labour* 2 (1):43–46.

Lansbury, R. D. 1978. *Professionals and management.* St. Lucia: University of Queensland Press.

———. 1979–80. Australian white collar unions in transition. *Industrial Relations Journal* 10 (4):31–42.

Lansbury, R. D., ed. 1980. *Performance appraisal: Managing human resources.* Melbourne: Macmillan.

Lansbury, R. D., and G. J. Prideaux. 1984. Industrial and organisational democracy: The Australian experience. In *International perspectives on industrial democracy,* edited by B. Wilpert and A. Sorge, 495–511. London: Wiley & Sons.

Low Beer, J. 1978. *Protest and participation: The new working class in Italy.* Cambridge: Cambridge University Press.

Mallet, S. 1963. *La nouvelle classe ouvriere.* Paris: Editions du Sevil.

Mukhi, S. K. 1982. Leadership paths and profiles. *Human Resources Management Australia* 20 (3):20–26.

Nichols, T. 1970. *Ownership, control and ideology.* London: Allen & Unwin.

Noble Lowndes—Cullen, Egan, Dell (CED). 1984. *Annual review of executive salaries in Australia.* Sidney: Noble Lowndes—CED.

O'Dea, J. 1964. Some features of the professional engineers' case. *Journal of Industrial Relations* 4 (2):92–107.

O'Loughlin, T. 1974. *Australian managers: Background and attitudes.* Unpublished Master of Arts thesis in political science, University of Melbourne, Melbourne.

PA Consulting Group. 1982–86. *Annual Salary Surveys.* Sydney: PA Consulting Group.

Pym, D. L. 1971. Social change in the business firm. *Australian Management and Society,* edited by D. Mills. Ringwood: Penguin.

Reform of the Australian tax system: Draft white paper. 1985. Canberra: Australian Government Publishing Service.

Report of the Committee on Policies for the Development of Manufacturing Industry (The Jackson Report), Vol. 1. 1975. Canberra: Australian Government Publishing Service.

Report of the Inquiry into Management Education (The Ralph Report). 1983. Canberra: Australian Government Publishing Service.

Royal Commission on Trade Unions and Employers Associations 1965–68 (Donovan Commission). 1968. London: Her Majesty's Stationery Office.

Short, R. 1984. Australia opts for graduate mania. *The Australian Financial Review,* March 28.

Snape, E., and G. J. Bamber. 1985. Analysing the employment relationship of managers and professional staff. *Current research in management,* edited by V. Hammond, 144–63. London: Frances Pinter.

Still, L. V., and J. M. Jones. 1984. Perceptions of the Australian woman manager. *Search* 15 (9–10):278–84.

Strachan, G. 1985. The quiet achiever: Equal opportunity and industrial relations. Proceedings of the Second Conference of Association of Industrial Relations Academics in Australia and New Zealand, September, Brisbane.

Towers, Perrin, Forster and Crosby, Inc. (TFP & C). 1982. Actuaries and management. *World Wide Total Remuneration*. New York: Tower, Perrin, Forster and Crosby.

Whitley, R., A. Thomas, and J. Marceau. 1981. *Masters of business: The making of a new elite*. London: Tavistock Press.

Wilenski, P. 1984. Equal employment opportunity: Widening the agenda. Proceedings of a Conference on Reshaping the Work Place, June 6. Sydney: University of Sydney.

Williams, A. J. 1977. The independent entrepreneur. In *The Worker in Australia,* edited by A. Bordow, 113–47. St. Lucia: University of Queensland Press.

5
New Zealand

DAVID F. SMITH

The fastest growing occupational groups in New Zealand are managers and administrators. The demand for managers, especially those with skills in marketing and finance, is being fueled by the continued expansion of New Zealand's economy into the tertiary sector and by shifts in the government's economic policies.

From an industrial relations perspective, managers and administrators as employees are a particularly interesting group to study. In this nation where the majority of the work force is unionized and terms of employment are set through a highly centralized system of statutory regulations, only a small percentage of managers belong to unions, and for the most part these are in the public sector. A provocative question is why are the terms of managerial employment in New Zealand not influenced more heavily by the collective bargaining system?

THE GROWTH AND COMPOSITION
OF MANAGERIAL EMPLOYMENT

Substantial changes in the industrial and occupational composition of the work force have occurred in New Zealand since 1956. These changes take the form of a decline in employment in the agricultural sector and a growth in the secondary (primarily manufacturing) and tertiary (i.e., service) sectors. Another prominent change is the distinct shift toward employment in white-collar occupations, paralleling the growth experienced by other countries (Price and Bain 1983, 46–58). Out of the 1.24 million workers in the occupied labor force in 1981, 531,448 were salaried white-collar employees in the categories of higher professionals, lower professionals, administrators and managers, clerical workers, sales workers, foremen, inspectors, and supervisors. Of these, 72,579 or 5.8 percent were administrators and managers.

During the period 1956–81, employment in white-collar occupations rose by 272,572 or 105 percent, and its share of total employment rose from 32.6 to 42.7 percent. By contrast, in the same period employment in manual occupations rose by 158,220 or 41 percent, and its share of total employment fell from 48.2 to 43.5 percent.

Table 5.1 illustrates the changing structure of New Zealand's work force, showing the growth indices for each occupational category and the changes that took place between 1956 and 1981. The number of white-collar workers more than doubled during that period. Administrators and managers have experienced the fastest rate of growth, followed closely by lower professionals.

Smith (1984, 109) found that for the period 1971–81 the growth in the numbers of administrators and managers was due to across-the-board increases in those occupations as well as expansion of the tertiary sector. Two-thirds of these workers were employed in that tertiary sector, the fastest growing area of the economy; the balance were employed in the primary and secondary sectors, which have been declining in relative size since 1966.

Included in the category of administrators and managers are the following occupations: legislative officials, government administrators, general managers, production managers, government executive officials, wholesale and retail managers, catering and lodging managers, farm managers and supervisors, medical and public health administrators, and dental administrators. These are commonly referred to as middle and senior management. Lower levels of management such as foremen and supervisors are included in the separate category of foremen, inspectors, and supervisors.

Although female full-time labor force participation grew from 29.6 percent to 45.8 percent between 1956 and 1981, and the female percentage of the labor force rose from 23.8 percent to 33.7 percent over the same period, women's proportionate share of administrative and managerial jobs remained small. This increased from 5.8 to 12.3 percent and in numerical terms represents a growth of over 400 percent; however, it should be noted that women still only account for a small proportion of workers in these occupations (see Table 5.2). Women who do enter the work force tend to do so at lower occupational levels.

Studies of female occupations (Smith 1983) indicate that little change has taken place in the degree of overall occupational segregation in New Zealand, as those occupations that segregate the most have also been growing at the fastest rate. An examination of occupations (Smith 1984) reveals that of the total occupied female white-collar work force in 1981, more than 50 percent were clerical workers. Three occupational groups—lower professionals, clerical workers, and sales workers—accounted for 92 percent of female white collar employment, only 2 percent less than twenty-five years earlier.

While some progress is being made at managerial levels (see Table 5.2), by 1981 women still only accounted for a small share of senior management positions. A recent report on the banking industry (Downey 1984), which is gener-

Table 5.1 The occupied population of New Zealand by major category, 1956–81

Occupational category	Number of persons in major occupational categories 1956–81				Percentage of total occupied population 1956–81				Growth indices 1956–81 (1956 = 100)		
	1956	1966	1976	1981	1956	1966	1976	1981	1966	1976	1981
Employers and self-employed	152,942	143,255	174,998	171,510	19.2	14.3	14.2	13.8	94	114	112
All white-collar workers	258,876	385,379	518,956	531,448	32.6	38.5	42.2	42.7	149	200	205
Higher professionals	16,447	21,650	34,275	36,072	2.1	2.2	2.8	2.9	132	208	219
Lower professionals	54,445	87,299	126,258	127,288	6.8	8.7	10.3	10.2	160	232	234
Administrators and managers	30,275	44,997	68,962	72,579	3.8	4.5	5.6	5.8	149	228	240
Clerical workers	93,913	137,034	171,210	175,131	11.8	13.7	13.9	14.1	146	182	186
Sales workers	44,761	68,382	73,695	78,552	5.6	6.8	6.0	6.3	153	165	175
Foremen, inspectors, and supervisors	19,035	26,017	44,556	41,826	2.4	2.6	3.6	3.4	137	234	220
All manual workers	383,265	472,952	535,206	541,485	48.2	47.2	43.6	43.5	123	140	141
Total occupied population	795,033	1,001,586	1,229,160	1,244,443	100.0	100.0	100.0	100.0	126	155	157

Source: Smith 1984.

Table 5.2 Women's share of top white-collar jobs*

Occupation	Percent of women					
	1956	1961	1966	1971	1976	1981
Scientists	15.4	16.2	9.6	9.7	9.6	13.6
Architects, engineers, surveyors	0.9	0.5	0.3	1.0	1.8	2.8
Doctors	13.1	11.3	12.9	13.2	18.0	20.9
Dentists	7.2	8.2	5.6	7.0	6.0	24.2
Accountants	8.3	7.3	6.3	4.7	8.9	13.0
Lawyers	6.6	4.4	3.1	4.9	9.4	18.8
Judges	—	—	—	1.4	4.6	5.6
Government officials	1.9	2.1	1.7	3.8	7.6	10.8
General and production managers	1.2	1.6	2.0	2.5	5.0	5.8

Sources: Smith 1981 and Department of Statistics 1981.
*Wage and salary earners only.

ally typical, found that only 1 to 2 percent of executives and 6 to 9 percent of those at the next managerial level in the four trading banks were women.

SHORTAGE OF MANAGERIAL TALENT

Despite the rapid growth of managerial employment, New Zealand has experienced a long-standing shortage of such workers resulting from the drain of managers to Australia, New Zealand's closest neighbor (Ruth 1985a, 1985b). Of the 8,243 people who left New Zealand on a permanent or long-term basis from June 1984 to June 1985, 20 percent were in professional, managerial, and technical categories. Most of these people emigrate to Australia because no immigration formalities exist between the two countries, jobs in Australia are readily available, and wages are higher there (see discussion of compensation below).

For those who remain in New Zealand, the job market is buoyant provided they have appropriate skills; for example, there is currently a high degree of occupational mobility in finance and computer areas. Some companies have been reassessing the qualifications required for certain positions because those wanted initially are not available. While many employers attempt to keep salaries high to retain staff, considerable job movement still occurs for greater job satisfaction and opportunities. Many key managerial positions remain unfilled, and companies are recruiting overseas. The main drain of managers is in the 30 to 45 age group; accountants, for example, begin to leave the country at about age 25.

There is a national shortage of graduates trained in finance, administration, and business. To make matters worse, most universities have restrictions on entry into commerce subjects, particularly business and accounting, because of staff shortages caused by high turnover and difficulties in recruitment. This problem has been exacerbated recently by poor salaries for university staff which, until September 1985, had not been reviewed for over four years. During this time, salaries had fallen dramatically behind those of comparable occupations in the private sector. An indication of just how much salaries had lost ground is the awarding of up to 38 percent by the Higher Salaries Commission to some university staff to bring them into line with increases in the private sector.

In addition to staff shortages, the university system has accommodation problems and a lack of suitable facilities and equipment. Those graduates that do appear on the employment market are thus able to command attractive remuneration.

Traditionally, job security in New Zealand has never been a problem. Those displaced in the labor market have easily found other work under conditions of full employment. Though unemployment has risen in recent years, it is primarily unemployment of school-leavers and unskilled workers. Even so, unemployment levels are well below those of most other OECD countries with which New Zealand compares itself.

MANAGERS AND THEIR BACKGROUNDS

In terms of their social status, education, and experience, administrators and managers cannot be considered a homogeneous occupational category. New Zealand managers have been classified by Franklin (1985, 23–27) into four types: self-employed, salaried, self-employed worker-managers, and self-employed manager-experts.

The self-employed managers are those who run their own small firms and businesses. As noted in Table 5.1, they are declining in number and are being replaced by the salaried managers who represent the fastest-growing occupational group. This growth is a result of the emergence of the large company, which has evolved from the increasing number of takeovers and mergers as well as the spread of multinational corporations to New Zealand. The top ranks of this occupational group are filled by executives of foreign multinationals, and senior executives of large New Zealand companies. The country's small size, coupled with the many interlocking directorships of companies (Fogelberg and Laurent 1974), means that the senior members of this group constitute a close-knit network. Along with farmers and senior public servants, the top echelons of company managers have emerged as a significant interest group determining the country's economic direction.

The third type of occupational category is the self-employed worker-manager, characteristically a very influential socioeconomic group in New Zealand, according to Franklin (1985, 25). Farmers are the best example, for although many spend a large portion of their time in heavy manual work, small business skills and knowledge are also important ingredients for farming success. Thus, manual work coupled with good judgment have often brought individuals from the worker into the self-employed category.

The fourth type of manager is the self-employed small-business professional, the manager-expert: accountants, lawyers, family doctors, dentists, architects, and consultants. Together with the worker-manager, they produce what Franklin (1985, 26) terms the "self-employed syndrome," people who are generally conservative in outlook and fiercely independent.

One of the few aspects of managers' backgrounds that has been studied is educational preparation. Hines (1972, 14–15) found that managers were little different from the general work force in their possession of formal educational qualifications. At the time of the study, it was noted that 72.6 percent of the total labor force had no formal educational qualifications at all, while 65.5 percent of managers were in that category. This finding is supported by a more recent study of production executives (those above foreman level in charge of manufacturing) undertaken by Turner and Radford (1981). Replicating a study carried out by Gill and Lockyer (1977), Turner and Radford found that the educational qualifications for this group gave "cause for concern" (p. 108). Comparing their findings for New Zealand with those for Britain, they commented that educational levels for production executives in New Zealand were worse than those of Britain, which were themselves considered by the authors of the British study to be poor. Furthermore, it was found that the perception of training needs was lower in New Zealand than in Britain.

Also according to Turner and Radford, production executives in higher technology industries had greater academic qualifications and lower vocational training levels than in other industries. However, there is a continuing trend toward higher levels of education in more recent times, as reflected in the finding that educational qualifications varied inversely with age (Turner and Radford, 110).

A study of New Zealand's managerial elite (senior executives who have attained the position of executive director) carried out by Fogelberg and Greatorex (1979) found that those at the top of New Zealand's largest companies had higher levels of education than both lower level managers and the population as a whole. Over half (52.7 percent) came from backgrounds where their fathers were business owners, managers, or foremen, or had professional occupations. Only 7 percent came from the lower socioeconomic strata where their fathers were unskilled, semiskilled, or farm workers. These findings led the researchers to conclude that members of New Zealand's business elite were members of a relatively closed social group.

INDIVIDUAL CONTRACTS OF EMPLOYMENT

Individually negotiated rather than collectively negotiated contracts of employment define the terms and conditions of most managers and administrators in the private sector. Employment contracts are not necessarily created by formal documents or even express agreements, written or oral, but can be made without any words by the conduct of the parties (Szakats 1981, 95). For this reason, the rights and duties of the parties must be ascertained from a variety of other sources, written and unwritten, and include terms that are either implied or expressed, or incorporated from legislation or work rules.

Most senior administrators and managers in the private sector rely on individual negotiation of their employment contracts to secure the most favorable remuneration or perquisites. Such contracts are negotiated in the light of market scarcities and ruling rates for skill. These may include profit-sharing and bonus or commission arrangements as well as expense accounts and retirement benefits.

Middle management workers may have to tailor their demands to fit an organization's existing salary structure, and their bargaining, although individual, may be more restricted than that of senior level employees.

COMPENSATION OF MANAGERIAL EMPLOYEES

From time to time, the wages and conditions of employment have been set by government edict. This mechanism was most recently used during the wage freeze that lasted from June 1982 to December 1984.

When not determined by government edict, wages and conditions are set differently for managers who are members of unions and those who are not.

Union Members

For workers in the private sector who are members of a union, legislation provides that a dispute of interest must be created. The dispute may then be resolved either through voluntary negotiation of an agreement between the parties, or conciliation proceedings resulting in a conciliated settlement or an award by the Arbitration Court. The resulting settlement binds the parties under pain of various penalties. In the case of an award, blanket coverage applies that binds not only the parties directly involved, but all other unions and employers connected with that industry within the area to which the award relates, or who enter the industry while the award is in force.

For workers in the state sector, membership in service organizations (unions) is usually voluntary. As with the private sector, the arrangements governing establishment of bargaining agents are designed to prevent the undue proliferation of unions. In the state sector, unions tend to be larger and more closely knit than in the private sector; they also tend to cover more than one occupation and span a range of industries. Most of the 270,000 state employees work for only nine employers: public service, health service, post office, education service, armed forces, railways, police, broadcasting, and fire service. State employing authorities are therefore large organizations with established hierarchical structures and well-defined personnel procedures.

Broadly speaking, bargaining over pay and conditions is carried out by negotiation between the appropriate union and the particular employing authority in the state sector. Reviews of salaries and conditions can be initiated either by the lodging of a claim or by the employing authority conducting a review, which it is required to do from time to time under the legislation. The State Services Conditions of Employment Act specifies the conditions of employment that may be prescribed and the criteria to be followed in determining remuneration, allowances, leave, hours of work, and severance and redundancy pay. The setting of wages and conditions takes the form of a determination issued by the employing authority. There is provision for review and appeal to a tribunal, which performs a role similar to that of the Arbitration Court in the private sector.

All rates of remuneration in the state sector are reviewed annually, and adjustments are made to reflect any general movement outside the state services. In practice, the nine organizations that make up the state services closely coordinate their activities in the personnel field. Such liaison is necessary to prevent one state employer paying a higher or lower rate for the same job than the other state employers and thereby creating anomalies and possible industrial conflict.

The key to state pay-fixing is comparability and "relativity" (i.e., the historical and customary differentials) with the private sector. The pay of state servants always lags behind similar occupations in the private sector for these reasons. Salaries of senior state employees, including senior administrators and managers, are reviewed from time to time by the Higher Salaries Commission to ensure that they are in keeping with similar occupations elsewhere.

So strong is the reliance on relativities that historical relativities may be reconfirmed, despite shortages or surpluses of skills in personnel, and often without regard to the ability of the employer to pay.

The New Zealand pay-fixing system is very centralized. Unionized workers have their rates of pay fixed at the national or industry level, and there are two or three trend-setting awards that determine the appropriate rate for subsequent national awards. However, since the mid-1960s, in-house or plant-level bargaining has become increasingly important, and this has tended to modify the rigidities of the centralized national system of pay-fixing in the private sector.

In the state sector, the degree of standardization of employment is much greater than in the private sector. The State Services Coordinating Committee (SSCC) has been established to advise government on all personnel matters, including the coordination of pay and other conditions for state employees.

Nonunion Compensation

For the majority of private sector managers who do not belong to a union, the negotiation of pay and conditions is carried out on an individual basis. Most employers have established salary scales for particular benchmark jobs that are often imported by foreign companies and adapted to local conditions, or developed locally if the company is a New Zealand one. Some salary scales, particularly those of larger companies, are linked to merit systems through performance appraisal or management-by-objective plans. Some also make use of job evaluation linked to salary scales.

Particularly important in the New Zealand context of salaries and conditions for nonunionized managers and professional groups are surveys on salaries, fringe benefits, and other practices carried out by management consulting organizations such as PA Greenwood Surveys and Hay Associates New Zealand, Ltd., two prominent suppliers of compensation information. These data are especially useful to the many smaller organizations that do not have a developed personnel function. Besides evaluating salary movements and trends, such surveys also offer information on appropriate fringe benefit packages, traditionally a vital component of managerial remuneration in New Zealand where high marginal tax rates operate at very low salary levels when compared with other countries. Recently, however, the 1985 law taxing fringe benefits has complicated compensation issues.

Table 5.3 reports the average basic salary for a group of benchmark occupations as of September 1, 1985.

As indicated previously, an important question in salary decisions is the relationship of pay levels between New Zealand and Australia. Table 5.3 also shows that for those same benchmark occupations, salaries in New Zealand are

Table 5.3 New Zealand salaries for selected occupations

Occupation	New Zealand average basic salary as of Sept. 1, 1985 ($NZ)	New Zealand average salary as percent of Australian average salary			
		1982	1983	1984	1985
Senior finance executive	42,290	91.1	89.6	84.9	97.8
Senior engineering executive	41,375	94.3	89.1	86.7	92.9
Senior manufacturing executive	39,770	92.8	91.8	85.9	93.6
Senior marketing executive	39,540	89.3	85.6	85.8	91.4
Senior personnel executive	37,980	89.4	87.9	80.1	91.0
Data processing manager	32,380	89.1	90.7	86.4	93.4
Chief accountant	31,870	91.4	89.1	87.5	92.4
National sales manager	31,440	80.6	80.8	77.3	90.1
Engineer, level 3	30,860	96.7	97.4	88.1	100.5
Scientist, level 2	24,430	94.4	90.7	86.9	90.9
Engineer, level 1	21,254	93.7	82.8	85.9	101.1
Design draftsperson	21,130	91.9	88.7	91.4	89.2
Production Supervisor—under 25 staff	20,540	91.3	86.8	81.1	83.3
Sales representative	19,180	91.1	89.2	88.1	87.8
Warehouse supervisor—up to 10 staff	17,770	84.4	79.5	77.4	81.0
Confidential secretary	17,580	89.9	89.0	86.5	90.7
General clerk, level 3	17,050	92.3	91.8	89.0	95.3

Source: PA Management Consultants (Salary Surveys), New Zealand. Used with permission.

generally lower. If we take into account differences in exchange rates that generally favor Australia, the gap between the two countries is even greater; in addition, this differential widened considerably during 1984, the period of pay freeze in New Zealand.

MANAGERIAL UNIONISM

Administrators and managers are the least-unionized occupational group. In 1981 (the latest year for which figures are available), 10,097 (13.9 percent) administrators and managers, from a total potential membership of 72,579 were union members.

Membership

Table 5.4 gives details of white-collar union membership and density (percentage organized) by occupation for 1971 and 1981. For both years, the highest degree of unionization is to be found among clerical workers and lower professionals. In terms of the contribution to overall growth in potential and actual union membership, lower professionals and clerical workers were the largest contributors, accounting for 56.2 percent in potential union membership and 72.4 percent in actual union membership. Higher professionals, administrators and managers, and foremen, inspectors, and supervisors accounted for 35.9 percent of the growth in potential union membership, but only 14.5 percent of the increase in actual union membership during the period.

The greatest degree of unionism (about 59 percent of the white-collar work force) is in the tertiary sector and concentrated among clerical and lower professional employees. Manufacturing is very poorly unionized, showing a total of 378, or 2 percent of the total potential administrators and managers and 16.7 percent of all white-collar workers belonging to a union.

Managerial Unionism and Collective Bargaining

Most administrators and managers in the private sector are not covered by a union. Even if they wish to be, many unions operate a salary bar to limit the coverage of an award; in addition, the membership rules of many unions exclude managers and administrators. There is no separate union for this occupational group in the private sector.

In the state sector, even though administrators and managers may be union members, little scope for bargaining exists because of the panoply of regulations surrounding state pay-fixing. Changes to salaries and conditions take place as a result of the system of review and adjustment, and all state servants receive these whether union members or not.

Any discussion of collective bargaining in the New Zealand context should note that few other democratic countries have relied as heavily on nonmarket

Table 5.4 White-collar union membership and density by occupation in New Zealand, 1971–81

Occupation	1971			1981			Change in density 1971–81 (percent change)	Percent of growth in membership accounted for by this occupation	
	Potential membership	Actual membership	Density	Potential membership	Actual membership	Density		Potential membership	Actual membership
Higher professional	25,388	8,049	31.7	36,072	12,917	35.8	+4.1 (+12.9%)	11.9	5.0
Lower professional	100,576	55,168	54.9	127,288	88,426	69.5	+14.6 (+26.6%)	29.7	33.9
Administrators and managers	56,482	6,344	11.2	72,579	10,097	13.9	+2.7 (+24.1%)	17.9	3.8
Clerical workers	151,342	87,610	57.9	175,131	125,427	71.6	+13.7 (+23.7%)	26.5	38.5
Sales workers	71,467	25,223	35.3	78,552	38,062	48.5	+13.2 (+37.4%)	7.9	13.1
Foremen, inspectors, and supervisors	36,389	12,282	33.8	41,826	17,844	42.7	+8.9 (+26.3%)	6.1	5.7
Totals	441,644	194,676	44.1	531,448	292,773	55.1	+11.0 (+24.9%)	100.0	100.0

Source: Smith 1984.

forms of wage and price control. Between March 1971 and July 1985, only eight months can legitimately be regarded as a period of free collective bargaining, since during that period the government sought by a variety of statutory and nonstatutory means to slow down the growth of nominal wages (Boston 1985).

Only during the past decade has the number of administrators, managers, technical, and professional workers seeking collective representation grown, although the unionization of managerial and supervisory workers was recognized by the Arbitration Court as early as 1903 in the case of *Shipmasters' Association of New Zealand* v. *The Registrar*.

Factors Affecting Managerial Unionism

Several factors have combined to produce this heightening of interest in unionization (Wilson 1983, 2). These include an awareness by white-collar workers that despite the strong demand for managerial employees, they are as vulnerable to dismissal and redundancy as hourly paid workers, but without statutory protections; that their role and status are changing as smaller enterprises have given way to larger; and that many rewards and benefits of salaried employees are being eroded by inflation and the aggressive bargaining of hourly paid workers' trade unions.

In addition, it has become clear to many administrative and managerial workers, especially in the private sector, that under New Zealand's industrial relations system, their interests are best protected through registration as an industrial union under the 1973 Industrial Relations Act. Without registration it is difficult, although not impossible, to obtain an award or collective agreement. This collective agreement protects wages and conditions, is a safeguard against unjustifiable dismissal, and provides the chance to obtain compensation following redundancy. Dismissal and redundancy are the areas where administrators and managers are especially vulnerable since most have only their individual contracts of employment to fall back on. For example, twenty-three redundancies were announced without warning in 1984 at International Computers Ltd. in New Zealand, and of these, three were regional general managers.

Legal Obstacles

Legal constraints on managerial unionism are an important factor influencing the low level of such associations in the private sector (Binnie and Smith 1984). Registration under the Industrial Relations Act is vital to union recognition in that it forces employers to negotiate with a group of workers. Some "unions" attempt to operate as voluntary associations of workers or incorporated societies in the form of staff or in-house associations. However, an examination of these in the private sector (Smith 1984) revealed that most could not be classified as unions since they did not negotiate wages or conditions.

The law relating to trade union registration protects established unions, especially where there is danger of new unions poaching on their membership.

A prospective union must comply with stringent criteria before it is granted registration by the Registrar of Industrial Unions. Such criteria restrict registration to workers in specific industries and occupations not already covered by a union, making it very difficult to establish unions for administrators and managers. This was demonstrated recently in the Arbitration Court's decision to deny registration to various managerial employees (*New Zealand Association of Professional, Executive, Scientific and Managerial Staffs* v. *Registrar*, 1983) on the grounds that the proposed union did not belong to a specified industry since potential members were spread horizontally across several industries.

Since collective bargaining, under New Zealand conditions, is so heavily reliant on union registration, and as the registration of unions for administrators and managers is so difficult to obtain, it may be expected that little collective bargaining takes place involving this occupational group.

Some managerial associations operate without registration, either as voluntary associations or incorporated societies. Most, however, lack bargaining strength, particularly those dominated by employers; ironically, such associations are often dependent on the employer's good will for their continued existence.

In the state sector, legislation is a less important influence on union registration and collective bargaining for administrative and managerial employees; in any case, recognition has already been granted to unions covering this occupational group. As already discussed, however, the degree of collective bargaining that actually takes place in the state sector is very limited and does not compare favorably with the private sector.

Attitudes of Employees

The question of managerial unionism is one that gives rise to considerable debate among managers themselves. Many undoubtedly believe they are different from other workers, having more in common with the owners of the business than with those on the shop floor. New Zealand is a small country with a small work force and with most managerial employees working in small organizations. Such organizations are frequently run along paternalistic lines with owners and managers working alongside one another. This size factor is thus another influence mediating against managerial unionism.

Government Actions

Government actions and pronouncements have an impact on the shape of trade unionism in a direct way through its industrial relations and employment policies, and through the political climate it creates (Bain and Price 1983, 12). Since 1949, government has been dominated by the National Party, the party of the small businessman, the farmer, and private enterprise. During this period, a Labour government has been in power for only two three-year terms until the election of the present Labour government in 1984.

Antithetical toward trade unionism, National governments have frequently been elected into office on an anti-union platform. Once in power, they have a record of introducing legislation that imposes constraints on the behavior of unions by increasing the restrictive provisions surrounding their activities—limitations on membership fees, restrictions on welfare payments, penalties for strikes and other industrial actions, and abolition of the closed shop. Furthermore, their public pronouncements on union matters do little to disguise their anti-union ideology. Labour governments, by contrast, have generally been much more sympathetic to trade unions, and most of the advances in union rights have been made on those rare occasions when a Labour government has been in power. It is probably not by chance that the greatest growth in union membership for both manual and white-collar workers took place between 1971 and 1976, coinciding with the period in office of a Labour government of 1972–75.

Employer Attitudes

Employer policies and attitudes toward trade unionism are less important in New Zealand, where union recognition is much more circumscribed by government action, than in countries where union matters are generally decided between employers and unions. Nevertheless, employer attitudes toward union recognition can influence potential members' willingness to join or form unions. Systematic evidence on employer policies and attitudes toward managerial unionism is difficult to obtain; however, some general observations may be made.

Substantial differences exist in attitudes toward the unionization of managerial employees on the part of employers in the state and private sectors. Though most state employees are not obliged to join unions (the exceptions being post office and railway workers), most do and are encouraged to do so by the employing authority. Even the most senior executives of state sector organizations join the appropriate unions, apparently without qualms. Procedures for consultation and negotiation are well established, and unions are generally well financed and organized, much more so than their private sector counterparts.

In the private sector, most white-collar workers, other than clerical and sales workers, are not unionized. Employers are generally opposed to unionization, and engage in the twin strategies of peaceful competition and forcible opposition (Bain 1970, 131–41) to prevent it. For example, many potential members, fearing reprisals, have refused to reveal their identities to the Society of Technicians, Administrators, Managers and Supervisors (STAMS). Like their colleagues, they are torn between the desire to be loyal to their company and the knowledge that their interests are not necessarily being safeguarded by their employer.

Management's Relationship to Political Processes

Curiously, the election of a Labour government in 1984 may herald a rise in managerial fortunes. Although traditionally a party of the workers and elected with powerful and overt trade union support, the government has made a radical departure from its socialist and working-class image. So swiftly has it moved to put in place its free-market policies, and so many changes has it made, that most interest groups have been left bewildered by the pace of developments. In one year, the government has attempted to cut spending and reduce unemployment, devalued the currency, removed subsidies from many commodities, presided over a doubling and in some cases a tripling of interest rates, ended a two-year wage and price freeze, increased social welfare payments to some families, and foreshadowed major income and consumption tax reforms.

In seeking a consensus for its reforms, one of the first moves of the new government was to convene an Economic Summit Conference of representatives from a broad spectrum of New Zealand society. The idea was borrowed from the Australian Labour Government, which carried out a similar exercise after its election, but this is not to demean its impact on New Zealanders. To most people, the new mood of consensus was a profound relief after the years of confrontational politics that typified the outgoing National Party Government of Sir Robert Muldoon. The incoming Labour administration chose as chair of the steering committee Sir Ronald Trotter, chairman and chief executive of Fletcher Challenge, New Zealand's largest company and biggest exporter.

Present government policies are firmly committed to export-led economic growth as a route out of New Zealand's current financial difficulties. And, in a world with substantial surpluses of New Zealand's traditional exports of meat and dairy produce, a new emphasis is being placed on diversification into manufactured goods, secondary processing of primary produce, and tourism. With this has come a new awareness of marketing and a premium paid for those with marketing skills. Market research and advertising agencies are growing in numbers and high salaries are being paid for those with managerial or creative talent in this field.

Company managers are strong advocates of free enterprise, competition, and the superiority of market forces. The new government has made significant departures from traditional New Zealand government policies of subsidies and protectionism in favor of a more market economy, strongly advocated by many of those in private enterprise for a considerable time. Thus, in their endorsement of government policy, and as the chief instruments by which the new economic policies will be put into place, company managers may be emerging as a new and influential elite, perhaps even replacing farmers whose fortunes have taken a severe downturn as a result of changes in government policies. The advent of a Labour government also may witness a rise in the fortunes of those managers who wish to unionize. Among its first official acts was the restoration of compulsory unionism, abolished during the term of the previous government. The passage of the Union Membership Act in 1985 honored a commitment to the trade union movement in return for its support during the election campaign. The Act restores the legality of unqualified preference clauses in awards and negotiated settlements, which have the effect of making union membership compulsory for workers within a specified period of taking up employment (postentry closed shop).

Encouraged by the supportive climate for unions, STAMS has begun lobbying the government for changes in the Industrial Relations Act to secure protection for nonunionized workers, particularly technicians, administrators, managers, and supervisors. STAMS officials estimate that there are at least 300,000 employees in New Zealand, many of them managers, who have no job protection against unjustified dismissal; only those workers covered by awards have the protection of the Arbitration Court. Accordingly, a proposal has been put to the Minister of Labour to amend the act so as to apply the personal grievance procedure contained in awards to all contracts of employment. This proposal is currently under consideration by the Parliamentary Select Committee on Labour and Education.

SUMMARY AND CONCLUSIONS

A substantial change has taken place in the composition of the New Zealand work force, resulting in a large increase of employment in managerial occupations. This change has been accompanied by intersectoral movements in the distribution of employment leading to a growth of employment in the tertiary sector.

The setting of wages and conditions for unionized salaried managers in both public and private sectors is closely prescribed by legislation, and the degree of collective bargaining that exists is very limited. However, most administrators and managers are not unionized and must negotiate as individuals directly with their employers. Unionization of administrators and managers is much greater in the public than in the private sector.

Managerial skills are in short supply in New Zealand, and those with appropriate qualifications command attractive salaries. Nevertheless, job mobility is high with managers looking in increasing numbers toward Australia for jobs where salaries are even more attractive and prospects for advancement greater. Job security in New Zealand has never been a problem under conditions of full employment and recurring labor shortages. Those displaced have easily found work elsewhere, and this may be part of the reason for the absence of any strong pressure for unionization. In any case, unionization is difficult for managers in the private sector where legislation favors existing unions over new ones, and makes it difficult for managers to form or join unions.

The demand for managerial talent seems sure to continue as a result of the changes brought about by new government policies; New Zealand is evolving from exporting primary produce toward a greater emphasis on manufacturing and secondary processing coupled with the development of new industries needing marketing and managing skills. It appears, too, that the recent change of government will contribute toward a rise in managerial fortunes that may ultimately be reflected in managers' remuneration and social standing.

REFERENCES

Bain, G. S. 1970. *The growth of white-collar unionism.* Oxford: Oxford University Press.

Bain, G. S., and R. Price. 1983. Union growth: Dimensions, determinants and density. In *Industrial relations in Britain,* edited by G. S. Bain, 3–33. Oxford: Blackwell.

Binnie, K. D., and D. F. Smith. 1984. Managerial unionism and the law in New Zealand. *New Zealand Journal of Industrial Relations* 9 (2):69–80.

Boston, J. 1985. Incomes policy and the 1985–1986 wage round: From non-market failure to market failure? *New Zealand Journal of Industrial Relations* 10 (2):65–82.

Department of Statistics. 1981. *Labour Force.* Vol. 4, *New Zealand Census of Population and Dwellings, 1981.* Wellington: Department of Statistics.

Downey, P. J. 1984. *Women in banking: A report on complaints of sex discrimination in the New Zealand banking system.* Wellington: Human Rights Commission.

Fogelberg, G., and C. R. Laurent. 1974. *Boards of directors of New Zealand companies,* Research Paper No. 1. Wellington: Department of Business Administration, Victoria University of Wellington.

Fogelberg, G., and D. S. Greatorex. 1979. Occupational origins and career paths of New Zealand's managerial elite. *New Zealand Journal of Business* 1:15–37.

Franklin, H. 1985. *Cul de sac: The question of New Zealand's future.* Wellington: Unwin Paperbacks.

Gill, R. W. T., and K. C. Lockyer. 1977. *The career development of the production manager in British industry,* Occasional Paper OPN 17. London: British Institute of Management Foundation.

Hines, G. H. 1972. *The New Zealand manager.* Wellington: Hicks, Smith & Sons Ltd.

Price, R., and G. S. Bain. 1983. Union growth in Britain: Retrospect and prospect. *British Journal of Industrial Relations* 21 (1):46–58.

Ruth, J. 1985a. Heavy drain of key people. *National Business Review* 16 (22):1.

———. 1985b. Worker loss may begin to threaten companies. *National Business Review* 16 (32):3.

Smith, D. F. 1981. Assessing the growth of New Zealand's white-collar work force. *Australian and New Zealand Journal of Sociology* 17 (2):77–84.

———. 1983. Occupational segregation amongst white-collar workers in New Zealand. *New Zealand Economic Papers* 17:37–49.

———. 1984. *An investigation into the growth and unionization of New Zealand's white-collar work force,* A Research Report to the Social Sciences Research Fund Committee. Wellington: Department of Business Administration, Victoria University of Wellington.

Szakats, A. 1981. *Introduction to the law of employment.* Wellington: Butterworths.

Turner, R., and R. W. Radford. 1981. The New Zealand production executive. *New Zealand Journal of Business* 3:105–125.

Wilson, M. 1983. The plight of professional, managerial, supervisory unions. *Direction: The Journal of the Society of Technicians, Administrators, Managers and Supervisors* 1 (1):2–8.

List of Cases

New Zealand Association of Professional, Executive, Scientific and Managerial Staffs v. *Registrar of Industrial Unions*. 1983. Unreported, Arbitration Court, 7 March (A C 19/83), Horn CJ.

Shipmasters' Association of New Zealand v. *Registrar*. 1903. BA 259 Vol. 4.

III
CONTINENTAL EUROPEAN COUNTRIES

6
Germany

EBERHARD WITTE*

In the nineteenth century, when many new companies were being established, the figure of the company executive did not exist. This is again the case today in the modern wave of company formation, especially in the field of advanced technology. The founder is an expert and an executive rolled into one; the need for persons of authority with the power to make decisions, who are, however, not the owners of the company, arises only with company expansion. The proprietor then tries to recruit trustworthy people to run the organization. This is why the rank of "procurator" exists in German law, signifying a person who is a caring representative of the company and is in close contact with the owner family. The Latin word stem (procurare = to care for, to tend, to administer) expresses this concept, while the legal definition establishes the right to legally represent the company through official appointment and judicial entry into a public registry. When property passes to the following generation, the procurator is often appointed executor of the will and, as such, must ensure that the inheritors of the company continue to run it according to the wishes of their predecessors.

Since the predominant criterion in Germany for selecting these leaders is not only expertise but loyalty to a company's owner, leadership figures have never characterized themselves as managers. However, the development of an employee prototype has been encouraged by trends toward a wider distribution of joint stock companies, diversification of products, and establishment of subsidiary companies. This type of employee emerged at the turn of the century and was clearly distinguishable from the remainder of the work force by the nature of the tasks he or she performed.

*Translated by Aileen Hooper.

Technicians, lawyers, and finance and marketing experts gradually made their way into company management. They were hired for their expert abilities, not because of personal ties with the owners. This development involved breaking the tradition that considered retired military officers, who were accustomed to giving orders and having them obeyed, as particularly suited to management positions. What remained was a certain elitist attitude, manifest in dress, social behavior, and politically conservative thinking, which still elevates executives above the level of managers who are merely specialists in their fields.

Not until after World War II did a new concept of the "manager" emerge. Traditional leaders, who considered themselves upper class, were replaced by managers whose qualities were judged entirely according to performance. This change occurred when the philosophy of the profession was being taken over by the principles of marketing and management, management style, organizational behavior, further professional training, and the internationalization of business events. The German executives now no longer hesitated to label themselves managers. Educational centers for further training in the profession called "manager academies" offered management techniques, and management achievement became a widespread notion.

In this development, German management and managers, to a great extent, have maintained their unique qualities in the background, education, and preparation of managers and in their roles within companies. These qualities were the subject of considerable controversy in a report commissioned by the Federal Economics Ministry, written by the consulting firm of Booz, Allen and Hamilton, and published in 1970. See the translation and criticism of the report in Hartmann (1973).

In this chapter, some of those unique and well-known qualities of German managers and management are reviewed, but more time is spent reporting on the growing body of information about the attitudes of German managers that gives a deeper insight into the conditions of their employment.

DEFINITION OF MANAGERIAL EMPLOYEES

White-collar employees in German organizations are stratified by law and custom in terms of the tasks they perform and their relationship to the management of the company or works.

The Structure of Managerial Employment

Table 6.1 illustrates the layers of managerial and nonmanual employees in a large manufacturing company. The executive board or *Vorstand* should not be confused with the types of boards of directors found in American companies. German companies also have another board of directors called the *Aufsichtsrat*, which appoints top executives to an executive board. This executive board names and promotes the *Leitende Angestellte* or upper manager.

Table 6.1 Levels of management

Managerial group	Management level	Task or job title
Spitzenfuehrungskrafte	1. Top or senior managers and executives who are members of executive boards	Executive Board (*Vorstand* in a publicly held company or *Geschaeftsfuehrung* in a privately held company)
Leitende Angestellte	2. Upper manager	Vice presidents (*Direktoren*)
	3. Middle manager	Department heads in large department (*Hauptabteilungsleiter*)
		Department heads in subdepartments (*Abteilungsleiter*)

Source: Lawrence 1980, 30–55.

The *Leitende Angestellte* and its subcategories are the focus of this study; however, comparisons will also be made to senior managers where appropriate.

Legal Distinctions

German labor law makes a broad distinction between workers and employees. Blue-collar personnel are the workers hired as craftspeople and mechanics. In 1985, there were 11 million of them, over half the work force of 20.5 million that is not self-employed. Employees, of whom there are approximately 9.5 million, were engaged as white-collar workers in the offices. Managerial workers on every level are generally included in the employee group. The difference between the two groups lies mainly in the fact that they are subject to different health insurance and retirement plans, that workers receive weekly wages while employees have a monthly salary, and that notification of dismissal is somewhat longer for employees (six weeks' notice as compared to two weeks' notice for workers).

No distinction is made between senior, middle, or junior employees. The only difference is that junior employees are hired on a fixed salary scale negotiated by unions and employer organizations, while middle and senior level employees have individual salary agreements.

When codetermination was introduced in Germany in the 1950s (1951 in the mining industry and 1952 in other large enterprises), incompany trade representation was reestablished for workers and junior employees only. Middle and senior level managerial employees, being part of company management, were not included.

The experience gained during twenty years of codetermination in Germany led to the reformation of incompany codetermination and the Law on the Constitution of Enterprises in 1972 (Fitting, Wlotzke, and Wissmann, 1976). An attempt was made to include middle and senior management, but not members of the executive board, in company constitutions. It was obvious the reorganizers took considerable care when drawing the dividing line between lower management and middle and upper management. The lower level employees remained classed with the workers under old codetermination laws, while middle and upper management were given the title of managerial employees to distinguish them clearly from lower management. Managerial employees were awarded certain rights and, in particular, were removed from the jurisdiction of the works council. This council, which represented workers and lower-level employees, had attempted again and again to have access to managerial employees' personnel files in order to draw them into its sphere of influence.

The law attempted to determine the dividing line by drawing up a definition of the managerial employee. The text from P5, Section 3, of the Law on the Constitution of Enterprises of 1972 reads:

> This law finds . . . no application to managerial employees, if they, according to position and contract,
>
> 1. have the power to independently hire or dismiss persons employed in the company or in any department of the company, or,
> 2. have general power of procuration or power of attorney, or,
> 3. on the whole, carry out responsible duties which are regularly assigned to them because of the importance of their role in the continuation and the further development of the enterprise, due to their particular experience and expertise.

This delimitation is of major importance for the definition of managerial employees as a social group within the company. The distinctions in the law are, for the most part, legally undefined and can, therefore, be interpreted restrictively or expansively, depending on intention. After this law came into effect in 1972, it was left up to the courts to make a decision, based on a large number of cases, concerning the limitation of its possible interpretations (Krumm 1983, 15). The courts were, however, able to retain considerable flexibility in the judgment of the determining features of a managerial employee (see Decision of the Federal Labor Court, No. 26, 36/1980).

The courts' definition of managerial employment has implications for the jurisdiction of the workers council. For example, the workers council has the right of codetermination in personnel matters such as dismissal or promotion only for persons who fall under the law cited above.

Empirically established criteria offer a better opportunity for the demarcation of the managerial employees group. In a study of more than 2,000 employees in 116 industrial and commercial companies beginning in 1973 (Witte and Bronner 1974, 120), the following features were sufficiently representative:

Power of attorney

Level of management (up to the fourth management level)

Yearly income

Responsibility for personnel (over 300 directly subordinate staff members)

Business responsibility for over 25 percent of total costs or 15 percent of total sales

With very few exceptions, all employees who are managers are described by these criteria.

THE MANAGERIAL EMPLOYEE AS AN INDIVIDUAL

The estimated number of managerial employees in Germany today is 500,000 (Witte and Bronner 1974). Earlier figures are difficult to determine, but it is safe to say that this group has grown since World War II in absolute numbers as well as in relation to the total number of workers and employees (Krumm 1983, 5); that is, from about 1 percent in 1957 (Grüll 1958, 42ff.; Hromadka 1979, 205ff.) to about 2.6 percent in 1979 (Borgwardt 1979, 14). The percentages naturally vary greatly across branches of industry, beginning at the low end with 1.4 and 1.6 percent in metal processing and construction, and reaching a high of 4.9 percent in the chemical industry (Borgwardt 1979, 18ff.; Witte and Bronner 1974, 46).

Personal Characteristics of Managerial Employees

The managerial cohort is described here in terms of age, sex, education, professional experience, and attitudes toward work.

Age
Several large-sample investigations indicate that the age structure of executives has changed very little over the years. Managers on the first level below the executive board have a mean age of 47, while those on the next lower level average 46 years old (Bertelsmann Foundation and Institute for Social and Economic Policy, hereafter called IWG, 1985, 18; Kienbaum 1984, Table 8; and Witte, Kallmann, and Sachs, also identified as WKS, 1981, 121). In large firms, where the career ladder has more steps and therefore takes longer, the average age of the managerial employee exceeds by six years that of an executive in a smaller company (Kienbaum 1984).

Sex
Although women make up about 40 percent of the German working population, they represent only 2 percent of the executives. This percentage is higher in positions that involve little contact outside the firm, such as personnel (9 percent), the legal department (7 percent), finance, and general administration (each 6 percent). The salaries of female executives indicate definite sexual inequality in German companies because women earn about 20 percent less than

their male counterparts (Tänzer 1984, 35). The representation of women in the managerial occupations and the compensation of women are not likely to improve quickly.

Education

The higher the position within the company hierarchy, the more university or college graduates one encounters. These graduates constitute 44 percent of managers on the second level (i.e., middle managers), 54 percent of executives on the level directly under the executive board, and 62 percent of managing directors (Kienbaum 1984, Diagram 2; Tänzer 1984, 4). If one contrasts these 1984 findings with those elicited by Witte in 1979 (Witte 1981, Table 2), then the generation turnover that has occurred in the intervening years becomes evident. On the level of managing director, the practically oriented figures of the postwar period have abdicated in favor of academically educated managers. On the first and second levels under managing director, the proportion of those with academic credentials has, however, decreased despite Kienbaum's observation that at all levels of the managerial hierarchy in the past ten years, there is a definite trend in favor of higher qualifications (Kienbaum 1984, 2).

The size of the company plays an important role in this respect, also. There is a balance between elementary school and university graduates in companies with up to 250 employees; however, those managers with a university background increasingly dominate over those with only elementary school education in the larger companies. In large firms with over 5,000 employees, the university/elementary school ratio even reaches 15:1 (Kienbaum 1984, 3). Furthermore, 31 percent of the executives with an academic background have doctorates. The number of PhDs is highest in natural sciences (57 percent), followed by law (34 percent), engineering (25 percent), and business studies (20 percent) (Kienbaum 1984).

Among managerial employees, one is most likely to encounter technical backgrounds, followed by natural sciences and business sciences. It is interesting to note that the emphasis is different among members of the executive board where business studies clearly dominate (Witte 1981, Table 3). Although lawyers constitute a small minority, it appears that they will continue to be represented at this minority level in the future also (Landsberg 1984, 40ff.).

Experience

A comparison between company affiliation and professional experience of managerial employees offers an interesting insight into company advancement practices. About one-third were placed directly in their position as managerial employee when they joined the company. The remaining two-thirds were recruited internally and have careers of varied duration behind them. Kienbaum's extensive investigation (1984, 4) found an average period of firm affiliation of sixteen years, eight of which were spent in the present position. Considering the average age of managerial employees, it seems that in the course of their careers there is usually at least one change of company.

Attitude Toward Work

In Germany, as in many other industrial nations, a change in the work morale of the population can be observed. To call this a shift away from values of duty and acceptance in favor of those of self-interest would be a strong simplification of the problem (IWG 1985, 8). It requires instead more differentiation, particularly in respect to the managerial employee under discussion here. As seen in Table 6.2, large-scale survey results show variance in professional attitudes among different population groups. Nevertheless, about 95 percent of the managers admitted in varying degrees to a conception of their profession in which work is considered as a duty that is not dependent on attractive financial gains, and that requires private affairs to take second place. This demonstrates that the traditional attitude toward the profession remains firmly anchored within the executive group. While the degree of concurrence with this attitude diminishes as those who were surveyed get older (IWG 1985, 13), the strength of the attitude among managers cannot be entirely ascribed to age because younger managerial employees generally hold more junior positions.

The relative importance of professional and private matters can serve as a further indicator of the general attitude toward work prevalent among managerial employees and executives. In the IWG survey, 36 percent stated that work usually has the highest priority, 51 percent said that professional demands and private interests are of equal importance, and 9 percent said that family or private affairs take precedence over the demands of work. Consequently, it is no longer possible to assume unconditionally, even for executives, that professional matters have complete priority over all other aspects of life. Table 6.3 shows, to the contrary, that a shift in priorities toward the private spheres of life has taken place among younger executives.

Forty percent of managerial employees aged 40 to 60 years, which is the majority of this occupational group, state that as a rule the profession still has priority for them; however, among those under 49 years of age, 29 percent think likewise. With retirement from professional life already on the horizon, it is easy to understand why those over 60 years of age devote themselves more to their private affairs and consciously try to disassociate themselves from their profession.

A similar pattern was produced by sorting the responses according to income groups. The influence of age and position then overlap, but the results indicate the need for a deeper understanding of the motivation structure of managerial employees.

When managerial employees themselves evaluate the significance of various factors that influence their motivation to work, it can clearly be seen that intrinsic incentives predominate, that is, those produced by the work itself (IWG 1985, 24). The picture changes, however, if managerial employees are asked what could incite them to change their jobs. An increase in salary is then most frequently mentioned, followed by opportunities for working independently and influencing the duties one performs (IWG 1985, 36).

Table 6.2 Evaluation of profession

	Occupational groups (percentages)					
Opinions	Skilled and unskilled workers	Specialized workers[a]	Nonmanagement employees and civil servants[a]	Managerial employees and senior civil servants[a]	Freelancers and the self-employed[a]	Employers and executives[b]
Opinion A I devote myself entirely to my profession and often do more than is required of me. My profession is so important to me that I make many sacrifices on its account.	28	35	34	61	80	90
Opinion B I perform my duties as is expected of me; therefore I cannot be accused of any neglect. I do not, however, think that I should need to exert myself particularly beyond this point. My job is not all that important to me.	61	49	47	19	8	8
Undecided/no statement	11	16	19	20	12	2

Source: Bertelsmann Foundation and IWG 1985, 15.

[a]Compiled by the Institut für Demoscopy Allensbach (IFD).
[b]Findings reported by Institut für Wirtschafts-und Gesellschaftspolitik (IWG).

Table 6.3 Relationship between professional and private interests

		Age in years (percentages)				Gross monthly income in DM (percentages)			
	Total	Under 39	40–49	50–59	60 and over	Under 4,999	5,000– 9,999	10,000– 19,999	20,000 and over
Family or private interests are more important to me than professional demands	9	11	8	7	15	17	8	8	3
Private interests and professional demands are of equal importance	51	57	50	51	42	64	58	42	58
As a rule, my profession is more important	36	29	40	40	32	17	34	49	39
No statement	3	3	2	2	11	1	1	1	—
N	1065	237	451	277	85	143	449	222	36

Source: Bertelsmann Foundation and IWG 1985, 16.

Concerning the question of enticements for changing jobs, the crucial issues have changed significantly over the last five years. Table 6.4 presents a comparison of survey results on this subject obtained by the IWG in 1985 and comparable data gathered in 1981 by Witte, Kallmann, and Sachs. It is obvious that income, authority, and independence are named less often, but the nature of the duties themselves as well as improved advancement and career opportunities are also offered less frequently as possible reasons for transfer. Significantly more frequent, however, is greater security in employment and income, while improved retirement provisions remain constant. Unemployment, which has risen dramatically in recent years, may have contributed toward this tendency for executives to think more in terms of security, although the unskilled workers have been most affected, rather than managerial employees.

Even though material incentives are not considered particularly important for performance, they are the most frequently mentioned reasons for a potential change in position. This seems to indicate the necessity for further investigation. According to a survey in 1985 (IWG, 41), 64 percent of managerial employees would continue to work as they have been doing even if they were financially self-sufficient. Only one-third would allow financial independence to influence their work habits, and only 10 percent would discontinue working entirely.

When asked what percentage their gross income would need to increase to motivate managerial employees to work 10 percent more than at present, one-third stated that they were already working to full capacity, while an additional 20 percent responded that greater willingness to work would be independent of income. In all, 57 percent of managerial employees could not be further motivated by financial means to perform better at work. For an even greater number (64 percent), work and material needs are not related. An analysis of responses according to the level of income of those questioned actually revealed that the effectiveness of material incentives decreases with increasing income. However,

Table 6.4   Changes in willingness to change jobs

Factors influencing the decision to change jobs	WKS 1981	IWG 1985
	(Multiple answers were possible)	
Higher income	42%	33%
More opportunities to apply ideas efficiently	—	28
More control, power of decision	38	30
Greater autonomy, independence while working	31	26
Better employment and income security	11	17
Change in style of company management	—	18
Improvement in image and goals of firm	—	17
Interesting tasks	26	19
Bettter advancement and career opportunities	23	14
Less rigid control over working hours	—	11
More opportunities to distinguish oneself through efficiency and achievement, and to be successful	—	9
Better retirement provisions	8	8
Better working atmosphere	3	5
More social recognition	—	2
No, definitely not willing	—	20
No statement	—	2
N	2,486	710
Date	1,979	1,984

Source: Witte, Kallmann, and Sachs 1981, 10; copyright by C. E. Poeschel Verlag; Bertelsmann Foundation and IWG 1985, 36ff.

nonmonetary incentives that go along with superior positions are obviously so crucial that high motivation can be presumed, even without added income incentives.

The percentage of financially saturated managerial employees is quite high. Forty-five percent of the managers responding to one survey indicated that they agreed with the statement, "Financially, I have on the whole achieved all I wanted to achieve. A higher income is no longer so important to me" (IWG 1985, 44). The variation by age for those who agreed goes from 31 percent of those under 39 years to 78 percent for those over age 60. By income, the range is 33 percent for managers earning under 5000 DM a month to 78 percent of those earning 20,000 DM or more a month.

THE MANAGERIAL EMPLOYEE'S POSITION
WITHIN THE FIRM

The position of managerial employees within the firm can be described in terms of the duties they perform, the salary they receive, and their satisfaction with both.

Duties (Qualitative)

The nature of managerial employee tasks is an essential factor both in the legal definition and in the empirical determination as to who is in fact such an employee. The only task mentioned explicitly in the Law of the Constitution of Companies is that of independent hiring and dismissing employees. However, as we have argued, in reality managers have much more significant accountabilities and decision-making responsibilities.

All definitions share the concept of the managerial employee as an executive. It is, however, considerably more difficult to define this executive role than it is to examine the number of employees for which a manager is responsible or the amount of material, costs, or revenue for which he or she is accountable. Alternatively, one can uncover the demands made on executives as a way of showing the essential duties of managers within a company.

To this end, Witte (1981) surveyed about 2,500 managerial employees and, for comparative purposes, a smaller group (121) of top or senior executives on executive boards. While the demands made on top executives were generally greater than those on managerial employees, distinctions between the two groups were evident in the following dimensions of interest: specialization of skills, intellectual capabilities, behavior, involvement in the company, and personality.

Although the educational background of managerial employees certainly leads to specific areas of concentration, the duties of a top executive require knowledge that reaches well beyond one field of specialization. In the case of managerial employees with technical backgrounds, for instance, knowledge of business matters is essential. Table 6.5 documents this point by presenting the specialization requirements, independent of position and educational background.

Specialization in business ranks first with managerial employees and top executives alike; foreign language skills and specialized technical knowledge are of equal standing. Legal specialization follows at a clear distance. A comparison with members of the executive board serves to reinforce the dominant role of business tasks over technical ones. In addition, foreign language skills are more important for the executive operating on an international basis than they are for the managerial employee, whose field of influence is usually regionally contained. The duties of a managerial employee demand intellectual capabilities that include, primarily, the capacity for creative and critical thought. It is surprising

Table 6.5   Requirements of managerial employment and top executive employment

Requirement	Mean values		
	Managerial employment	Top executives	Mean differences
Required specialization			
Business	5.6	6.2	+0.6[a]
Foreign language skills	5.2	5.9	+0.7[a]
Technology	5.2	5.0	−0.2
Law	4.4	5.2	+0.8[a]
Required personality traits			
Physical endurance	5.7	6.2	+0.5[a]
Self-confidence	5.4	5.9	+0.5[a]
Strength of will	5.2	5.9	+0.7[a]
Willingness to compromise	5.4	5.5	+0.1
Required intellectual capabilities			
Creative thinking	5.7	6.2	+0.5[a]
Critical thinking	5.7	6.1	+0.4[a]
Verbal expression	5.2	5.6	+0.4[b]
Expected behavioral requirements			
Leadership ability	6.0	6.5	+0.5[a]
Ability to work in a group	5.7	6.0	+0.3[c]
Negotiating skills with customers, suppliers, etc.	5.5	6.2	+0.7[a]
Getting on well with employee representatives	5.6	5.7	+0.1
Getting on well with colleagues	5.2	5.6	+0.4[b]
N	2490	121	

Source: Witte 1981, copyright by C. E. Poeschel Verlag.
[a]Significant at the .10% level.
[b]Significant at the 1% level.
[c]Significant at the 5% level.

to find physical endurance rated on the same level as these intellectual requirements, particularly since it outranks features that determine bearing such as self-
confidence, strength of will, and willingness to compromise. The large gap
between managerial employees and top executives in the importance of strength
of will is especially obvious.

As seen in Table 6.5, the major significance assigned to leadership ability
proves again that this task distinguishes the managerial employee from coworkers. Socially important talents for teamwork and cooperation within the company are only a shade less sought after. It is also obviously taken for granted that
the executive will get along well with colleagues and superiors since this trait
rates last on the list of expected behavioral requirements.

What distinguishes the managerial employee from a member of the executive board is reflected in the findings concerning the investments expected of
executives. Willingness to make decisions and shoulder responsibility are less
developed in managerial employees, and they are also quicker to admit that

professional concerns take a back seat to private interests. One gets the overall impression that a higher proportion of operative tasks exist in the spectrum of a managerial employee's duties than in those of an executive. Managerial employee tasks also tend to be restricted mainly to internal affairs, whereas members of the board of directors or the board of managers carry out more representative and leadership tasks. The expectations vary, of course, according to the field of activity and the position within the company (Witte, Kallmann, and Sachs 1981, 82).

Pullig and Stührenberg's (1985) longitudinal analysis of job offers during 1951–83 gives further insight into the development of the demands made on managerial employees. The requirements of dynamism, a sense of responsibility, capability of teamwork, motivation potential, foresight, and resilience appear with increasing frequency, while features such as self-confidence, integrity, authority, and a self-assured manner occur less often. The style of management preferred by a certain company can be assessed over a period of time by observing the relative frequency of assertiveness, negotiation skills, and persuasiveness.

Figure 6.1 serves to illustrate this development. The advances made by the feature persuasiveness since the late 1960s are remarkable, as is the former rise and present decline in assertiveness. At present, the same order of rank exists as up to the mid-1960s, with negotiating skills rated above assertiveness and persuasiveness.

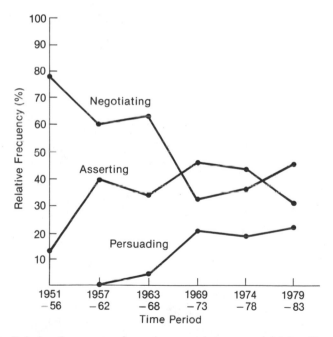

Figure 6.1 Relative frequency of requirements in managerial job offers, 1951–83 (*Source:* Pulling and Stührenberg 1985, 5).

Duties (Quantitative)

Two comparable studies (IWG 1985, 21; Witte, Kallmann, and Sachs 1981, 74) have indicated that half of all managerial employees work 45 to 55 hours per week. In comparison, 54 percent of all employers work more than 55 hours per week (IWG 1985, 20). Contrary to expectations, however, the number of managerial employees with a working week of fewer than 45 hours has decreased. Only 1.3 percent of the total number can enjoy the 40-hour week granted to the remainder of employees. Further reductions in weekly working hours, which are being sought by German trade unions, are likely to bring no relief to managerial employees. In the last five years, if not even before then, average weekly working hours for management have increased, and this situation is gradually approaching the pain threshold. Managers who work average work weeks of 57 hours indicate that their private interests were suffering severely.

This problem could be offset by the generous amount of yearly vacation awarded in Germany. There has been no significant change in this aspect for either managerial employees and other workers in recent years: Annual vacation time has remained at approximately 30 working days. Hierarchy of position has almost no influence on this figure, and it is only slightly affected by age. When the actual number of vacation days taken is compared with the number of days set out in the managerial employee contracts, it appears once again that management works harder than the average worker. Whereas 25 percent of managerial employees state that they have a right to over 30 days vacation, only 17 percent actually use this number of days. In fact, 11 percent even admit to taking no more than 20 days vacation a year (IWG 1985, 23).

Salary

The rewards for all this dedication vary considerably. The salary scale (gross income) for managerial employees extends from 50,000 DM to 200,000 DM annually (Tänzer 1984, 34). There is a concentration between 70,000 DM and the 110,000 DM mark; however, more than one-third of managerial employees earn over 110,000 DM a year.

Five years previously (1979), this third constituted only 14 percent of the total number (Witte, Kallmann, and Sachs 1981), thus showing the significant increase in salaries since then, even if the rate of inflation is taken into consideration. This is an interesting observation because in the 1979 study managers expected their salaries to increase at a rate lower than that of collectively agreed earnings (Witte, Kallmann, and Sachs 1981, 58).

Salaries vary, of course, by the level of one's position within the hierarchy of a company. The relationship between level and salary is presented in the Kienbaum Wage Structure Investigation, an annual confidential report compiled by a consulting firm. It shows that a member of the executive board of an industrial firm with approximately 1,500 workers earns about 225,000 DM per year, a managerial employee on the next lower level earns 125,000 DM, and a person on the second level has a salary of 102,000 DM (Kienbaum 1984). The figures presented are based on gross earnings. Contributions to social security, obligatory in Germany, added to the high tax rates that rise progressively with income, combine to produce substantially reduced and greatly diversified net incomes. These may be estimated for the example chosen at 142,000 DM for the board member, 82,000 for the executive on the first level, and 71,000 for the manager on the second level (married, no children).

Salary increases in recent years cannot be entirely attributed to the improved economic situation. It certainly facilitated an increase in that part of salary which is success related, but in the last ten years or so there has been an unusual tendency to determine fewer and fewer salaries in these terms as well as a diminishing portion of salary for those who have performance-based compensation. Whereas only 30 percent of managerial employees had a fixed income in the mid-1970s, by 1984 the percentage had grown to 48 percent, almost half the total number! The average amount of salary dependent on profit sharing sank simultaneously from 28 percent to 14 percent of total earnings (Tänzer 1985, 34).

When considering these mean figures, it should be kept in mind that profit sharing is more common on the upper levels; at the rank of the executive board, for example, it is almost taken for granted. In 1984, the percentage of managerial employees on the second level beneath the board of directors, whose salaries were in part dependent on profits, was estimated to be 45 percent. Their colleagues on the first level were estimated at 60 percent, while those on the managing director level comprised 70 percent (Tänzer 1984, 5). Of course, it should be remembered that salary structure varies considerably in different departments. Profit sharing is far more prevalent in sales than, for instance, in personnel. On the whole, however, the trend toward higher and more stable salaries continues to be obvious and remarkable.

Company size is among the major determinants of salary level. All available studies indicate that managerial employees earn more in larger companies (Tänzer 1984, 3). The reason for this finding is often considered to lie in the very size of the company and the number of departments it contains, both of which make greater demands on management expertise. This is also coupled with more personnel responsibility (Tänzer 1984, 3). Taking into account that the standard of education among managerial employees in large companies generally exceeds that in smaller firms, the relationship between income and education shown to exist in several studies can be better interpreted. No significant disparities in salary, which might be ascribed to different levels of education, can be determined for managerial employees who have positions on the same level in companies of comparable size. Table 6.6 demonstrates this for first and second level managerial employees.

There is, however, a direct relationship between age and income. Even in management positions, experience is rewarded. As a rule, newly appointed members of management have a lower remuneration than colleagues of equal

Table 6.6   Gross income (in 1,000 DM)
of managerial employees according to education

Level of educational attainment	First level	Second level
Elementary school	105.5	85.6
Middle school	113.7	90.6
High school	123.7	100.7
Technical college	113.3	93.8
Business college	113.3	89.4
University without PhD	128.0	106.7
University with PhD	139.9	108.2
Total	119.3	94.2

Source: Kienbaum 1984.

rank who were hired earlier. Only after years of proving their worth can new managers attain the regular salary level. However, the influence of company size may make itself felt in this regard also, since the average age of managerial employees in larger firms tends to be higher. In addition, these companies also pay their managers better (Kienbaum 1984; cf. Witte, Kallman, and Sachs 1981, Figure 4, for the relationship between standard of education, position, and income; also Tänzer 1984, 4).

Bonuses and fringe benefits have become much more important than they used to be. The number of managers with company pensions has risen continuously and stands today at 90 percent of the managerial employees and members of executive boards. However, considerable differences exist in the size of the pension between levels. Employees on the second and third levels can count on a company pension of 35 to 40 percent of their last basic salary, whereas executives on the first level look forward to 50 to 55 percent of theirs (Tänzer 1985, 35). The company car (one provided by the company that may also be used privately) has become increasingly popular. Even outside the board of directors, where the company car is obligatory, 45 percent of department head managers and 25 percent of all managers are supplied with one (Tänzer 1985, 35).

The explanation for the rise in fringe benefits may be found in the existence of the high taxes and burdening social security deductions placed on cash compensation.

Managerial Employee Job Satisfaction

Overall satisfaction with work is exceptionally high among managerial employees: 68 percent of all managerial employees questioned by the IWG stated that their work was totally satisfactory in every way, 29 percent admitted to being partially satisfied with work, while a mere 1 percent confessed to complete dissatisfaction. These findings correspond well with the results of a representative survey by the Institute of Demoscopy in Allensbach showing that job satisfaction reaches this level among no other occupational group except farmers.

There is also a marked increase in job satisfaction for older managers, probably because of their better working conditions. Because older employees have usually progressed further along their career paths, their working conditions are characterized by greater autonomy and creativity considered so essential by executives for their interest in the profession. Indeed, data compiled by IWG (1985, 32) indicate that the degree of individual autonomy and freedom has more effect on managerial job satisfaction than a change in income level. Further estimations by the IWG showed that overall work morale increases and work motivation remains high with growing job satisfaction, even when financial motivation is absent.

Workers' satisfaction with the details of their jobs is reported in Table 6.7. Based on a seven-point scale, in 1981 satisfaction with the duties themselves clearly ranks highest, while satisfaction with superiors and management is lowest. Also ranked low is satisfaction with income. One aspect of their employment that is particularly difficult for management employees to accept is the ratio of income to performance between themselves and members of the executive board. Dissatisfaction on this dimension produces particularly critical managerial employees as subordinates.

Table 6.8 reports on an attempt to identify the hindrances affecting managerial performance and thus job satisfaction. Managers were asked to indicate on a four-point scale (with 4 equaling the strongest) how strongly they were hindered by various constraints on their jobs. Clearly, the factors seen as the greatest hindrances by managers on their autonomy and probably their creativity are aspects of the work environment beyond the control of either the manager or the company.

MANAGERIAL EMPLOYEES AS A GROUP

Managerial employees have worked to establish themselves as a distinct group within the occupational hierarchy.

Self-image of Managerial Employees

As a group, managerial employees have problems in developing their own separate identity, distinct from the traditionally accepted groups of senior executives and all employees. The title managerial employee already signifies their intermediary position, located as they are between management and the wage and salary earners. Group cohesion, however, demands clear delimitation of members and nonmembers of the group.

Survey research (Witte, Kallman, and Sachs 1981, 11) shows 11 percent of managerial employees count themselves among employees, while 48 percent are equally convinced of their affiliation with company management, and 41 per-

Table 6.7   Satisfaction with management situation

Aspects of managerial situation	Satisfaction scale = 1 to 7
Duties	5.4
Are very interesting	6.0
Allow me to apply my talents	5.6
Leave room for the application of my own ideas	5.2
Are not restricted by unnecessary organizational regulations	4.6
Require too much work so that my private life suffers	4.3
I enjoy them	5.7
Income	4.5
Is in line with performance	4.8
Is satisfactory when compared with the income-performance ratio in the collective-agreement area	4.4
Is satisfactory when compared with the income-performance ratio of board members	3.7
Is satisfactory when compared with the income of most of my acquaintances with the same level of education	5.2
Colleagues	5.2
Are competent in their field	5.6
Are open to change	5.1
Are very helpful	5.1
Are very likeable	5.0
Superior	4.4
Manages very well	4.6
Provides much stimulation	4.1
Is very well informed of field of work of coworkers	4.5
Keeps coworkers well informed	4.0
Includes coworkers in decisions	4.4
Supports coworkers	4.5
Is very popular	4.3
Board of Directors, Management	4.3
Runs the company very well	4.9
Represents the company well in public	5.1
Informs managers thoroughly	4.1
Actively supports claims of managers	3.5
Enjoys very high esteem among managers	3.9
Overall management situation	4.7

Source: Witte, Kallmann, and Sachs 1981, 98, copyright by C. E. Poeschel Verlag.

cent feel that they are located somewhere between these two groups. Basically, this middle group alone can form the basis for a separate class representation.

Although almost half the surveyed managers identify with the company's top management, the two groups differ on several beliefs. Managerial employees feel strongly that they are bound by directives and are financially dependent on

Table 6.8 The effects of various hindrances on willingness to work and performance capacity

	Total	Employer	Employee
Too much bureaucracy	2.74	2.97	2.63
Rules and regulations	2.35	2.77	2.13
Demotivating tax load	2.30	2.30	2.29
Defective economic policies	2.18	2.51	2.03
Union confrontation strategies	1.91	1.98	1.90
Public misjudgment Defamation of management	1.78	2.01	1.61
Hindrances due to coworkers/ colleagues/superiors	1.73	1.79	1.67
Unjust payment for performance	1.73	2.07	1.59
Co-management laws	1.72	1.65	1.76
Insufficient willingness for co-operation by works council	1.55	1.50	1.62
Private disagreements	1.52	1.84	1.36

The question was formulated: "I have here a series of hindrances which could conceivably influence your willingness to work and your performance capacity. Would you please tell me if the individual hindrance affects you strongly ($=4$), noticably ($=3$), slightly ($=2$), or not at all ($=1$)?"

Source: Bertelsmann Foundation and IWG 1986, 17.

the company like other employees. However, although these middle managers believe that their thoughts and actions are management oriented and that they are exceptionally dedicated to their jobs, executives on the boards hold these views even more strongly.

History of Intercompany Managerial Employee Associations

It was not until after World War I that managerial employees began to develop a sense of unity in Germany. Riots during the strike of the Berlin metal industry employees in November 1918 and the imminent enactment of a Collective Wage Agreement combined to set the stage for the foundation of the first independent organization, the Association of Managerial Employees in Trade and Industry (VELA) (Höfchen 1920, 83ff.; Stöve 1918, 21ff.; Zellien, 1953, 29ff.). Until then, only trade organizations had been formed; with this act, a managerial employee organization was established on the basis of functional issues. The League of Employed Chemists and Engineers (BUDACI) was founded a short time later, which has been called since 1925 the Alliance of Employed Academics in Technical and Science Professions (Hromadka 1979, 120ff.). VELA regarded itself as the trade union of employees, while BUDACI considered itself a professional organization, especially for scientists and technicians with academic backgrounds. Both organizations assumed that the interests of their members conflicted with those of the rest of the work force and pursued these interests independently (Krumm 1983, 2ff.).

The importance of these two organizations for the group-forming process of managerial employees is reflected in the membership quotas they reached. In 1932, VELA had about 31,000 members and BUDACI about 10,000 (Totschek 1932. 2ff.). By the mid-1930s, like all organizations, they were forced to conform or be completely disbanded during the Third Reich (Müller 1966, 81ff.). Collective self-help and the establishment of unions were incompatible with the concept of national community between employers and employees which, following the idea of the business community as defined by the Nazi regime, had taken over from the traditional conception of social opposites.

After World War II, in 1947, the first managerial employee association to reappear was the Association of Senior Mining Officials e.V. (registered society) (VOB). Other associations followed, and eventually joined together to form an umbrella organization. The title changed several times, but since January 1, 1951 it has been known as the Union of Managerial Employees (ULA) (Hromadka 1979, 194ff.; Krumm 1983, 3ff.). In the following years, a series of other organizations combined with ULA. Today it has nine member associations and sees itself as a leading managerial employee organization whose member associations have retained their independence. It considers its function to be first and foremost the collective public representation of interests, especially before employers.

The basic demands of the ULA have changed very little since its founding. On one hand, they are directed toward the specific position the managerial employee holds both within the company and in the overall situation of labor and social security regulations; on the other hand, these demands are aimed at securing financial guarantees for managerial employees through appropriate remuneration, adequate protection against dismissal, and retirement provisions (Grüll 1958, 44ff.; Grüll 1960, 44ff.). Although painstakingly positioning itself alongside the remainder of the work force and its organizations, the ULA never considered itself a trade union. Today, ULA associations together can claim about 40,000 members (Rollwagen 1984, 4; Witte, Kallman, and Sachs 1981, 28). This is equivalent to the number of VELA and BUDACI members combined in 1932, and in relative terms represents a considerable decline in the portion of the cohort that belongs to such associations, which now stands at a mere 8 to 10 percent.

Managerial Employees in Company Constitutions

From their inception, managerial employee organizations demanded recognition as an autonomous group and separate status within each company constitution. Because the Law of the Company Constitution excluded them, even though legally they were considered employees, the associations sought legislation to establish a separate company body called the spokesman committee to represent the interests of managerial employees. In 1968, the ULA went so far as to draw up a "Law Outline for the Legal Standing of the Managerial Employee in Company Regulations" (Anon. 1968; also, Gumpert 1968, 1487ff.) It succeeded in winning support for the initiative from the major political parties, but failed to obtain the necessary legislative recognition and judicial rulings to obtain its goals.

The Codetermination Law of 1976, which provides for the inclusion of employees on the supervisory board, was the first law to introduce special protection for the managerial employee minority. However, it does not regard them as a separate group distinct from workers and employees but a special category within the employee group. Yet managerial employees can select their supervisory board candidates autonomously. From two preselected candidates, all employees together then must elect a candidate to the supervisory board (Fitting, Wlotzke, and Wissmann 1976, 68). For this reason, managerial employees have greeted this law as a breakthrough (Hromadka 1979, 307). Their high participation in the election of the supervisory board—over 85 percent—is proof of their great interest in being represented in the company constitution.

Some companies have exceeded the legally stipulated managerial employee representative on the supervisory board by admitting a second managerial employee to the board. In a small number of cases, a managerial employee has become a member of the presiding committee of the supervisory board or deputy chairman of the board. In almost one-third of all companies, managerial employees are members of various committees of the supervisory board (Krumm 1983, 111ff.). Thus, they have gained recognition and may take advantage of the opportunities these positions offer. Despite the low rate of organization among managerial employees in general, almost 30 percent of their representatives on the supervisory board are members of the ULA, and a further 13 percent are members of the German Employee Trade Union/German Trade Union Federation (DAG/DGB) (Krumm 1983, 232).

In addition, several companies have actually founded spokesmen committees for managerial employees. Such committees, although not legally required, can still be formed by individual contracts and incompany rulings as an exercise of the parties' freedom of contract, as long as the action does not violate legal rulings. In 1968, the first were established. By 1973, there were 100 spokesmen committees in existence, and by 1979, about 250 (Borgwardt 1979, 28ff.; Hromadka 1979, 288). In a 1982 investigation, spokesmen committees were seen in 42 percent of all large companies questioned (Krumm 1983, 75ff.). In some cases, additional regional subcommittees and managing boards were set up.

These spokesmen committees had an average membership of just under seven. In almost all cases, they were accepted by the board of directors and even initiated by them in some instances. In 44.5 percent, committee activities were actually based on a formally established agreement with the board of directors (Krumm 1983, 83). Spokesmen committees assembled irregularly in most cases, averaging a little over six times annually (Krumm 1983, 87ff.). Representatives of managerial employees, however, came together with company management for formal discussions more than seven times a year. There is a wide variation in the ways in which these committees function and the types of issues they deal with.

Managerial employee participation in the governance of the organization is also possible through employee assemblies. Although such assemblies are not legally determined, 47 percent of large companies have them (Krumm 1983, 123) and over 70 percent of managerial employees participate in their meetings.

DEVELOPING ISSUES

Previous to 1914, talented young people chose the civil service, the army, scientific professions, and large agricultural enterprises as their career fields. It was not considered highly desirable for a young person to seek a career in business, for according to the humanistic ideal of education, industry and trade were less intellectual fields of occupation. However, after 1945, large farming operations located mainly in East Germany were cut off, the military no longer existed, and the civil service forfeited much of the respect it once enjoyed because of its political character between 1933 and 1945. Therefore, science and business alone presented themselves as potential careers. Because there were relatively fewer career opportunities in science, bright young people (including those returning after the war) preferred to enter business. Indeed, it was the availability of this pool of younger and talented workers that gave such a strong impulse to the German economic miracle of 1948–60.

Management successes that followed World War II were also facilitated by a population inspired with a common will to rebuild and form a new prosperity. There was agreement within companies among superiors and subordinates on the goals, thus permitting a high level of efficiency and avoidance of dysfunctional conflict. The growing gross national product, as well as the addition of new business opportunities stemming from Germany's involvement in the Common Market and overseas expansion, helped to assure that all groups experienced a rise in their real income.

In the 1970s, however, the self-image of management began to change. The contrast between top managers and staff, formerly not generally realized, became more clear. One cause for the change was the growing polarization between political parties; another was the increasing influence of trade unions over such issues as the extent of state social policies, equality in education for all groups, and environmental protection. In the public debate on these issues, managerial employees had to decide for themselves whether they sympathized more with the arguments of the employers or with those of the trade unions.

To deal with this inner conflict, managerial employees came to consider themselves as a third group as they began to identify their own specific interests. They resisted being drawn in by one side or the other. This was most pronounced when they refused to allow themselves to be categorized according to the duties they performed or the money they earned. Instead, they considered their interests to lie in the successful growth and continuation of the company as the focal point of a prolonged means of existence.

This stable and independent role of managerial employees grew even more important at the close of the 1970s, a time when the German economy grew slower. Rises in the income of certain population groups could no longer be financed by the developing economy, but instead were determined by conflict between workers and employers, pensioners, and the state. Today, the interest of all participants is no longer focused on rising income and portioning of the gross national product, but rather on job security, coping with technical advancement, and continuing education.

Currently, managerial employee organizations still guard themselves carefully from establishing an adversary attitude toward coworkers or employers. For example, they do not accept responsibility for negotiating pay settlements for their members with the employers. In addition, managerial employees have proved resistant to fashionable intellectual trends. They support environmental protection, but refuse to use it as an argument against economic development. They are more sensitive about energy wastage, yet will not fight industry with the issue. They certainly support retirement provisions and health insurance, but value economic viewpoints over social ones.

The new era of slower economic growth has particular significance for managerial employees. Through the 1970s, newly trained entrants into management positions had no difficulties obtaining management positions. Not only were businesses growing, but large companies increased the number of managers disproportionately in response to the introduction of new technologies, the internationalization of business, the need to respond to social and personnel matters, and complicating marketing practices.

By the 1980s, however, unusually large numbers of children born in the 1950s were seeking entry-level positions in management but were confronted by managers who had been installed during the 1970s. The career prospects have been lessened even further by a wave of business mergers that have reduced the number of independent companies and possibly the number of managerial jobs. Normal retirements do not represent enough positions or the right types of positions to solve the problem. Some companies are discouraging employed managers from remaining in the profession until they have reached 65 by allowing them to retire at 60, or even 58.

The prospects of younger workers may be improved by the apparent trend in which experienced technicians and sales experts are leaving management positions and founding companies of their own. This seems to be taking place in several industries, not just in the field of advanced technology. Through the influx of newly founded companies, a rejuvenation is taking place that to some extent will allow new, vital, and expandable companies to develop. It remains to be seen, however, how many managerial positions can be created through such growth and how managerial employees will respond to these newer types of opportunities.

REFERENCES

Anon. 1968. Gesetzentwurf der ULA. *DLA* 18 (11):183ff.

Borgwardt, J. 1979. 2,6% der Gesamtbelegschaft sind Leitende Angestellte (Managerial employees comprise 2.6% of the total work force). *DLA* 29 (4):28ff.

Fitting, K., O. Wlotzke, and H. Wissmann. 1976. *Mitbestimmungsgesetz—Kommentar* (*Codetermination law—a commentary*). Munich: Verlag Franz Vahlen.

Grüll, F. 1958. Der Leitende Angestellte in der betrieblichen Praxis (The managerial employee in management practice). *Union* 8 (3):42ff.

———. 1960. Die Notwendigkeit des Zusammenschlusses der Leitenden Angestellten (The necessity of the amalgamation of managerial employees). *DLA* 10 (3):44ff.

Gumpert, J. 1968. Gesetzentwurf uber die Rechtsstellung der Leitenden Angestellten (Bill on the legal position of managerial employees). *Betriebs-Berater* 35/36:1487ff.

Hartmann, H. 1973. German management. *International Studies of Management and Organization*. International Arts and Sciences Press, Inc. Spring-Summer.

Höfchen, C. 1920. Die Vereinigung Leitender Angestellter in Handel und Industrie (VELA) (The union of managerial employees in trade and industry (VELA)). *Betriebs-Berater* 1920:83ff.

Hromadka, W. 1979. *Das Recht der Leitenden Angestellten* (*The rights of the managerial employee*). Munich: Beck.

IWG (Institut für Wirtschafts und Gesellschaftspolitik). 1985. *Die Arbeitsmotivation von Führungskräften der deutschen Wirtschaft* (*Executive job motivation in the German economy*). Bonn/Gütersloh: The Bertelsmann Foundation.

Kienbaum Vergütungsberatung (Kienbaum Payment Advisory). 1984. Gehaltsstrukturuntersuchung Leitende Angestellte 1984 (The salary structure of managerial employees in 1984). Gummersbach: unpublished manuscript.

Kleine, K. H. 1960. Die Union der Leitenden Angestellten. Struktur und Organisation (The union of managerial employees: Structure and organization). *DLA* 10 (9):156ff.

Krumm, A. 1983. Das Einflusspotential der Leitenden Angestellten: Eine empirische Untersuchung (The influence potential of managerial employees: An empirical investigation). PhD diss., University of Munich, Munich.

Landsberg, G. von. 1984. Strukturwandel der Akademikerbeschäftigung in der Wirtschaft (Structure changes in the employment of academicians in business). *Personnel Report*. Munich: Institut für Mensch und Arbeit.

Lawrence, P. 1980. *Managers and management in West Germany*. New York: St. Martin's Press.

Müller, R. 1966. Die Verbände der Leitenden Angestellten in der Bundesrepublik Deutschland. Entwicklung—Aufbau—Aufgabem (Managerial employee associations in the Federal Republic of Germany: Development—structure—task). PhD diss., University of Cologne, Cologne.

Pullig, K. H., and R. A. Stührenberg. 1985. Die Anforderungen an obere Fuhrungskrafte (Requirements for top executives). *Personnel Report*. Munich: Institut fur Mensch und Arbeit.

Rollwagen, G. 1984. Ein wichtiges Ziel: Manipulationsfreie Abgrenzung (An important goal: Delimitation without manipulation). *DLA* 34 (11):4.

Stöve, H. 1918. Die Arbeiter und Angestelltenausschüsse, Tarifverträge, Schlichtungsausschüsse (*Worker and employee commissions, wage agreements, arbitration boards*). N.p.

Sturzenecker, W. 1965. Der leitende Angestellte in Theorie und Praxis (The managerial employee in theory and reality). PhD diss., University of Münster, Münster.

Tänzer, A. 1984. Was verdienen Führungskrafte? (What do executives earn?). *Personnel Report*. Munich: Institut für Mensch und Arbeit.

_____. 1985. Manager—Gehälter: Der Aufstieg macht sich bezahlt (Manager salaries: Promotion pays). *Personnel Report*. Munich: Institut für Mensch und Arbeit.

Totschek, C. 1932. Der Begriff des Leitenden Angestellten (The concept of the managerial employee). PhD diss., University of Leipzig, Leipzig.

Witte, E. 1981. Spitzenführungskrafte im empirischen Porträt. in: *Die Führung des Betriebes* (Top executives: An empirical portrait. In *The company management*), edited by M. N. Geist and R. Kohler, 165ff. Stuttgart: Poeschel Verlag.

Witte, E., and R. Bronner. 1974. Die Leitenden Angestellten: Eine empirische Untersuchung (*The managerial employee: An empirical investigation*). Munich: Beck Verlag.

_____. 1975. Die Leitenden Angestellten (*The managerial employee*). Vol. 2. Munich: Beck Verlag.

Witte, E., A. Kallmann, and G. Sachs. 1981. *Führungskrafte der Wirtschaft* (*Business executives*). Stuttgart: Poeschel Verlag.

Zellien, R. 1953. Von der VELA zur Union der Leitenden Angestellten (From VELA to the Union of Managerial Employees). *Union* 3 (2):29ff.

7
Sweden

KARL-OLOF FAXÉN AND HÅKAN LUNDGREN

CONTENT AND DEVELOPMENT OF MANAGERIAL WORK

The work of managers at low and middle management levels involves many different tasks. Principally, one can distinguish between first-line managers (supervisors) and middle management. Within middle management, some managers, who are positioned somewhere between senior executives and supervisors, have direct subordinates, and some managers hold staff or specialist positions. Not all managers in this category need to have subordinate personnel, but their work does include decisive or rather important influence over some operative decisions.

The most homogeneous of these subgroups is the first-line managers, who all have direct personnel management responsibility. Production supervisors in general have previously been operatives, and their area of responsibility is generally easier to define than that of middle managers.

Within middle management, a person is either a superior manager over other managers or a specialist. Within middle management, the managerial functions are often less clear than those of top management and those of first-line managers. The area of responsibility and the results expected of middle management are seldom distinctly formulated.

While job descriptions for each middle manager are a basis for compensation decisions, the actual working conditions of managers vary widely and are determined by a variety of different circumstances, both within and outside the individual managerial area. Among these circumstances are the nature of the business, the technical equipment, the geographical location of their area, the number of subordinates and their qualifications, their own authority and competence, their own administrative functions, and access to staff and specialist units and to top management.

On these or the other factors that we take up in this chapter, there is hardly any significant difference between Swedish-owned and foreign-owned companies in Sweden. There are, naturally, considerable differences from one company to another, but the differences are probably greater within these two groups than between them (Lindestad and Jeffmar 1984, 50–54).

Recent Trends

In this section we look at some trends of the past fifteen years that have had implications for the conditions and content of managerial work.

Cooperation and Work Practices

The ability of employers and employees to cooperate is a typical feature of Swedish working life. There are good relations between management and employees in business enterprises.

At the end of the 1960s, the country went through a process of rapid change in working practices, organization, production systems, and methods of consultation in business enterprises. Greater independence for small units, flow-oriented production layouts, richer jobs, and closer day-to-day cooperation are characteristic features of this process.

In the early phase, discussions on this topic were heavily influenced by the views and theories of behavioral scientists. Group organizations became a central concept. Job rotation and job enrichment were discussed and even tried.

Parallel to this, there was a lively debate on the content and development of the managerial role. In particular, supervisors were criticized for their lack of competence and their way of handling managerial functions. From some quarters, the need for supervisors was questioned; and in some firms self-managing groups without supervisors were tried.

However, the managerial function was soon restored in these companies, in a modified form. Managers—including supervisors—acquired a key role in the development of cooperation and codetermination in business enterprises. Recruitment of subordinates, utilizing their competence, and focusing their efforts on the central goals of the business became important aspects of a new style of management.

Employee Board Representation

Under the Law on Board Representation for Employees passed in 1973, and revised in 1988, unions nominate two regular board representatives and two deputies in companies with more than 25 employees, regardless of the size of the board. In companies with more than 1,000 employees unions nominate three regular board representatives and three deputies. In most cases, one regular and one deputy board member are nominated by the salaried employees' union locals. The overall experience with this system after more than ten years is encouraging. In the main, the employee representatives have made valuable and positive contributions to the work of company boards, but on rare occasions public displays of conflict have occurred between employees and corporate presidents on such issues as dividend increases and decisions to merge.

It should be mentioned that Swedish boards normally consist of representatives of stockholders or groups of stockholders and outside legal or financial experts. Only the president and, occasionally, the chairman are employees of the company in addition to the union representatives.

Codetermination and the Responsibility of the Employer

On January 1, 1977, the Act on Codetermination at Work came into effect after having been preceded by some years of discussion and inquiry. Among other things, the law contains rules regarding the employer's responsibility to negotiate with a local labor union organization before making decisions on important changes, as well as a far-reaching obligation to provide information.

According to the preparatory work, the Codetermination Act was really intended to provide support for the further development of consultation and decentralization. However, many of the law's provisions were so formulated that they had a quite different effect. Formal negotiations between employers and local labor union organizations became the most important channel of influence. Many new issues relating to the organization and administration of the company could be referred to central negotiations between the labor market organizations and even to the Labor Court.

In many companies, there was a trend in which questions that had previously been dealt with by consultation between first-line managers and their subordinates became matters for negotiation between top management and the union locals. This led to some issues going over the heads of middle and first-line managers. The act thus released powerful centralizing forces.

One reason for this problem was that both the law and some companies in implementing codetermination tended to copy the traditional collective bargaining system for wages. However, it is one thing to negotiate the application of national wage agreements to a company, and quite another to negotiate how to organize and manage a company.

To counter the trend toward centralization and increased bureaucracy, many companies concentrated on decentralizing the organization and management responsibility. Managers at first-line and middle management levels were given authority to accept responsibility on behalf of the employer for obligations under the Codetermination Act within their area. These managers thus gradually assumed a more markedly employer role.

As a result of the changes that have taken place, the criticism of many managers and managerial functions in the late 1960s was gradually transformed into the recognition that a stronger, modernized, managerial function was needed. It was realized that managers should take responsibility for the development and results of their own area, for involving their subordinates in dealing with problems, for developing and creating commitment, and for following up on the demands they place on subordinates.

Agreement on Efficiency and Participation

The Codetermination Act and some other labor laws, which were passed in the 1970s, resulted in formal rules and procedures replacing a great deal of healthy, informal collaboration that had been built up in companies. The well-known Swedish spirit of cooperation had ceased to apply.

However, in many companies, management and employees sought to overcome the growing bureaucracy by developing or returning to informal methods of practical cooperation, which focused on the business activities of the firm. In companies today, the cooperation between management and employees and union locals is better than it has been for many years.

In 1982, these new practical methods of cooperation were confirmed by Sweden's central labor market organizations, the Swedish Employers Confederation (SAF), the Swedish Trade Union Confederation (LO), and the Swedish Federation of Salaried Employees in Industry and Services (PTK) through the *Agreement on Efficiency and Participation*. The agreement recognizes that developing and improving the efficiency of enterprises and safeguarding employment are matters of common interest to a company and its employees. Both sides agreed that the efficiency, profitability, and competitiveness of business enterprises must be improved in order to create employment, security, and development at work. Under the terms of the agreement, efforts will focus principally on three fields: the organization, technical development, and finances and resources of the company. The agreement also provides opportunities to replace the formalistic provisions of the Codetermination Act with practical methods of cooperation and participation, if the parties at the local level agree (SAF-LO-PTK 1982).

In this process, managers assume a key position, for they will be making use of the competence of their subordinate employees and will create opportunities for individuals to develop. Managers also will represent the employer on various consultative issues, and have the final responsibility for the result of the activities within their respective areas.

Decentralization and Delegation

In many companies, decentralization and delegation were key themes during this period. These principles were seen as a way of meeting demands both to improve the efficiency of the business and to give the employees more influence. Important aspects of this trend included the following:

1. Increasing the self-sufficiency and the capacity for self-regulation of small organizational units.
2. Heightening the orientation to customers and commercial activities.
3. Emphasizing commercial-mindedness and results in the design of managerial jobs.
4. Developing the managerial role at all levels, so that managers can effectively manage the activities of their own units and fulfill their employer role vis-à-vis their respective subordinates.
5. Creating employee involvement.

Managerial Strategies for Coping with the New Demands

A company shapes the organization of its management and the roles of individual managers to take into account the specific requirements made by the nature of the company's operations. Thus, there is no standard model showing how a managerial function should be structured and developed within an enterprise; the characteristics of management will vary from one company to another and they will change as the business changes.

However, all managers must concern themselves with at least three broadly defined functions: (1) to represent the company, (2) to manage the business, and (3) to develop the business and subordinate employees (Lindestad and Jeffmar 1984).

In executing these duties, Swedish managers are adhering to a set of developing principles and beliefs. They are:

1. To build up organizations and working methods that emphasize commercial-mindedness and the interest of the customers.
2. To strengthen line managers at all levels in the enterprise, even though the number of managerial levels is reduced.
3. To build up managerial areas with independent profit responsibility so that, as far as possible, managers can function as top executives in their own areas.
4. To increase decentralization and delegation to subordinates, giving managers enough authority so that they can influence and consult with all employees in the company.
5. To create a management function in which managers accept responsibility for helping all employees understand the company's operations, as well as responsibility for channeling information from top management to the employees.
6. To build a comprehensive integrated management function in which corporate culture and loyalty to the company are developed, and where everybody is pulling in the same direction.

EMPLOYMENT AND DEMOGRAPHIC CHARACTERISTICS

This section provides a brief statistical picture of the age and sex structure, training, and professional competence of lower and middle managers based on data collected by the Swedish Employers Confederation.

Table 7.1 shows the age and sex of middle managers, supervisors, other salaried staff, and blue-collar workers. As one might expect, managers tend to be older than nonmanagerial employees. There are also clear differences in the median age of male and female supervisory workers. According to Table 7.1, 25 percent of female middle managers were below 35 years of age compared to 12 percent of male middle managers.

Table 7.1 Age and sex distribution of all employees[a]

Age	Below 35		35–50		Over 50		All ages	
Group	Male	Female	Male	Female	Male	Female	Male	Female
Middle manage-ment	8,980	1,180	46,200	2,850	21,390	680	76,570	4,710
Other salaried staff[b]	55,430	43,740	71,780	52,550	38,900	24,260	166,110	120,550
Supervisors	7,160	250	25,350	710	15,680	490	48,190	1,450
Blue collar	350,000	75,000	230,000	60,000	140,000	45,000	720,000	180,000

Source: SAF, 1983b, 48–49.
[a]The figures include part-time workers.
[b]Excluding supervisors.

Given Sweden's reputation for equality, it is surprising to note that females make up only about 6 percent of all employees in middle management. More detailed data on the distribution of male and female employees is reported in Table 7.2, according to the level of the job based on the Swedish national system of ranking white-collar occupations (identified by the Swedish acronym BNT). Levels 4, 3, and 2 signify middle managers upward; levels 7 and 8 refer to manual white-collar occupations, such as clerical workers. Conspicuously, the highest occupational level has no females in 1970, 1975, 1980, or 1985, and the next highest level has a miniscule representation. Still, looking historically, there are signs that females are entering higher ranking occupations since 1970. Progress has been greatest in the areas of personnel services, marketing and sales, and financial administration (SAF 1980, 23). As females have entered the managerial professions, they have evidenced stronger commitment to the labor force,

Table 7.2 Percentage of men and women in salaried occupations: 1970–85

	Job level						
Year	2	3	4	5	6	7	8
Male Salaried Employees *(Including Supervisors)*							
1970	1.2	4.9	13.4	29.8	34.3	14.1	2.3
1975	1.2	5.3	15.6	33.8	31.7	10.8	1.7
1980	1.3	5.9	17.8	35.7	29.3	8.8	1.2
1985	1.1	6.3	20.2	37.1	27.0	7.3	0.9
Female Salaried Employees *(Including Supervisors)*							
1970	0.0	0.1	1.0	5.7	17.9	43.3	21.3
1975	0.0	0.2	1.5	8.0	24.1	46.0	20.3
1980	0.0	0.3	2.6	12.1	30.7	42.0	12.2
1985	0.0	0.5	4.0	16.7	36.5	36.2	6.0

Source: Data provided by SAF.

as illustrated by the fact that the mean age of female salaried employees rose from 28 to 35 between 1970 and 1980 (SAF 1980, 26).

Table 7.1 also shows that on average there are just under 20 subordinate personnel for each supervisor, and that around one-quarter of the salaried employees as a group, excluding supervisors, can be placed in the middle management category. Unfortunately, only limited inferences about the comparative importance of middle managers can be made from these data, because many managers included in that category are not actually managers and these relative figures say nothing about the span of the area controlled by each manager.

Table 7.3 shows the educational background of those in supervisor and other salaried staff positions. The most prominent feature in this table is the large proportion with a technical education in all three categories. Among supervisors and other salaried staff, most have less than 12 years schooling, but a relatively large proportion has some technical education; among supervisors with any form of education, technical training is the dominant background. Technical education is most pronounced for middle managers.

Men and women salaried white-collar employees tend to have different educational backgrounds. The education of males is usually technical in nature; the education of women tends to be directed more toward commerce and economics.

Table 7.4 shows the breakdown of the managerial occupations in several areas of operation. The largest group of middle managers is employed in construction design and R&D, whereas the largest group of salaried staff is employed in the areas of administration. Unfortunately, apart from the area of production management, it is not known how many salaried managers are actually supervisors.

Table 7.3 Educational background of managers and salaried staff

Educational group	Middle management	Supervisors	Other salaried staff	Total
Graduate engineers and Bachelors of Science, 15 years or more	14,380	180	6,820	21,380
Certificate of technical education, 12–14 years	25,910	6,610	39,100	71,620
Business administration, law, social science, 15 years or more	5,200	10	3,340	8,550
Certificate of commercial education, 12–14 years	5,570	170	20,000	25,740
Other, 12 years or more	2,510	150	6,080	8,740
Less than 12 years education, incl. vocational training	27,740	42,530	211,470	281,740

Source: Data provided by SAF.

Table 7.4 Employment by occupational field

Occupational field	Middle management	Supervisors	Other salaried staff	Total
Production management	9,670	49,630	5,540	64,840
Technical methodology incl. planning, control, service and industrial preventive health care	8,310	—	37,010	45,320
Construction and design, R&D	22,410	—	41,570	63,980
Business & commerce	20,670	—	91,500	112,170
Administration incl. financial, data processing and personnel	18,720	—	107,490	126,210
Other	1,520	—	3,550	5,070

Source: Data provided by SAF.

PREPARATION AND EDUCATION

Several different types of programs offered by many institutions and companies are found under the rubric of management education in Sweden. Examples of the ways in which such education is organized are presented below.

Among the variety of educational experiences are open courses, customized management training/education programs for individual companies, training consultation for individual companies, and on-the-job training. In addition, there is specialist training in various functional fields, which, strictly speaking, is not management education as such, but provides an important foundation of knowledge for managerial work. Most of this functional education is associated with universities.

Outside Educational Institutions

The largest organization in the field of management education for supervisors and middle management is the Swedish Management Group, a wholly owned subsidiary of the SAF. Some sections of the Swedish Management Group's program are also directed toward top management, particularly in small and service companies.

The scope of programs offered by the Management Group covers the general area of management education as well as functional training courses as illustrated by the following list of course offerings in 1988:

Company management and business development
Management and leadership development
Company management in smaller companies
Training of supervisors
Women career leadership

Production
Industrial engineering vocational training
Quality development
Development of personnel administration
Recruitment
Finance development
Remuneration employer/employee law, contracts
Career and competence development for secretaries

Two notable trends are in evidence in the educational programs of the Swedish Management Group and other educational institutions. Traditionally, management education for middle managers has consisted of courses with open enrollments that emphasized functional and specialist training. More recently, emphasis has shifted toward general management education.

Another trend is that customized management training programs for specific companies are becoming increasingly important, while open courses are decreasing in extent. For the training institutions, this requires that they achieve greater integration between management education and educational consulting. For the enterprise, it means that external and in-house training activities must be integrated.

Behind these developments lie changes in the business sector's demand for training. There is a clear tendency for the purchasing of management education programs by firms to be handled by line managers and less by specialists and corporate staff functions.

In 1984, the external courses run by the Swedish Management Group for supervisors and middle management catered to some 16,500 participants during some 41,000 "participant days," and in-house training for companies accounted for 40 percent of total activities.

If each manager in Sweden takes part in only one open course a year, then one in every eight lower and middle managers is reached by the Swedish Management Group's courses. Since there are many other institutions that engage in management training, it would appear that Sweden enjoys a high volume of management education.

The largest training institution for top management education in Sweden is the Institute of Management, which is closely associated with the Stockholm School of Economics. The principals of the Institute are the Swedish Association of Schools of Economics, the Swedish Employers Confederation, the Swedish Association of Graduate Economists, the Swedish Association of Graduate Engineers, and the Federation of Swedish Industries.

The Institute also offers courses directed toward managers at middle management levels of organizations. Education programs for top executives are heavily oriented toward basic business economics. Like those of the Swedish Management Group, the Institute's courses include programs in general management as well as more functionally oriented training. Examples of the first category from the Institute's recent programs include:

Seminars for presidents
Business management
Developing your company
Development programs for small firms
Management Institute College—a one-year executive development
program

Examples of more functionally oriented courses include:

Financial analysis and control
Accounting and financing
Financing analysis
Marketing
Long-term organizational and personnel policy

MIL, Management in Lund, is an independent foundation that provides
advanced management training programs in close association with the University of Lund and the business sector. The MIL Foundation has 150 public and
private sector sponsoring companies that elect its board. MIL's training programs are directed toward senior executives in business enterprises and government departments and seek to provide participants with general competence in
business management. An important feature of MIL's programs is its emphasis
on project work dealing with the problems of the participant's company.

Sweden's universities and similar institutions provide no organized or
planned management education. According to the prevailing view, the purpose
of a university education is to provide basic training in various fields, which in
turn will create an environment for further training in management.

Apart from the institutes mentioned, many training and consulting companies are active in offering management training and consulting services in the
training field. Among these, too, a trend can be observed toward integrating
general management and customized training for firms, namely, tailored management training programs for individual companies.

In-house Management Development Programs

No comprehensive description and analysis about training within companies are
available. This is especially the case for middle-management, a professional area
hardly researched at all in Sweden. One reason is probably the large number of
widely varying functions and areas of activity that are embraced by the term
middle management. What follows are general observations and experiences
based on discussions with various companies.

In part because in-house training and on-the-job training are assuming
growing importance in management education, companies have been able to
better integrate training with the needs of the organization.

Many companies achieve integration by utilizing systematic management
succession programs. These programs cover such matters as the demands that

will be made on managers in the future, what the characteristics of successful managers will be, and how systematic programs for recruiting and developing managers can be created and applied.

In the same vein, many companies also have individual development and succession plans for their "potential managers." They may involve alternating training and practice, career patterns planned in advance, and training in a range of skills through being given posts in a variety of functions and types of business. Interestingly, Arbose (1982) showed that Swedish companies are the least likely of all European companies to have formal succession plans for filling jobs internally. However, it is our impression that, assuming his findings to be accurate, in just a few short years Swedish employers have taken to succession planning and individual development plans.

Recruitment

If a systematic description or analysis of recruitment policies and methods were available, it would document the wide differences in practices from company to company. Some companies have a stated policy of giving priority to internal recruitment, while others focus more on recruiting from outside.

Still, there are marked differences in recruitment and career patterns between supervisors in production and managers in middle management. Supervisors in production are recruited to a considerable extent from among the operatives. Therefore, they generally are experienced in the work they are expected to manage. For the vast majority of supervisors, however, this position is the last stop on the line in their careers. It is therefore rather unusual for supervisors to be promoted to a managerial post in the middle management bracket.

Middle managers, on the other hand, are not recruited from among the supervisors but enter from the outside. Common sources of recruitment include a variety of specialist functions such as production engineering, time and method units, finance departments, laboratories, and so on. Sometimes middle managers are drawn directly from universities or high schools. This pattern is, of course, not general, but it can be fairly widely seen. As a result of these practices, large groups of middle-level managers lack experience in the direct supervision of workers.

This systematic difference in the recruitment method used to obtain and develop supervisors and middle managers has given rise to some problems. For one, many supervisors cannot look forward to a career at higher levels of the organization. Equally important is that it is more difficult to create consistent management functions across levels of the firm, especially where changes in technology and organizational structure require a unified managerial hierarchy. Closing the gulf will not be easy because of differences in the educational background of supervisors and middle managers.

UNIONIZATION

One unique feature of Swedish managers is the high degree of unionization and the considerable bargaining power of salaried employees in the private sectors. Among supervisors, the degree of unionization is estimated at over 90 percent, and in middle management, at over 70 percent. It is not easy to explain why this is so, but a historical review might contribute to an understanding.

Historical Overview*

Labor unions of manual workers were first formed in the 1880s and 1890s, and the practice of collective agreements for workers was established without much legal controversy. The Swedish Trade Union Confederation (LO), a central labor union organization, was established in 1898 and its contemporary counterpart, the Swedish Employers Confederation (SAF) in 1902.

From the very start, SAF was more highly centralized than other existing employer organizations and derived its power from three pillars of strength: (1) the existence of conflict insurance to aid member companies; (2) the right of veto over collective agreements by member firms; and (3) the power to direct any member firm to lock out its workers.

SAF's constitution dealt exclusively with the relationship between member companies and their nonsalaried workers, leaving the relations of a member firm to its salaried staff as an individual matter between employer and employee.

In an agreement known as the December Agreement of 1906, SAF recognized manual workers' unions in exchange for the LO's recognition of management's right to manage, and LO permitted employers to continue a policy of regarding first-line supervisors as representatives of the employer.

As employer representatives, first-line supervisors could not belong to a workers' union. This principle of SAF was generally accepted and was made part of the 1936 legislation on the rights of association. Supervisors were salaried staff with the same privileges as other staff groups in the form of better employment security, full pay during sickness, and so on. Salaries were monthly, whereas most workers were paid hourly wages.

The Swedish Union of Foremen and Supervisors (SALF) had already been set up in 1905 as an independent labor union for supervisors. For other salaried personnel, a staff association, the Association of Salaried Employees of Industrial Estates, was formed in 1909. The more aggressive Swedish Union of Clerical and Technical Employees in Industry (SIF) was formed in 1920. A private sector central organization for salaried employees, DACO (the Employees Central Organization), was formed in 1931.**

---

*This section draws heavily upon de Geer (1986), in particular part 3, pp. 237–312.

**SIF absorbed the staff association of 1909 in 1940, and DACO merged into the Central Organization of Salaried Employees (TCO) in 1944.

In the banking and insurance industries, two sectors originally not covered by SAF membership, salaried unions originated earlier. The Swedish Association of Bank Employees had already been set up in 1887 and was reorganized as a labor union in 1919. Its employer counterpart did not start until 1937.

To ensure SAF's control over all agreements (not only those for manual workers) at the industry, company, and plant levels, SAF's constitution was amended in 1930 to give it explicit power to prevent member associations or individual employers from making agreements with SALF or SIF without SAF's approval.

Gradually, SAF's opposition to managerial unionism softened. In the late 1930s, SALF was given partial recognition. SAF's constitution was revised (most significantly in 1948) as salaried employees gained strength. By 1963 workers and salaried employees had achieved a parallel status under SAF's constitution. This meant that SAF could order employers to lock out not only workers but also salaried staff, thus making it possible for SAF to muster its full strength in support for a member firm earmarked for attack by a union of salary employees.

Finally, in 1966, SAF published a proposal for a new bargaining procedure, indicating that the unions of manual workers and salaried employees were now considered equally important bargaining partners. SAF had abandoned its earlier policy to bargain first with LO and then with salaried unions and wanted now to meet both groups simultaneously and on the same footing.

In 1974, a confederation of salaried unions was formed, known as the Swedish Federation of Salaried Employees in Industry and Services (PTK), containing members from SIF, SALF, the Swedish Union of Commercial Employees (HTF), SACO, and several smaller white-collar unions. PTK joined with LO in 1977 to bargain against SAF but has preferred to bargain separately until 1986, when the SAF/LO and SAF/PTK agreements were reached simultaneously on April 10 and 11.

PTK has more than 500,000 members, and LO around 2 million, of which 900,000 are within the jurisdiction of the SAF. Inside PTK, SIF has 275,000 members, HTF has 105,000, SALF 70,000, and the Swedish Association of Graduate Engineers (CF), a SACO union, has about 40,000 members.

The Pension Issue

A major aim of the Association of Salaried Employees of Industrial Estates when it began in the early part of this century was to improve pensions. Since 1920 pensions to salaried employees in private corporations have been financed through insurance in the Swedish Staff Pension Society (SPP), although some direct supplements to the Society's pension by employer's have been made. From its beginning, the society's board has had salaried unions' employees as members. Currently, there is equal representation for employers and employees on the Society's board.

For a long time, finding a solution to the pensions issue was the dominating problem for salaried unions. The existence of this central insurance scheme has undoubtedly facilitated both the growth of salaried unions and their acceptance by employers. It was not, however, until 1960 that pensions were actually regulated by collective agreements as a private supplement to the National Supplementary Pension System.

Positions of the Salaried Unions

The central policy of salaried unions has been to maintain the relative pay position and pay differentials with manual workers. This puts them in opposition to point four of SAF's policies, "Fair Pay," which states that "it must be possible for pay differentials between various groups and individuals to be changed all the time. Historic pay differentials must not be the basis for setting pay rates" (SAF 1979). Pay relationships have also been a source of tension between the salaried unions and the LO, which has sought to close the gap between the pay levels of manual and salaried employees. Over the past fifteen years, this competition over pay and the positions of the various large blocks of workers has had important implications for public policy and has been a significant source of cost escalation in Sweden.

Various methods to control this competition by linking wages and salaries have been tried. However, the interpretation of those linkages has often turned out to be exceedingly controversial. In fact, all four open conflicts during the central negotiations between SAF and LO or PTK in 1977, 1980, 1981, and 1983 were caused by such wage-wage or wage-salary linkages.

As for salary structure, the policy objectives of salaried unions depend on internal tensions as well as relations with other unions. In SIF's program for 1978, reductions of salary dispersions, minimum salaries, and equal salaries for equal work were emphasized. On the other hand, SALF in 1986 wanted increased differentiation of salaries among supervisors. CF underlines the need for adequate income differences to facilitate recruitment of good managers and executives (Lundberg and Hellstrom 1985, 32–33).

The unions of salaried employees have shown themselves to be skillful and innovative negotiators who compete successfully with the unions of manual workers (Giesecke 1985, 169). Examples of their accomplishments include various insurance agreements and a five-year salary agreement in 1969.

Employers and the salaried unions have had longstanding disputes over the responsibilities and loyalties of unionized salaried employees. Employers have always upheld the principle that executives cannot strike or belong to a union and that executives' salaries should be determined individually without union interference. The issue came to a head in September 1976 when PTK announced an overtime ban during negotiations on pensions. The unions wanted the definition of executives to be much narrower than the employers considered possible. There was even a strike at the Alfa Laval plant in Lund on the issue of the definition of "not organizable executive personnel" and it was a subject of bargaining in 1977, 1979, and 1981. In April 1986, PTK struck again on this issue, this time at SKF in Gothenburg, suggesting that the subject is still controversial.

According to SAF principles, even if the agreement on general conditions of work is valid for both organized and nonorganized salaried employees, only organized salaried employees may take part in lockouts or strikes. In comparison, nonorganized manual workers are locked out together with the organized ones.

Coverage

Union representation of managers is a complex issue influenced by three factors. First, salaried staff agreements do not apply to employees in high level jobs, defined as those jobs above level 2 in the job classification system.

Second, employers can demand that their executives do not belong to a salaried union. However, the concept of executive is not defined in any greater detail than to include private secretaries of executives as well as personnel who represent the employer in dealing with the conditions of employment of salaried staff. A reasonable interpretation may be that executives have a general responsibility for the overall activities of the enterprise, whereas the responsibilities of middle management are limited to a defined part of the enterprise. Thus, according to PTK, a manager responsible for a plant with 1,500 employees belonging to a 10,000-employee corporation is not an executive. He or she belongs to middle management. On the other hand, a member of a management board, a group consisting of individuals responsible for various functions of the corporation under the chairmanship of the president or the chief executive officer, is an executive.

Third, the employer has a right to exempt executives from participating in strikes and lockouts. Employers logically seek a broad definition of exempted managers; PTK, for its part, wants to restrict exemptions to the president of a corporation and very few ancillary men and women.

As a practical matter, exemptions are defined when SAF defines those groups of workers who may not be locked out during a work stoppage. When serving lockout notices, SAF has always excluded a majority of the middle management as well as supervisors. In 1986, the following groups were excluded from lockout notice on the grounds that they are always exempt from taking part in conflicts.

1. Senior executives who are part of a top management group or who occupy leading positions as follows:
   a. The top executive—managing director or president and his deputy or the equivalent.
   b. Salaried employees who are responsible for individual units within the company, such as site managers (managers of local administrative units), divisional chief executives, members of management groups at divisional level or the equivalent.

    c. Salaried employees who represent the company in its relations with workers on matters concerning terms of employment or codetermination on general questions.

    d. Secretaries of managing directors, secretaries of their deputies, or the equivalent.

2. Leading salaried employees in specialist positions whose ordinary work includes:

    a. Dealing with long-term projects and such development work and research that an interruption could cause long-term damage.

    b. Handling personnel questions that affect workers not covered by the conflict action.

3. When no salaried employee in any of the above-mentioned categories is present, one salaried employee is always exempted.

4. Salaried employees who are required for the running and maintenance of power stations and electrical supply installations.

5. Salaried employees who are needed to:

    a. Inform customers, suppliers, associate companies, and foreign representatives about the extent of the lockout and about action to which the lockout gives rise.

    b. Observe periods of legal notice to deal with the authorities.

Thus, the controversy over the unionization of management personnel is a rather fluid one, subject to variance over time and across companies. For example, in January 1988, middle managers who were members of SIF struck at those corporations hit by a work stoppage. On the other hand, a lockout in February 1988 in companies that were members of the Engineering Employers' Association did not apply to the groups listed above. Perhaps the lesson to employers in other countries is that recognition of salaried unions makes it necessary to reach an agreement on the executives who will not be allowed to organize; otherwise, problems in this area will recur.

The Council of Employment Security

The SAF-PTK Council for Employment Security was formed in 1973. The purpose of this organization is to promote employment security among salaried employees by financing in-house education and retraining, assisting unemployed salaried employees in finding new jobs or in starting new businesses of their own, and, as a means of last resort, to finance early retirement from age 55 (compared to 60 in the government-financed superannuation system). The council also finances severance pay contributions through an insurance system.

Currently, the Council for Employment Security is an important and very active organization. It stated in its 1984 report that 4,000 employees of 89 companies were subject to action to prevent redundancy and 4,600 new cases of clearing of unemployed salaried employees for new employment came up during the year (Trygghetsradet 1985). Of the clearing applicants, 800 salaried employees were helped (probably mainly middle management) to start their own firms at a cost of SEK 33 millions. In addition, 3,700 applications for severance pay were dealt with, compared with 6,000 in the years 1982–83.

There were 193 cases of severance pay for salaried employees above 55 years, of which 156 came from companies that had gone bankrupt. In light of the accelerating pace of change in technical and market conditions for business, the Council for Employment Security is carrying out practical trials to avoid future overstaffing by increasing both the competence and the transferability of salaried employees in business enterprises.

CONDITIONS OF EMPLOYMENT AND COMPENSATION

Collective bargaining with salaried unions is concerned first with general conditions of employment and second with annual salary adjustments.

Nonsalary Matters

Agreements on general conditions of employment originate from the 1930s when SALF reached its first industrial agreement with the Swedish Engineering Employers' Association. At the present time, all SAF's member associations have collective agreements on general conditions of employment with SIF, SALF, HTF, and others with practically the same content, and negotiated by SAF.

These agreements regulate such items as vacations, sickness and overtime pay, periods of notice for layoffs and redundancy, employment security, pensions, working hours, and bargaining procedures. Technically, working hours, pensions, and the SAF-PTK employment security agreement, as well as the agreement on employees' rights to innovations and patents, are regulated in separate agreements.

Process of Setting Salaries

Only annual adjustments to salary levels are subject to collective bargaining. The starting salary for a newly hired salaried employee is a matter of individual bargaining between employee and employer.

The collective agreements on salaries often contain, first, a general salary increase for everyone and, second, certain "kitties" as bases for individual distribution either to all salaried employees or to particular groups, such as women or elderly employees. The agreements also include clauses relating to what are known as age and qualification supplements. Where applicable, promotion supplements can also be paid, although these are not covered by the salary agreements.

Table 7.5 illustrates the workings of the system. As the table shows, this system allows considerable scope for individual differentiation in local bargain-

Table 7.5   SAF-PTK agreement for 1982

Sources of salary increase	Percent of salary bill
General salary increase	1.0
Kitty for individual distribution, overall	1.8
Kitty for individual distribution to job levels 6–8	0.5
Kitty for individual distribution to supervisors	0.5
Total contractual salary increase	3.1
Salary drift	2.6
Total increase in salary level, standardized for age distribution, job pattern, and working hours	5.6
Age supplements	0.6
Supplements for qualification and promotion	0.5
Total increase for a "cohort" of identical salaried employees	6.7
Add: unstandardized increase in salary level 6.1%	6.1

Source: Data provided by SAF.

ing between the employer and the salaried union locals. Out of a 6.7 percent overall increase, only 1.0 percent is a general salary increase, the remaining 5.7 percent can be redistributed among individual employees. Of the total increase, 0.6 percent is an adjustment for age. This reflects the generally held opinion that all employees deserve higher salaries as they get older. The kitties for age as well as for promotion and qualifications are calculated for the company as a whole; their distribution, however, is on an individual basis (Klevmarken 1980, 10).

Table 7.6 shows that the kitties are in fact distributed widely. Of the 6.7 percent increase in 1982 for identical salaried employees, 15 percent of all employees received less than 4.0 percent and 17 percent more than 10 percent.

Table 7.6   Distribution of salary increases in 1982

Percentage salary increase	Percent of all full-time salaried employees
Below 2.0	3
2.0–3.9	12
4.0–5.9	33
6.0–7.9	24
8.0–9.9	11
Above 10.0	17
Total	100

Source: Data provided by SAF.

The agreements also embody the principle that salaries are individual and differentiated. Furthermore, it is stated that salaries will be set in relation to the level of responsibility and the degree of difficulty of the job and the manner in which the employee concerned satisfies the job requirements. The sex of the employee in no way affects the salary setting.

Of particular interest for the salary policy of middle managers is, in the language of the 1985 SAF-PTK agreement, the fact that "for senior executives, both managerial and specialist, factors such as managerial capability, judgment and initiative, financial responsibility, ability to work together with others, and richness of ideas and innovative ability are of particular importance to the setting of individual salary levels" (Lundberg and Hellstrom 1985, 20).

A policy of highest priority for the union of supervisors and foremen (SALF) is that the salaries of employees with responsibility for subordinate personnel are set and adjusted with due regard to the pay level of subordinates.

The annual adjustments negotiated locally between the employers and the local salaried unions are based on the elaborate BNT position classification system (SAF 1983a; 1984), written in 1955 and more recently revised in 1975, and used by SAF, SIF, SALF, and HTF (SAF 1983b; SAF et al. 1975 and 1981). The classification system is based on two concepts: the task and the difficulty of the task. Jobs are defined by a system of four-digit codes detailing the occupational field, job family, job level (degree of difficulty), and position description (SAF et al. 1981, 9). BNT contains approximately 280 four-digit "position types."

In local salary bargaining, each individual salary is compared with data on salaries compiled through a survey of all employers in the business sector. Comparisons are based on the median and the upper and lower quartiles of salaries for the same position type (four-digit code), age group, and geographical region to which the employee belongs. Beginning in the mid-1950s, SAF as well as each of the salaried unions distributed statistical abstracts to member firms or union locals with this information. These abstracts also show the age supplement for each individual.

For instance, one salaried employee may have 86 percent of the comparable median salary and another 115 percent. The employer can thus compare an estimate for the efficiency of one of the employees in question to his or her relative pay position. Salary kitties for individual distribution should be used to increase salaries for employees whose relative pay is judged to be low in relation to his or her individual efficiency. Furthermore, a salaried employee whose relative pay position is judged high should be given a less than average amount from the kitty for individual distribution, or nothing at all.

Presently, SAF policies emphasize the need for each employer to develop and communicate its own culture—that is, norms and practices—with respect to salaries. While the BNT and the agreements based on BNT restrict salary flexibility in the short run, it is felt that considerable room exists to increase individual motivation and performance by adjusting salary relativities and differentials in the long term. An expression of these ideas is found in Lundberg and Hellstrom (1985).

The Process of Setting Salaries

According to current research (Nilsson 1987), both employers and unions use operational points of reference in the same region or industry when negotiating local wages and salaries. As one would expect, however, employers seek to maintain their salary position in relation to other firms to remain competitive in the labor market. The unions, for their part, have other salary objectives. SIF and CF locals rely on joint salary statistics for the nation or for the region. SALF locals insist that salaries for supervisors should be set and adjusted with due regard to the pay levels of subordinates in the same firm.

Considering the many components that make up both salary levels and yearly increases, it may be helpful to describe the processes of salary negotiations at the local level in greater detail. This section draws heavily from Klevmarken's review of wage revisions at the local level (1980, 5–6).

At the local level, the process of revising salaries can be organized in different ways, depending on such factors as the size of the company and the strength of the union. Generally, however, the process begins when the employer conducts a salary review with each staff organization. The review, which is also a preliminary negotiation, tends to include the centrally negotiated agreement, the previous year's salary statistics, and special analyses. These discussions form the basis for demands by both the union and the company for possible changes in the relative salary positions of particular groups.

It is common in these negotiations for the company and union to agree on the total sum available at the local level based on the centrally negotiated total as well as special kitties applicable to the company and on the distribution of these funds to the members of the represented unions as well as the unorganized portion of the company. After reaching this division of the pool, no transfer of funds takes place among groups of unionists. Thus, there is a premium for one union to wait to see how all the funds are distributed before signing an agreement.

Big companies utilize a relatively sophisticated system of distributing the total sums negotiated over sections, departments, and individuals. Preliminary proposals for distribution are prepared by staff departments and sent to department heads for review and subsequent refinements. The influence of department heads compared to the influence of the staff specialists in setting wages will vary from company to company.

The role of staff organizations and unions in these decisions will vary, but tends to be one of watching and reacting, restricting their active contributions to special cases.

The company, after verifying the final salary recommendations with the total amount available for increases, will place the recommended salary levels before the local union for final negotiations, leaving itself some additional funds to accommodate the union's requests for selected higher increases. The agreed-upon distributions then form a salary agreement that the local union signs.

A 1988 strike settlement between SIF and the Engineering Employers' Association created salary-setting procedures that are worth noting. Under the agreement, when local salaries are adjusted, the employer is supposed to discuss those adjustments with the union. If agreement is not achieved at the local level, further discussions are held at higher levels between the union and the Employers' Association. These discussions may be followed by discussions at the level of the Salary Council, which has equal representation from the union and the association. In a very novel step, the parties created a "Supreme Council," which can review the decisions of the Salary Council. While SIF called the strike in part to gain a greater say in local wage decisions, SALF and CF did not participate in the work stoppage because they were satisfied with the amount of local influence they have traditionally exercised.

In small or medium-sized firms and for local unions with comparatively few members, individual raises are commonly negotiated directly without the preliminary negotiations to identify the totals going to particular groups.

In really small companies, there is no need for negotiations and salaries are set through informal processes.

Salary Relationships

During the first fifteen years of its existence, this system (BNT in combination with central agreements defining general increases and salary kitties for individual distribution) led to a slow reduction in salary spread among the occupational levels. The total spread—as measured by the coefficient of variation—for levels 2 to 8 decreased from an index level of 112 in 1958 to 110 in 1967. After that, the decline has been much faster. In 1972, the index for the total spread was 100, and in 1983 it was 85 (Jonsson and Siven 1986, 13; Lundberg and Hellstrom 1985, 16).

During the 1970s, salaries continued to compress. The average salary for job levels 2 and 3 in relation to jobs at levels 6 through 8 declined from 260 percent in 1969 to 169 percent in 1982. Salaries for jobs at levels 4 and 5 declined in relation to those at levels 6 through 8 from 156 to 139 percent in the same period. Table 7.7 provides an illustration of the compression experienced by selected occupations during the 1970s.

Naturally, such compression was a matter of concern among employers. Furthermore, employers feared that they would have difficulty setting subordinate salaries fairly when their own salaries were being set by collective bargaining. Partly due to those concerns, in 1983 the adjustment of salaries above SEK 130,000 per year (about 150 percent of the wage for an adult male manufacturing worker) was exempted from collective regulation. A similar limit was agreed in 1984. However, in 1986, at the request of the unions, the SAF-PTK salary agreement again applied to all employees.

Table 7.7 Salaries as percentage of wages
of adult male manufacturing workers

Occupation (code)	1972	1983
Supervisor (1206)	123	115
Production manager (1104)	195	166
Sales manager (8003)	257	233
Design engineering manager (3102)	315	263

Source: Data provided by SAF.

Along with the compression of interoccupational salary differentials, the system of setting salaries just described has had other consequences for the structure of managerial compensation.

First, there have never been any significant or systematic salary differentials from one industry to another, after standardization for differences in age distribution and job patterns. Industry differences in salaries do not play any significant role in discussions between the bargaining partners, unlike the situation for manual workers' unions.

For instance, textiles and clothing had a relative salary ranking of 98 to 100 in 1962 as well as in 1970, and 101 in 1981 to 83. The relative wage level (unstandardized) for the same industry was 76 to 82 in 1964, 79 to 85 in 1970, and 85 to 90 in 1982.

Second, age profiles—the relationship between age and salary level—have flattened during the 1970s, in part because of a higher than average drift in starting salaries and because of more salary drift for younger salaried employees.

Third, interregional differentials have been reduced (Jonsson and Siven 1986, 18).

Finally, differentials have narrowed within job levels. Analytically, it is attractive to assume that these observed reductions in salary differentials within job levels have the same causes as the overall reduction in interoccupational differentials. This may be interpreted as a consequence of the improved quality of information that has resulted in a more efficient labor market, or it may be the result of strong union influence over salaries.

The total effect of this elaborate statistical system is a strong tendency toward compression of all salary differentials. The fact that such statistical comparisons are made exercises a strong psychological impact to even out what appear as irregularities in the salary structure. It takes a good deal of courage for an employer to increase the relative salary of an employee from 120 to 125 or to reduce it from 80 to 75, even if the former employee is four times as efficient in the same position type as the latter.

It must be noted that the BNT does not include position descriptions for executives' positions within industry and business and other high level positions. As a supplement to BNT, therefore, SAF has recommended the SKF Position Class System (SAF 1979b) which covers executives who report directly to the chief executive officer of the corporation. However, it also can be applied to such middle management positions as export manager or technical salesman (reporting to a marketing manager), or divisional controller (reporting to a divisional manager). The SKF system is based on an evaluation of ten factors, including education, experience, influence on results, and size of the unit.

With all its sophistication and elaborate detail, the combination of BNT and central salary agreements has created a body of knowledge accessible only to a limited number of specialists. Most corporate executives (with the exception of personnel managers) and most salaried employees do not care about the elements and components in salary increases; they look only at the final level of their increase. According to an SAF study in two regions, most small and medium-sized employers do not apply all the sophistication described above, but follow in broad terms the leading employer in the region.

Considering that the salary drift accounted for 40 percent of total salary increases during the 1980s, the Swedish method of compensation is not ready for export as a method of macroeconomic control.

MANAGEMENT AND CORPORATE POLICY

Is There a "Low and Middle Management Ideology"?

To what extent do managers at low and middle management level absorb the policy and ideology of top management? Is there a coherent management philosophy through all management levels in the firm and can corporate cultures be created to fill in the ideological gaps? It is clear that there is no general, unambiguous answer to these questions.

By tradition, first-line managers have often regarded themselves as sitting on the fence between top management and their subordinates. In view of their background and methodology of recruitment, this is understandable. See Delamotte (1985, 3) for the most recent statement of the strong line of demarcation between supervisors and managers.

Most observers looking at this demarcation focus on its implication for management of the shop floor. The other side of the problem, the role of the middle manager, also has been very important in Sweden. Middle managers must also straddle the fence between subordinates and supervisors. While their status may be marginal, the first-line managers are at least a relatively homogeneous group, and therefore relate more easily to the middle managers.

Moreover, since the 1960s, intense discussions and efforts to improve first-line managers have taken place in response to the introduction of codetermination and other trends in Swedish industrial relations. As indicated, many companies have devoted considerable attention to managerial development and management training. First-line managers now regard themselves as representatives of company management within their area of responsibility.

Middle management personnel, on the other hand, often have an unclear identity. They do not regard themselves as representatives of top management, and are often uncertain about company policy, management ideology, and what level of performance is expected of them. At the same time, many middle managers are specialists and often feel a greater identity with a particular professional group than with top management. This is reflected in and reinforced by much of the management education that is directed toward middle management. It is to a great extent still functionally oriented and thus tends to focus more on specialist functions than on management functions in general.

One consequence is that middle-level managers find it difficult to communicate company policy, business ideas, and management ideologies to their subordinates. They seldom formulate distinctly what results are required and they do not follow up the results in their area of responsibility. Also, their area of responsibility is often less clearly formulated than at other management levels.

While Sweden has no comprehensive and systematic studies of these issues, they nonetheless are the complaints that always come up in discussions and interviews with managers and organizational specialists. Naturally, this creates some problems. Unclear managerial functions and lack of management identity can create blockages that impede or make it impossible to build up a comprehensive management system. There is a risk that many employees are thus cut off from company policy, business, ideas, and the expectation of results.

A Consistent Management Function

To address the ideological gaps existing across the managerial hierarchy, many top executives are working systematically to develop a specific corporate culture as well as to foster a corporate identity throughout the entire company. These efforts generally start with an identification of the qualities top management sees as being important. From these a coherent management system that supports these qualities is developed and the jobs of individual managers more defined. Toward this end, many Swedish companies are relying on such approaches as management development programs or quality campaigns in which company goals, company philosophies, and company culture are emphasized. However, a great deal still remains to be done. In this connection, it is useful to note the resolution of a recent Congress of SAF which encouraged employers to abolish distinctions between manual and salaried employees and toward a concept of "co-worker" (SAF 1987).

An important question in this context is what importance union membership and the increasing centralization and collectivization of salaried formation has for the identity problem of middle management. Ideally, pay systems should be used to communicate with and reward middle managers for desired traits or performance. However, a collectivized pay system makes this very difficult and weakens identification with the company and the corporate style. A new trend toward a decentralized pay system may be developing.

Although union membership for managers and supervisors has not been a major problem in recent years, it is difficult to see how the roles now being desired of managers can be achieved when pay and conditions of employment are set through collective negotiations. The long-term effect of this double message on the loyalty and commitment of managers, and ultimately the effectiveness of the managerial function, remains an open question at this time.

REFERENCES

Arbose, J. R. 1982. Succession planning: An international perspective. *International Management* 37 (May):48–52.

de Geer, H. 1986. *SAF i Forhandlingar—SAF i Samhallsutvecklingen (SAF in negotiations—SAF in the development of society)*. Arlov: Swedish Employers Federation.

Delamotte, Y. 1985. Managerial and supervisory staff in a changing world. *International Labour Review* 124 (1):1–16.

Giesecke, C. S. 1985. SAF's Utveckling och andrade roll under aren 1947–1977 (Development and changed role of SAF during the years 1947–1977). *Fred eller Fejd. Personliga Minnen och Anteckningar (Peace or conflict. Personal memories and notations)*. Stockholm: Swedish Employers Federation.

Jonsson, L., and C. H. Siven. 1986. *Varför Löneskillnader? (Why wage and salary differentials?)*. Stockholm: Swedish Employers Federation.

Klevmarken, A. 1980. *Age, qualification, and promotion supplements: A study of salary formation for employees in Swedish industry*. Research Report 1980:3. Department of Statistics, University of Göteburg.

Lindestad, L., and C. Jeffmar. 1984. The first-line manager. SAF/SALF Committee for Supervisory Training.

Lundberg, U., and T. Hellstrom. 1985. *Lonekultur: Individuell Lonesattning for Tjänsteman (Salary culture: Individual salary determination for salaried employees)*. Stockholm: MGruppen.

Nilsson, C. 1987. Lokal Lönebildning och Löneinflation. (*Local Wage and Salary Formation*). Stockholm: Trade Union Institute for Economic Research, Research Report No. 15.

SAF. 1979a. *Fair pay: A pay policy program; premises and principles*, Doc. No. 182. Swedish Employers Federation.

———. 1979b. *The SKF position class system: Workbook*. Stockholm: Office of Statistics, Salary Statistics Section, Swedish Employers Federation.

———. 1983a. *Befattningsvardering. Hogre tjansteman. SKF-systemet (Job evaluation: Higher salaried staff. The SKF system)*. Stockholm: Swedish Employers Federation.

———. 1983b. *Pay of salaried employees*. Stockholm: Swedish Employers Federation.

———. 1984. *BVT-systemet. befattningsvardering. tjänsteman (The BVT-System. Job evaluation: Salaried staff)*. Stockholm: Swedish Employers Federation.

———. 1987. Creative Sweden, a resolution adopted November 6, 1987.

SAF-LO-PTK. 1982. *Agreement on efficiency and participation: Progressing together, development agreement*.

SAF, SIF, SALF, and HTF. 1975. *Position classification system: Salaried*. Stockholm: Swedish Employers Federation, The Swedish Union of Clerical and Technical Employees in Industry, The Swedish Union of Supervisors and Foremen, and The Swedish Union of Commercial Employees.

SAF, SIF, SALF, HTC, and CF. 1981. *Salary statistics for salaried employees, 1980*. Stock-

holm: The Swedish Employers Confederation, The Swedish Union of Clerical
and Technical Employees in Industry, The Swedish Union of Supervisors and
Foremen, The Swedish Union of Commercial Employees, and the Swedish Association of Graduate Engineers.

Trygghetsradet (Council for Employment Security). 1985. *Arsberattelse 1984* (*Annual Report 1984*). Stockholm.

Wheeler, C. 1975. *White-collar power: Changing patterns of interest group behavior in Sweden*. Champaign: University of Illinois Press.

8
France

JACQUES ROJOT

DEFINITIONS

The terms and concepts of industrial relations frequently vary between countries. This is especially true of the definition of managerial employees in France. The closest approximation is the term *cadre*. Used nearly exclusively in France and some other French-speaking countries, cadre has no English equivalent when it refers to a person and not a group. Moreover, cadres as a class of workers are not homogeneous (Rojot 1978).

Cadres can be managers with very different levels of responsibility, such as salaried professionals and technical specialists, at different levels of the organizational structure. Like the Italian *dirigente,* the German *Leitende Abteilung,* the American executive, or the Swedish free-circle employee, French cadres are members of top management up to the president or *directeur general* (equivalent to an American chairman of the board). However, cadre also refers to middle and junior management personnel, including staff or technical specialists, researchers, and professionals.

Excluded from the definition are board members, who are considered non-salaried officers of the company elected by the shareholders. Also excluded are junior programmers, laboratory technicians, and supervisors who constitute an intermediate category labeled the *techniciens and agents de maitrise,* as well as clerks and blue-collar employees. References are also made to employees who are "assimilated to cadre" or "assimilated to *agent de maitrise*" to designate persons who do not quite fully belong in these two categories.

All of this makes it confusing to focus on that group of French employees broadly classified as the managerial and professional staff. Statistics on the cadres, because they encompass white-collar employees at different levels of the organization, may be only broadly comparable with data on managers in other countries.

Cadres as a Social Group

Even if the limits of the cadre group are not sharply delineated, the consensus among employers and unions is that cadres have achieved recognition as a distinguishable and high-status group within French society (European Association for Personnel Management 1979, European Trade Union Institute 1982). In fact, French society has conferred so much status and legitimacy on cadres and the management function in general that managers are used as role models in advertising campaigns.

Within the cadre grouping, Boltanski (1984, 373) identified several subgroups based on their career trajectories, type of education, social origins, and characteristics of the enterprise they are employed in. One subgroup contains people with a good family background and relevant social contacts, usually educated in the *grandes écoles* (elite graduate schools), where family support and educational background help them pass the grueling entrance examination and ensure that they are successful in business and industry. Those in this subgroup constitute the main source of top management and executives. While these managers have replaced the traditional employer-owners in France, they tend to share with these owners common social origins, educational experiences, and attitudes (Greffie de Bellecombe 1969, 6; Monjardet 1972; Savage 1976).

At the other extreme are self-educated cadres with no formal qualifications or degrees. They tend to be from lower social classes and usually enter the ranks of the cadres through promotion. Because they lack the social contacts of higher-ranking cadres, later in their career these persons may suffer unemployment and wage loss or have to accept positions of lesser responsibility in smaller enterprises (Boltanski 1984, 418, 420–26).

Legal Definitions

Because French law grants cadres a wide range of employment-related benefits, and because many people seek the social status of being identified as cadres, a precise legal definition of the term should be a necessity. However, the legal definition of cadre is not clear-cut, having been developed by combining several elements and criteria (Despax and Pelissier 1985, 205).

The Act of January 18, 1979, which deeply overhauled the French Labor Courts, also created a special court section for cadres with magistrates who are lay judges elected by their peers. For the court's purposes, cadre was defined by going back to concepts developed earlier:

1. Graduate engineers, whether or not they have power of command over other employees, or employees who have equivalent training with or without degrees.
2. Employees with technical, managerial, legal, or business training who have power of command over other employees by delegation of the employer.

3. Traveling sales personnel functioning as independents (Despax and Pelissier 1985, 207–10).

Other previous legal definitions have relied on these criteria as well:

1. The delegation of the power of command over other employees.
2. A graduate degree in various fields such as engineering or business.
3. Formal or informal training resulting in knowledge equivalent to that of
   a person with a graduate degree.
4. A great amount of initiative and responsibility, even though the employer has not delegated the power of command.
5. Certain pay levels that may automatically qualify employees for a special
   cadre retirement system, although they may not qualify for other cadre
   benefits.

In addition, it is not clear whether an employer can give the status of cadre
to employees just by issuing individual contracts of employment that label them
as such.

In summary, the legal definition of cadre is far from complete and fuzzy at
best.

Statistical Definitions

Although several statistical definitions exist of varying occupational scope, the
National Institute of Statistics and Economic Studies (INSEE) census and the
biannual surveys of employment have utilized perhaps the most encompassing
definitions. Until 1982, INSEE defined a cadre as someone belonging to two
major socioprofessional categories of its official occupational scheme—categories 3 and 4. Category 3 was high-level cadres (*cadres superieurs*); Cateogry 4 was
middle-level cadres (*cadres moyens*). Foremen were not considered part of either
category but were included in category 6 for blue-collar employees; other white-
collar employees were classified in category 5.

Category 3 also included self-employed professionals (nonwage earners),
professors and high-school teachers, persons in literary occupations, scientific
employees and engineers (who are engineering cadres with or without a graduate degree, but not mechanics, skilled craft workers, machine operators, or
repair workers), and high-level administrative cadres. Category 4 included
grade-school teachers, persons in occupations of an intellectual nature, medical
and social workers, technicians, and middle-level administrative cadres. Categories 3 and 4 encompassed civil servants and other public sector employees as well
as those in nationalized companies.

In 1982, a new classification system with slightly different categories was
started. The occupation labeled cadre and high-level intellectual professions
replaced the category called high-level cadres. The category known as middle-
level cadres is now called the intermediary occupations.

Other statistical agencies use more restrictive definitions. The Ministry of

Employment conducts a yearly survey on the structure of employment, based on compulsory reports filed by enterprises employing over ten people, excluding civil servants but including some of the nationalized enterprises whose employees fall under the labor laws. Because of differences in the definition and coverage of the Ministry's survey and the INSEE, the number of cadres reported in the Ministry's survey is generally smaller.

Another source of information on private sector employment is provided by AGIRC (*Association Generale Interprofessionnelle des Retraites Complementaires*), a special retirement system for cadres in the private sector established by an interindustry collective agreement in 1947. AGIRC classifies as cadres all employees qualified as such in industry-wide collective agreements, plus all employees whose pay-grade coefficient are above the level of 300, as specified in a national pay-grade collective agreement. The number of cadres reported by AGIRC may be a bit misleading because non-cadre employees with a pay coefficient between 200 and 300 may also be covered in the retirement system.

Because of the difficulties in defining cadres, different groups in society use the definition that is most politically expedient. For instance, some unions of cadres prefer the most extended definition. This helps them claim a wider membership within the occupation and give an impression of growing importance as cadres become more numerous in the labor force. Conversely, some political parties observe that a broad definition of cadre is an attempt to obscure the privileges received by the few overpaid top managers among a larger mass of workers.

STRUCTURE OF THE POPULATION

One of the dominant characteristics of French industry is the large number of small businesses and the relatively small number of companies that dominate some sectors. For instance, in 1981, 56 percent of the 11,567,177 employed persons worked in firms employing fewer than 500 employees. Only 12.4 percent of all employees worked in the 42 companies employing more than 10,000 or more employees. These facts have important implications for the terms and conditions of employment for cadres.

Number of Cadres

Tables 8.1 and 8.2 provide estimates for the number of cadres under the various definitions used above. Depending on the definition, the cadres represent from 7 to 27 percent of the labor force. However, whatever the definition, the proportion of the labor force employed as cadres has been increasing, albeit less so recently.

French companies more than others have historically employed a large

Table 8.1　Number of cadres, 1982*

Occupation	Number
All cadres and high-level intellectual occupations	1,808,362
Self-employed professionals	212,127
Cadres from the public sector	218,114
Intermediary occupations	
Grade-school teachers	3,813,000
Health and social workers	590,000
Clerical workers	59,000
Public and civil service employees	222,000
Enterprise, administrative, and commercial staff	923,000
Technical staff	656,000
Foremen	550,000
All persons in the labor force	23,525,000

Source: INSEE.
*Based on the wide definition used by INSEE in 1982.

number of individuals in staff, managerial, and administrative capacities. Maurice, Sellier, and Silvestre (1979), for instance, in comparing metalworking companies in Germany and France, found that German enterprises had more blue-collar workers, but that French enterprises had more nonproduction employees in such occupations as technicians, foremen and supervisors, middle managers, and other white-collar jobs. This might partially explain why the size of the cadre population is growing faster than the overall number of wage earners.

Table 8.2　Other estimates of the number of cadres for selected years

	1974	1977	1981
	INSEE's pre-1982 definition		
Total high-level cadres	680,800	779,420	861,723
Engineers and technical cadres from production	168,502	179,064	196,342
Cadres in services	512,298	600,356	665,381
Total technicians and middle-level cadres	772,811	854,835	945,389
Technicians in production	431,019	456,229	493,162
Technicians in services	341,792	398,606	452,227
	AGIRC's definition		
Cadres and others above 300 points	1,207,742	1,370,117	1,626,487
Noncadres from 200 to 300 points	260,174	295,490	318,012
All cadres	1,467,916	1,665,607	1,944,499

Sources: INSEE and AGIRC.

Industry

According to data provided by the National Association for the Placement of Cadres, APEC, and its report (APEC 1986), the representation of cadres varies greatly among different industrial sectors. The ratio of cadres to all wage earners is lowest in the leather and clothesmaking industry (3:10) and highest in oil, construction, and natural gas (19:36). Pharmaceutical, electrical construction, printing, insurance, and banking generally range between these extremes.

Firm Size

As the following data from APEC indicate, the ratio of cadres (using APEC's relatively restrictive definition) to all employees also varies by the size of the firm.

Number of employees	Percentage cadre in 1981
11–19	8.7
20–49	21.4
50–99	14.5
100–199	13.7
200–499	16.5
500–999	9.8
1,000 and more	15.1

Clearly, there is a threshold above twenty employees, perhaps due to economies of small-scale operations. Variations above this threshold are probably due to a variety of factors, including differing requirements of the labor law that are applicable to firms of 10, 50, 300, and 1,000 employees. These provisions require the firm to hire additional cadres to comply with legal provisions mandating employee representation, reporting, and tax and fringe-benefit administration.

In addition, the function and job of a cadre differs in the small and large enterprise.

Age

The distribution of cadres by age is shown in Table 8.3, which reports AGIRC data separately for all cadres above the 200- and 300-point pay grades. Looking at only those above 300 points, female cadres appear to be younger than male. This does not mean that younger women have better access to jobs as cadres than younger men, or that affirmative action has been successful, but rather that women have had access to cadre positions in large numbers more recently. At least for those under 25 years of age, it probably reflects the fact that entry into the occupation is delayed for males who participate in a system of national service.

Table 8.3 Age of cadres* by sex, 1980

	Cadres with 300 or more pay-grade points		Cadres with 200 or more pay-grade points	
Age	Men	Women	Men	Women
Total	100.0%	100.0%	100.0%	100.0%
<25	0.9	2.9	1.1	2.1
25–29	7.5	12.6	6.6	6.9
30–34	16.6	19.8	12.4	10.1
35–39	16.6	15.1	15.8	10.7
40–44	15.1	12.7	12.9	8.0
45–49	14.8	12.2	11.9	6.9
50–54	13.9	11.1	11.6	7.7
55–59	11.0	9.1	7.5	6.7
60–64	3.3	3.2	4.6	6.5
>65	0.9	1.3	15.6	34.4

Source: APEC 1986.
*Based on the AGRIC's definitions of cadre.

If we use the less restrictive cut-off of 200 points, the distributions get older. To some significant extent this reflects the practice of allowing a faithful employee with extensive service (and age) to be part of the cadre's more advantageous retirement system, even though these employees did not carry the cadre label during most of their career.

Under both definitions used by the AGIRC, the age distributions indicate a population much older than the labor force or wage-earning population as a whole. Cadres are older because they tend to remain in school longer and because some may obtain the position of cadre after a period of employment as a non-cadre.

Education

Table 8.4 shows the formal educational attainment of the cadres for 1981 in terms of persons broadly defined by INSEE to be in the occupational group. Only half the high-level cadres and professionals hold a degree from a university or an engineering or administrative *grandes ecole*. Boltanski (1984, 363) estimates that 30 to 70 percent of the cadres in the private sector are self-educated, hold no degree, or hold continuing education diplomas. On the other hand, most of the high-level cadres in the private sector who have an engineering or administrative degree come from the *grandes ecoles*. Many of the university graduates remain in lower positions or hold high-level positions in the public sector.

Education and training in management have long been generally absent from the French scene. The major exception has been some schools like the *Ecole des Hautes Etudes Commerciales* and *Ecole Superieure des Sciences Economique et*

Commerciales specializing in training students at the outset of their careers. However, even this limited amount of managerial training was outside the university system, and the schools providing it were mostly established by Chambers of Commerce.

The situation changed drastically during the late 1960s. First, several business schools were created by the Chambers of Commerce, the *ecoles de commerce*.

Table 8.4 Educational attainment of cadres, by sex and occupation, 1981*

Occupation and sex	No degree	Vocational degree at level of jr. high school or below	Vocational degree at level of a high school or degree (French Baccalaureat)	BA completed	MA or above (graduate degree)
All labor force					
Men	26.5	54.4	9.4	3.8	5.9
Women	21.3	54.7	11.8	2.8	4.4
Middle-level cadres					
Men	5.2	47.7	27.7	15.6	5.8
Women	3.4	32.7	26.6	30.9	6.4
Technical staff					
Men	5.2	52.6	26.5	13.8	1.9
Women	5.9	44.0	21.7	24.1	4.3
Administrative middle-level cadres					
Men	5.6	58.8	24.1	5.7	5.8
Women	3.9	57.9	26.9	7.6	3.7
Self-employed professionals and high-level cadres					
Men	3.7	21.9	19.7	10.0	44.7
Women	2.4	16.4	16.6	14.5	50.1
Engineers					
Men	1.5	13.3	15.1	9.6	60.5
Women	1.8	7.1	17.7	10.9	62.5
Administrative high-level cadres					
Men	4.9	35.8	22.3	8.5	23.5
Women	3.2	38.7	24.9	9.4	23.8

Source: INSEE.

*Based on INSEE's definition of cadre.

The *grandes ecoles* also began to offer curricula in administration and business along with more traditional subjects like engineering. Training in managerial skills has been introduced into the universities both at the undergraduate and post-graduate levels.

Second, most schools of business have established continuous (or mid-career) training programs. This was facilitated by the passage of the 1971 law requiring employers to contribute 1.2 percent of their payroll toward continuing education of their employees. While it is not known for sure, it is thought that a significant share of those funds was spent in the management area.

Third, the government has supported training in management skills. In 1969 it established the National Foundation for the Education in Management (*Fondation Nationale pour l'Enseigement de la Gestion des Entreprises*) which has undertaken to provide training for trainers.

Even with this expansion, there are still problems (Michaud 1983). Some of the *grandes ecoles* do not devote much attention to instruction in managerial skills, and other existing programs are still maturing.

Women

In theory, female and male employees enjoy exactly the same rights at work. Several successive waves of statutory laws have removed legal discrimination between the sexes and provided incentives for nondiscrimination as well as civil penalties for acts of discrimination. The latest legislative effort began in 1982 with the passage of the Act of July 13, 1983 (No. 83635), but at this point it is still too early to evaluate its impact. However, under the previous legislation very few suits were brought to court by female plaintiffs (Rojot 1985).

Also, participation of women in the labor force, although not a recent phenomenon (31 percent in 1901), has recently increased tremendously, going from 33.2 percent in 1958 to 52 percent in 1980.

According to a study in APEC (1981), *The Female Cadre,* the wages paid female cadres are noticeably below those of men in equivalent categories. Female wages in the labor force as a whole average 33 percent less than men. For the category of high-level cadres, the differential is 37 percent; however, for middle-level cadres it is 26.4 percent. Moreover, these differentials do not appear to be narrowing, even though a modest reduction of 3 percent has taken place over a ten year period. Interestingly, 85 percent of women surveyed by APEC answered that they believed a man in their same job would be paid an equal amount, possibly because women tend to enter the lower paying occupations.

The APEC study also found that men and women who enter the labor force with similar educational credentials are hired into different jobs: Women are concentrated more in the lower ranking occupations and the public sector. The differences in male/female earnings, of course, reflect these patterns.

LEGAL STATUS OF CADRES

As employees, cadres enjoy all the legal rights granted employees by statutory law, applicable collective agreements, and individual contracts of employment. Cadres also have a special legal status.

They can bring a case against their employer (or be sued by the employer) in a special section of the Labor Court where the employee lay judges are also cadres. This ensures that their case will not be decided by lay judges associated with either employers, blue-collar employees, or other white-collar employees. These suits cover the application of the labor laws to such matters as dismissal and salaries. In addition, the courts have decided that the cadres should not receive overtime pay (see Despax and Rojot 1979 for further details).

An Act of January 3, 1978, tried to create a degree of consultation between employers and cadres beyond the general requirements of the works councils. The law made no specific consultative actions compulsory, but employers with over 500 employees must issue a yearly report on consultation with the cadres. To date, the law has had little practical effect.

Within the works councils, for enterprises with more than twenty-five employees, a seat in the employee section must be reserved for cadres. Also, one or two seats must be reserved for cadres on the nonvoting delegation of the works council that attends the board meetings of incorporated companies.

In the area of training, cadres enjoy comprehensive educational benefits under the program financed by the compulsory contributions of employers. Cadres undergoing training receive stipends for longer periods than other employees in training, and they are more likely than other types of employees to take a leave for training or education.

Beyond statutory law, collective agreements may grant specific benefits to cadres. Under French labor law, once an employer signs a collective agreement, it applies to all employees, unionized or not. Very often these agreements contain a specific addendum detailing a higher minimum wage for benchmark positions and persons holding graduate degrees. These addenda also may grant other privileges such as earlier notice of layoffs, higher severance pay, longer vacations, or a longer guarantee of employment in case of lengthy illness.

In case of unemployment, cadres are referred to the Association for the Placement of Cadres (APEC), a special placement system different from the one operated for regular employees.

Finally, even though under French labor law all employment relationships are based on an implicit or explicit premise of an individual contract of employment, such contracts for cadres are almost always in writing. They may give additional benefits to a cadre beyond those granted by the collective agreement.

Not all the special legal treatment given cadres would be considered beneficial. The courts have held that a manager can be dismissed more easily than other employees. Wrongfully dismissed employees may collect only damages, and are not entitled to reinstatement, excluding those who are union officers or employee representatives. Dismissal of all employees must be for "real and serious cause." However, in two particular areas, the courts have held that cadres can be justifiably dismissed for reasons that would not be sustained against non-cadres: One is the employee's obligation of loyalty to the employer, where the smallest demonstration of disloyalty by a cadre is adequate grounds for dismissal; the other is the employer's loss of confidence in a cadre, as for example when that person publicly opposes a business decision.

Cadres who directly carry a command by delegation of the employer may incur specific penal responsibilities. They can be held responsible and sentenced in criminal courts for offenses against the labor law such as hindering the functioning of the works committees or the functions of a union or personnel delegate. Also, such a cadre is personally responsible in cases of work-related injuries caused by violations of the occupational health and safety laws. If a plant manager has delegated responsibility, authority, and means of control to a subordinate, both can be held jointly responsible for these offenses.

Finally, collective agreements and written individual contracts of employment often contain provisions that are more restrictive for cadres. For instance, the trial period, during which an employee can quit or be dismissed without severance pay, delay of notice, or damages is much longer than for regular employees. Also, covenants of noncompetition after employment, which can be quite restrictive under French law, are often applicable to cadres (see Despax and Pelissier 1985).

ECONOMIC AND SOCIAL TRENDS

"The Malaise"

Beginning in the early 1970s, the French media began talking about the "malaise" or ill feelings among the cadres. Stories told of a general disquiet, a feeling of lost status and lost power among the managerial and professional staff.

Perhaps the most perceptive study was done by Crozier (1978), who found that the malaise was real and deeply felt but did "not correspond to an apocalyptic vision of a disintegration of values" (p. 14) during the social upheaval following the disruptions of May 1968. Crozier pointed out that the main problems were the companies and their system of organization. Cadres were "in the midst of a very difficult transition from an administrative model of the business enterprise based on loyalty, compromise, and, especially, limited communication that granted [the cadres] both security and power to a system based on rapid exchange of information, competition, and collaboration" (p. 16). The central cause of the change was France's entry into the Common Market, which prompted adoption of new, more competitive conditions.

Significantly, the malaise developed at the apex of postwar economic growth, before the oil shocks of the 1970s and the economic crisis of the 1980s. These events have been associated with, and may have contributed to, rising unemployment among the cadres, the erosion of their salary and social status, and the stabilization of cadre employment patterns.

Unemployment

Statistics on the unemployed (reported recently in APEC 1986) are collected for the following categories of workers: all individuals looking for employment at the end of every month and registered with the national placement and employment agency ANPE (*Agence Nationale pour l'Emploi*); all persons receiving unemployment benefits from the unemployment compensation system; and all cadres registered with the Association for the Placement of cadres (APEC). Along with the usual problems of interpreting such data, we also should take notice of some special limitations. For one, the coverage of the unemployment compensation system has been modified in recent years, thus making time-series unemployment data unreliable. Information on APEC registrants is similarly flawed because cadres are not required to register with the agency. Although registration is mandatory with the ANPE, and its data generally more reliable, data from ANPE also exclude some categories of the workers.

The average monthly number of cadres and total number of workers looking for employment from 1971 to 1984 are reported in Table 8.5. Even though the data for the entire labor force are only roughly comparable to those for the cadres, it is clear that the oil shocks of 1973–74 and 1979 had a serious impact on the level of unemployment among the cadres. Their unemployment is cur-

Table 8.5 Unemployment of cadres, 1971–84

Year	Number of cadres looking for work[a] (in thousands)	Number of all workers looking for work[b] (in thousands)
1971	13.9	329.1
1972	19.0	376.6
1973	20.6	393.8
1974	25.0	493.4
1975	39.7	840.0
1976	47.2	943.9
1977	53.5	1088.3
1978	57.0	1165.5
1979	63.3	1348.5
1980	62.9	1446.7
1981	64.9	1762.7
1982	64.7	2007.2
1983	59.3	2039.8
1984	62.0	2307.7

Source: APEC 1986.

[a]Restrictive definitions, seasonally adjusted average for month of persons looking for work at the end of that month.
[b]Average number looking for work, not seasonally adjusted.

rently much higher than historical standards and has increased 4.5 times since 1971. If the possibility of unemployment is now a significant threat to cadres, they still are better protected than the general labor force. The average number of persons seeking work each month increased 8.8 times since 1970.

Obviously, these figures are averages and represent very different situations for individuals depending on their geographical location in France, their industry, age, technical qualifications, and experience.

The relative gains in unemployment among cadres may be too small to have significance for macroeconomic or labor market policies, but it is now recognized that unemployment constitutes a factor to be taken into account when people make their career plans. Thus, other things held constant, younger workers have become less mobile and easier to recruit.

Other Labor Market Conditions

As the demand for cadres has trailed off and as unemployment has become more likely, the career patterns of cadres have stabilized.

Mobility

Using the restrictive AGIRC definition (i.e., cadres plus other employees over 300 points), an APEC study shows that the rate of new entrants into the ranks of the cadres has fallen from 10.3 percent in 1973 to 7.1 percent in 1983. New entrants included those who become cadres by promotion or entry into the labor force, the so-called first-hired (APEC 1986). New entrants in 1983 were actually below the number of cadres leaving the labor force. The rate of leaving in 1983 is also the highest since 1973, 8.10 percent against 6.6 percent. Equally as significant is that in 1983 the rate of mobility (those who have changed jobs) was the lowest since the first oil shock. Cadres, it would appear, are staying longer with their employers.

Another study (APEC 1983) confirms the deterioration of the labor market for young cadres. Fewer and fewer graduates with higher education degrees are being hired directly into jobs as cadres, in what might be called "direct access" to cadre positions. Rather, they are hired as white-collar employees and are promoted to positions as cadres a few years later. The drop in direct access appointments between 1972 and 1978 was particularly significant—71.2 to 59.0 percent. However, the graduates from the *grandes ecoles* kept their relative advantage in obtaining positions as new cadres (Boltanski 1984).

Employment Security

The traditional model of employment for cadres represented the exchange of job security for total loyalty. The economic changes discussed above resulted in a major reevaluation of company policies toward cadres. While the era of presumptive job security may be over, it has not come to a complete end. Unemployment among cadres is still below the labor force as a whole. The socially well-connected graduates of the *grandes ecoles* are still protected. However, even though some fare better than others, it appears that all employees must now prove themselves after entering the white-collar positions.

Salary Erosion

In 1983–84, the principal unions representing cadres argued over how much their members' salaries had actually increased. One union claimed that the real wages of cadres had increased 1.8 percent for 1982, while another said that real wages dropped after taxes by 0.5 percent in 1983. A third union alleged that for cadres in the private sector, under the AGIRC's narrow definition (those with 300 and more points), real wages had improved only 0.65 percent. More than anything, the debate was actually over the definition of the relevant population, for nearly everyone agreed that the available data unambiguously demonstrate that cadres, however they are defined, have lost ground to other occupational groups in the labor force.

The Center for the Study of Revenues and Costs reports (*Le Matin*, 1983) that mid-level and high-level cadres (based on INSEE's definition) experienced a loss in purchasing power of 0.8 and 9.4 percent, respectively, between 1974 and 1982, whereas the purchasing power of the legal minimum wage, by comparison, increased by 37.3 percent. If 1970 equaled 100, disposable income by 1980 had risen to 136 for all workers, but only to 120 and 122 for high-level and mid level cadres, respectively.

Also, such benefits as monthly wages, five-week vacations, and yearly bonuses, once granted exclusively to cadres through collective bargaining, now have been granted to other occupational groups through law or separate interindustry agreements covering all the labor force. These developments have further eroded the social status or special position of the cadres.

UNIONIZATION AND COLLECTIVE BARGAINING

As wage earners, cadres enjoy the legal right to organize and join unions as granted by the preamble of the Constitution of the Fifth Republic (Despax and Rojot 1979, 122ff). Unionization among all workers in France is no more than about 20 percent, the lowest in the EEC (Goetschy and Rojot 1987); however, among cadres the rate is generally considered to be lower.

Precise estimates of union membership are generally difficult to obtain in France because of the legal prohibition of union security clauses. For cadres, membership figures are even less precise for two reasons. First, everyone does not agree, including the cadres unions themselves, on the exact definition of the population eligible to be union members. In this regard, different unions of cadres claim different occupational jurisdictions. Second, because a major source of statistics on membership are the cadre unions themselves, such statistics are usually subjective estimates and sometimes the result of political manipulation. Indeed, the unions' self-reported membership estimates described below, if added together, imply that French managers have a strong interest in trade unions. The best way to view these organizational claims, therefore, is as "guesstimates."

Cadres unions follow the principle of pluralistic unionism found in the French labor movement. There is no rule of exclusive jurisdiction: Several labor organizations represent the same group of employees at the national, company, or plant levels (Despax and Rojot 1979, 123ff). The law, however, does make a distinction between representative and nonrepresentative unions, which among other things means that a union has the right to enter into a collective agreement. A further distinction is made between those unions that represent cadres exclusively and those that represent all categories of employees including cadres.

Cadres themselves are divided on whether or not they should belong to mixed unions. Grunberg and Mouriaux's (1979) 1974 survey of cadres (defined broadly to include those occupations subsumed under the INSEE definition plus civil servants and agricultural employees), of whom 16.9 percent were union members, found that 40.6 percent of the sample wanted to be organized solely in cadres unions but 29.1 percent considered that they should be organized with other wage earners. Interestingly, 15.4 percent of the sample thought cadres should not be organized because they shared the authority of top management, and 7.9 percent considered that professional associations satisfactorily represented cadres' interests.

Unions

Union membership of the cadres is spread among several organizations: one independent organization exclusively for cadres, four others affiliated with the major labor federations in France, and several organizations that are nonrepresenting bodies.

CGC

The oldest cadre union is the General Confederation of Cadres (*Confederation Generale des Cadres,* abbreviated as CGC), which was created in 1944 but has earlier roots in prior associations of graduate engineers and social Catholic associations. Recently, it changed its name to the *Confederation Francaise de l'Encadrement-CGC* (CFE-CGC) after deciding to open its rank to all cadres from top management to those normally belonging to the foreman or *maitrise* (supervisor) ranks.

Like all French unions, CGC is organized along dual lines—geographical and industrial. Basic unions at the local level join industry federations as well as departmental or regional groupings. All intermediate industrial or geographical bodies are also affiliated with the confederation.

At the time it was created, CGC was opposed to the two dominant ideologies of its era, economic liberalism and Marxism. Instead, it proclaimed itself in favor of reform and evolutionary change, and focused on what it defined as the common interests of its members.

The major goals of CGC currently include the following. First, it seeks to reform the business enterprise to obtain more power for cadres at all levels of decision-making; for example, it was involved in the 1978 agreement on commissions of consultation between cadres and top management discussed above. CGC demands extending the power of these consultative arrangements. It also demands improved representation for cadres in employee representative bodies such as the work council and the board of directors.

Second, CGC seeks a just hierarchy within the organization. At all levels, it wants to equate a manager's power, authority, knowledge, and degree of responsibility with wages. The union strongly opposes egalitarian and utopian proposals such as flattening of the wage hierarchy.

Third, CGC advises that the standard of living and purchasing power should be maintained for all categories of employees, but particularly for cadres, who have been the victims of wage compression as well as social taxation policies that have benefited other groups at their expense.

Finally, CGC advocates that the social security system should be limited to a compulsory insurance system and not be used as a tool for transferring wealth to the lower part of the income ladder. The union particularly desires the maintenance of some special benefits for cadres that were first achieved in 1947.

CGC claimed 100,000 members in 1947; 280,000 in 1973; 302,000 in 1979; and 300,000 in 1982. However, it is often said that only about one-half of these members pay their dues.

UGICT

The *Union Generales des Ingenieurs, Cadres et Techniciens* has a Marxist ideology and, although it has no institutional links with the French Communist Party, many of its top officials also are high officials of the party and many officers at lower ranks also join both UGICT and the party.

UGICT is a separate organization for cadres who have joined the *Confederation Generale du Travail* (CGT); its members belong to both. Recently, UGICT petitioned the government for status as a separate representative organization, but the request has not been granted and seems unlikely to be granted in the future.

In terms of its potential membership, UGICT is the most wide-ranging and encompassing of the cadres' unions. Among the groups it organizes are graduate engineers (historically separated from administrative and managerial cadres but who have the quality of cadre notwithstanding), all cadres within the definition of the two categories of the INSEE, technical staff, foremen, supervisors, and civil servants in selected grades.

Ideologically, the UGICT follows all the positions of the CGT. UGICT defines itself as a class organization opposed to class collaboration with the owners of capital, takes a position in favor of extensive nationalization, and advocates the exclusive and extensive representation of unions in the various decision-making bodies within the company.

Because of this ideology, UGICT's status as a union solely for cadres has raised a serious problem for CGT. According to Marxist philosophy, existence of a growing intermediary class between the workers and owners of capital is theoretically impossible. However, this group does exist and has specific needs requiring the attention of unions. After serious debate, UGICT determined that it represents a "layer" of employees that creates added value and is an ally of the working class. As such, the union is available to address the specific needs of these workers.

UGICT claims 320,000 members in both private industry and the public sector, where it is well represented. In the private sector, it seems to gather support mostly from lower cadres—those with no university degrees, those who do not directly supervise other workers, and those who come from working-class families (Boltanski 1984).

UCC

The *Union Confederale des Cadres* is affiliated with the *Confederation Francaise Democratique du Travail* (CFDT), which was created in 1967. UCC draws its membership from only one grade of civil servants, engineers and high-level cadres in the private sector (a group close in definition to that used in the more restrictive definition of the AGIRC). It expressly excludes from membership all technicians and foremen. Members do not belong to a specific organization for cadres; they are regular members of their company section or local union, which in turn joins the national union for the industry. These national unions register their cadres' membership with UCC. UCC, therefore, was created to represent the interests of cadres at the federal level.

To some degree, UCC plays (or wants to play) the role of a research laboratory of ideas for CFDT. It originated nine proposals issued by CFDT in 1979 to efficiently control the introduction of new technology, especially computer-based technology, at the company level. In 1970, CFDT declared itself in favor of "self-managerial socialism," reflecting its desire to change economic exploitation and address the alienation and domination of lower-ranking workers by higher-ranking workers. After the 1978 legislative elections, in which left-wing parties suffered considerable losses, CFDT adopted a recentralization of its policies. This has meant reorienting its programs to emphasize the needs of employees at the plant level. Accordingly, the union has declared itself in favor of limiting wage differentials and encouraging employment by reducing the duration of work.

UCC claims 45,000 members within its own restricted definition of cadres. Most are in the public sector and nationalized industries. UCC also claims the largest number of members with graduate degrees (between 60 to 88 percent). There are probably more engineers than administrative and managerial cadres among UCC's members, 28 percent of whom hold jobs in production and 32 percent in research and development.

UCI

Created in 1970, the *Union des Cadres et Ingenieurs* is the cadre organization of the CGT-FO (*Confederation Generale du Travail—Force Ouvriere*) which split from the CGT in 1947. Each national union of the FO defines eligibility in

UCI; membership, therefore, is highly varied. The cadres join a local or union section and are duly registered with the UCI directly by the national industrial unions.

UCI adheres to the ideological orientations and policies of FO. More specifically, it seeks strict independence of unions from government, political parties, and churches; defends collective bargaining; and believes in strikes as the main tool of the working class. It endorses a mixture of the labor movement's anti-capitalist traditions with very strong anti-communism—a blend that favors reformist policies and gradual changes with a desire to bolster employees' rights and working conditions.

The UCI contends that, even though cadres have needs in common with other wage earners, they also have specific objectives. These include limitation of working time, retirement systems, and preferential receipt of information.

UCI claims to have 60,000 members and is strongest in the civil service, public and nationalized sector.

UGICA

The *Union Generale des Ingenieurs, Cadres et Agents de Maitrise* (UGICA) is affiliated with the *Confederation Francaise des Travailleurs Chretiens* (CFTC), the federation with the lowest membership. Formed in 1974, UGICA is composed of about 5,000 cadres belonging to one of the national unions affiliated with CFTC federation; all these unions, however, are not required to register their cadre members. Like the CFTC, UGICA adheres to Catholic social doctrine.

Other Organizations

In addition to the organizations discussed above, cadres may belong to several nonrepresenting unions. The most important one exclusively for cadres is the *Union Syndicale des Cadres Dirigeant,* which is more of a club or discussion group than a union. Top managers also have their own organizations, such as the *Centre des Jeunes Dirigeants,* the *Association des Cadres Dirigeants de l'Industrie pour le Progres Social et Economique,* and *Enterprise et Progres.* These are not cadre unions, but serve as centers for reflection and research in which top managers may interact with the owners of companies.

Finally, teachers in the state system and professors, as well as public education system administrators and employees, belong to their own organization, the *Federation de l'Education Nationale,* which has about 500,000 members. The largest part of the educational system is state run in France, and the degree of unionization is very high for primary and secondary school teachers as well as administrators, but is much lower at the university level, especially among full professors.

Industrial Action and Relative Influence

Work-place actions, such as work stoppages, are of limited value to cadres for the following reasons. First, cadres do not constitute a homogeneous group with consistent interests, and as such are not a well-organized, efficient pressure group. Second, some cadre categories are too clearly identified with top management. Third, many cadres in positions of intermediate authority have little bargaining power because they can be easily replaced by subordinates, or their tasks can be carried out by superiors. Fourth, many cadres consider their social status incompatible with an industrial action, and especially with a strike.

For these reasons, except in circumstances dealing almost always with plant closures when the jobs of all are threatened, there are very few instances of industrial action by cadres at the plant level. A good case in point took place during the closure of plants of the Boussac Group in the northeastern region of Vosges in 1977–78.

On the other hand, the cadres constitute a powerful and growing group of voters. To that end, cadres' unions have turned to political pressure to ensure that their points come across. For example, on May 27, 1977, CGC joined with other cadres' and workers' unions calling for a general strike against the Prime Minister's plan to dampen inflation through wage restraint. This demonstration was intended to show the government the discontent of the cadres, even if only a few of them actually stopped work on that day. On October 4, 1983, another demonstration against government policies, called to protect the cadres' wage and standard of living, was successful enough to drum up 80,000 to 100,000 demonstrators.

Apart from mass demonstrations, CGC has also used other original forms of action. In 1980, it organized in several companies the General Assembly of Cadres, through which cadres were to meet in each company and discuss issues. In 1981, it threatened to back a "cadres'" candidate in the Presidential elections.

The other cadres unions act mostly through the federations to which their members belong, but press for their own set of demands acting jointly or sometimes separately.

The influence of cadres unions may also be measured by the results of those social elections regularly conducted for various purposes (e.g., works councils, labor courts, social security) in which unionized and nonunionized cadres may vote for candidates nominated by the unions. The relative strength of the unions can be gauged by the percentage of votes they get from people who may be members.

When the malaise of the cadres was first noted in the 1970s, a massive turn to unions was not deemed likely. Rather, it was felt that cadres would express their protest politically by voting against the center-right government then in power (Rojot 1978). This they did to some extent in the legislative elections of 1978 and even more so in the presidential elections of 1981. A Socialist Party leader estimated that 30 percent of the upper grade of cadres and 60 percent of the lower grade had voted for the candidate of the left in 1981 (Quilés 1982).

The 1983 elections to elect lay judges to the cadre section of the labor court give some insights into the preferences of cadres for the various unions seeking their allegiance. The CGC candidates received 41.4 percent of the vote, UCC-CFDT was a far second with 17.1 percent, CGT and FO third and fourth with 13 percent and 11.6 percent respectively, and CFTC fifth with 9.1 percent.

Table 8.6 Election to the works councils, 1983

| | Percent of votes cast | |
Union	When supervisors and technical staff vote with cadres	When cadres vote alone
CGT	11.2	2.9
CFDT	18.2	12.0
CFTC	5.1	4.4
FO	9.6	6.6
CGC	24.0	44.6
Other	6.4	7.2
No union (after second ballot only)	25.0	21.7

Source: Ministry of Labor.

Nonrepresentative unions taken as a whole claim 8.1 percent of the vote (Goetschy and Rojot 1987).

The predominant appeal of CGC is also seen in the results of within-company voting for representatives to works councils, even though considerably fewer employees vote in these elections than vote in social or legislative elections. Table 8.6 shows the affiliation of 2.2 million votes received in works council elections in 1983. Employees may vote in "colleges" representing different classifications of workers in each company. In this election, when cadres voted within such colleges, nearly 45 percent voted for CGC candidates. When cadres voted in colleges along with other supervisory and technical staff, CGC candidates were still the most desired, but the percentage of votes received was only 24 percent.

To summarize, almost no plant-level actions occur against employers because very few cadres are unionized and most of the collective settlements governing cadres are negotiated at the industry or national levels. In addition, unionized cadres have sought to obtain their objectives in the political arena.

PERSONNEL MANAGEMENT POLICIES

While the treatment of cadres is heavily influenced by statutory law, interindustry national collective agreements, and industry-wide agreements, corporate management is not overly constrained in personnel policies regarding them. Externally imposed constraints serve as a broad framework and constitute the minimum protection for cadres (see Rojot 1985 for additional material on this point). The employer, however, can always go above that floor and provide additional benefits either unilaterally or by agreement, collectively at the corporate or plant levels or individually through separate employment contracts. Also, with a few notable exceptions, because the labor unions have been relatively weak at the plant level, management has considerable room to manage cadres as employees. The 1981 law which imposed an annual duty to bargain at the plant level has not yet been vigorously enforced and is limited mostly to wages. Hence, it has not yet had a significant impact on the terms and conditions of employment for cadres.

General Policies Toward Cadres

Personnel management practices in France are not highly developed, partly because of the many small family-owned businesses. The function is more systematically conducted and progressive in the larger or nationalized companies but is sometimes backward in the family-owned, small manufacturing concerns located in semirural areas. Of course, there are a few progressive small firms. The present head of the French Employers' Federation used to run a medium-sized company, Radiall, which had a high degree of participative management. One consequence of these different practices, however, is that there are very few data collected on personnel systems and policies. Instead, it is necessary to describe the nature of personnel systems by referring to the practices of a few companies studied by the author.

At one extreme are the policies of a large French subsidiary of a very large U.S. multinational corporation. In this case, the multinational has adopted a headquarters' model of organization with the visible goal of establishing policies of the country of origin, to the extent this is possible.

Still, the company has put in place a very sophisticated system of personnel management. First, except when the law and extended collective agreements require otherwise, the distinction between cadres and other employees is ignored.

Second, job descriptions are consistent with a detailed job evaluation system used by the company worldwide.

Third, even though pay levels must take into account across-the-board wage increases negotiated at the industry level, pay is related to performance within a strict system of performance appraisal and management by objectives.

Fourth, a large range of established policies are at the disposal of managers, at all levels, to ensure that the relationship between manager and employees remains the essential relationship at work, without the intervention of third parties, as far as legally possible. Among the tools available to managers are the maintenance of a low span of command, internal guidance procedures, discretionary rewards at the disposal of the manager, counseling, suggestion plans, quality circles, and so on.

Fifth, promotion is strictly from within and no layoffs for economic reasons ever take place. The efficient and actual implementation of this model is ensured by an effective set of procedures that include compulsory yearly training in management of human resources at a school run by the corporation, a program of assigning foreign staff to either the headquarters or other subsidiaries, and frequent meetings at all levels.

In comparison, there is the case of another large multinational that has its headquarters and substantial production facilities in France. Its personnel management, and in particular the management of the cadres, has been described in the words of its present chief executive officer as "artistic fuzziness." No job descriptions, pay scales, or formal procedures exist, much less are made known internally or externally. Each manager or cadre is left in a vacuum to define his or her power, responsibilities, and field of action, and to negotiate wages and conditions with peers and superiors.

The company is known for having a deep veil of secrecy surrounding all its activities, whether it is research, production, or management. Actual power, it appears, is very much concentrated in the hands of the chief executive officer.

Between these extremes is another French multinational containing a diversified group of companies. This company, known for its progressive attitude in human resources management, has pioneered several innovations. A set of formal policies has been established and published within the company for the management of the cadres; it also has the goal of permitting cadres to manage their own careers within the company, subject to the constraints dictated by needs of the business.

A set of human resources management tools are used to fit the enterprise's strategy with individual goals. These include a system of performance appraisals designed mostly to allow a dialogue between cadres and their superiors. Under this system, the year's activities are reviewed against objectives, and the career development goals of individuals discussed.

Along with performance appraisals, the career of each cadre is followed by a management committee consisting of his or her immediate superior and all those in a position to have a considered opinion. The committee studies the appraisal and gives feedback to the cadres.

In addition, a file is kept on each cadre that contains information on previous jobs within the company, as well as pay and status.

This company also maintains a special monitoring system for high-potential or fast-track cadres, namely those who on the basis of their performance are identified to be promoted faster. About 10 percent are identified for this program but are not told of their selection.

All vacant job positions at this company are internally advertised within the corporation based on their location within the firm and their job-evaluation grade.

A computerized data file includes all the essential elements of the cadres' curricula vitae and makes it easier to compile monthly statistics on employment and internal mobility and to determine whether an existing employee might be qualified to fill a vacancy. In addition, the company is presently moving toward replacement tables, a form of succession planning.

Recruitment and Selection Processes

In 1985, the Agency for Employment of Cadres (APEC 1985) conducted a survey of the recruiting practices of 80 enterprises employing over 50 employees. Its main findings were that these companies did not follow a common set of practices. Recruitment procedures tend to vary with the size of each organization as well as the type of jobs to be filled. Also, apart from the widespread use of the employment interview, selection procedures were different for technical or commercial staff, beginners or experienced managers.

Ads in the national press were the most used in recruitment practice; the larger the firm, the more likely it was to advertise, although most enterprises did not name themselves in the ad. Ads in the regional press are also mostly used by middle-sized enterprises and are a last recourse for enterprises over 2,000 employees.

Fifty-nine percent of all enterprises in the sample used personal or professional relations as a source of top managers; 42 percent of those seeking average-level cadres and 28 percent of enterprises seeking beginners relied on personal or professional relations. Bigger firms were less likely than smaller firms to use this mode of recruitment; Parisian companies used it comparatively more than those in the provinces.

Recruitment agencies (management search firms) are mostly used for experienced managers (in 56 percent of the enterprises) and rarely used in filling inexperienced positions (16 percent). Mid-sized enterprises with between 300 and 500 employees, enterprises in the provinces, and enterprises trying to fill several positions at once are most likely to utilize this recruitment technique. Spontaneous candidatures (what Americans call walk-ins) are not common practice when experienced personnel are being sought.

The Agency for Employment of Cadres was used by 37 percent of enterprises for average level cadres, 21 percent and 23 percent, respectively, for top managers and beginners. It is used mostly by middle-sized enterprises and the ones in the Paris region.

Only about one-third of the companies recruit entry level cadres through on-campus recruiting. Alumni associations of top schools are used by 19 percent of enterprises seeking beginning cadres. Not surprisingly, this source of information is mostly used by the larger enterprises where the number of degree holders (presumably from the same schools) is the highest.

Among the pool of recruited candidates, it is almost universal to request a copy of one's curriculum vitae. However, as the following data reported in the APEC study indicate, firms follow widely different practices of selection:

58 percent verify the contents of the curriculum vitae
59 percent check the references
49 percent use an application blank
41 percent contact the latest employer
36 percent use graphological analysis
31 percent use personality tests
28 percent use technical tests
16 percent use group candidate interviews
 2 percent use simulation exericses

Large enterprises use the largest variety of methods. Small enterprises use fewer methods, with more than 50 percent relying only on a contact with the last employer, and one-third checking the elements of the curriculum vitae. When a top manager is being considered, most companies dispense with these traditional methods and resort to one interview.

According to the APEC study, it takes on average one to two months to fill a vacancy for a cadre, and most vacancies are filled in anywhere from fifteen days to three months.

Wages

Each year, several wage surveys from a variety of sources appear in the popular or business press; companies and unions conduct their own surveys as well. Shell, IBM, and other large companies are in a group of organizations that share compensation information. Compensation consulting firms, such as the Hay Group, are very influential. Even though these surveys lack the precision and accuracy of a wage study performed by a specialized consultant or government agency, they constitute an important and interesting indicator of trends.

Several compensation developments and trends are currently in evidence. More than one cadre out of two in 1983 had his or her total wages tied to some sort of incentive system linked with financial results ("*Le Salaire des Cadres*" *1984*). This is confirmed in a UCC survey for 1984 and 1985, which shows that 43 percent of the managers received "individual" wage increases, representing approximately half of their salary increase (FIET 1986, 11). The best paid cadres are middle-aged men heading large successful companies.

Education is clearly an important determinant of salary levels. Only a small minority of the 170 best paid cadres out of a sample of over 7,000 in 435 enterprises (*Le Salaire des Cadres 1984*) did not have a university education (compared to about 50 percent in the general cadre population); the *grandes ecoles* were heavily represented in this segment of the sample. Beginners could earn between 70,000 FF and 170,000 FF, depending on the school they had attended.

As indicated by the following salary ranges for persons considered managers (as reported in *Le Salarie des Cadres 1984*), salaries tend to vary across functional areas.

Job	FF (thousands)
Financial manager	260 to 620
Legal department manager	158 to 462
Accounting manager	180 to 387
Export manager	214 to 540
Marketing manager	290 to 524
Personnel manager	230 to 580
Computer manager	224 to 474

Within each functional area, the salaries of cadres vary directly with the size of the enterprise. Salary is positively correlated with turnover rates and age as well. The UCC study (FIET 1986) found that managers less than 30 years old enjoyed a 5 percent increase in their purchasing power in 1984–85, but those over 50 recorded a loss of 4 percent. It would appear, therefore, that even though salary levels increase with age, the value of an increased year of age (and possibly job tenure) has diminished recently.

CONCLUSION

The cadres are no longer the few superior employees gathered around the employer and representing him or her in all respects before the work force. Their number has grown, and they have developed new occupational specialties. Historically, the employment of cadres was characterized by high status and high degrees of job security, which was granted in exchange for loyalty to the employer. However, since the mid-1970s, rapid economic growth and foreign competition have produced a new model of cadre employment. Under this model, the employer still demands loyalty, as Boltanski (1984) has noted, but he also has subjected the cadres to higher expectations of performance and greater degrees of competition.

Contributing to the new situation facing the cadres, especially since the first oil shock, has been increased unemployment, deterioration in their job security, wavering job market prospects, decreased real wages, and a lower standard of living compared to other wage earners. At least with respect to job prospects, however, the cadres have fared better than the labor force as a whole.

So far, in the face of these worsening conditions, the managers and professional employees have shown little militancy other than to shift their voting preferences in national elections. They have been attracted to unions in very limited numbers.

REFERENCES

APEC. 1981. *Les femmes cadres (The female cadres)*. Paris: Agence pour l'Emploi des Cadres.
_____. 1983. *Les cadres dans les conventions collective (The cadres within collective agreements)*. Paris: Agence pour l'Emploi des Cadres.
_____. 1985. *Recrutement et integration des cadres (Recruitment and integration of cadres)*. Paris: Agence pour l'Emploi des Cadres.
_____. 1986. *Quid des cadres (All about the cadres)*. Paris: Agence pour l'Emploi des Cadres.
Boltanski, L. 1984. *Les cadres, la formation d'un group social (The cadres, the formation of a social group)*. Paris: Les Editions de Minuit.

Crozier, M. 1978. Attitudes of French managers regarding the administration of their firm. *International Studies of Management and Organization* 8 (3):39ff.

Despax, M. and J. Pelissier. 1985. *La gestion du personnel. Aspects juridique (Legal aspects of personnel management)*. Paris: CUJAS.

Despax, M., and J. Rojot. 1979. France. In *International encyclopedia for labor law and industrial relations*, edited by R. Blanpain. Deventer: Kluwer.

European Association for Personnel Management. 1979. *Management unionization in Western Europe*. London: European Association for Personnel Management.

European Trade Union Institute. 1982. *The unionization of professional and managerial staff*. Brussels: The European Trade Union Institute.

FIET. 1986. *Newsletter*. Geneva: Federation Internationale des Employes Techniciens et Cadres (July):10–11.

Goetschy, J., and J. Rojot. 1987. France. In *International and comparative industrial relations: A study of developed market economies*, edited by G. Bamber and R. Lansbury. London: Allen and Unwin.

Greffie de Bellecombe, L. 1969. La participation des travailleurs à la gestion des entreprises en France, données de base du problèms (The participation of workers in the management of the firm in France, getting to the bottom of the problem). *Bulletin de l'Institut International d'Etudes Socials.* (6):6088.

Grunberg, G., and R. Mouriaux. 1979. *L'univers politique et syndical des cadres (The political and trade union world of the cadres)*. Paris: Fondation Nationale des Sciences Politiques.

Maurice, M., F. Sellier, and J. J. Silvestre. 1979. La production de la hierarchie dans l'entreprise: recherche d'une effet societal comparaison France—Allemagne (The production of hierarchy in the firm: Research on the societal effect comparing France and Germany). *Revue Francaise de Sociologie* (20):350ff.

Michaud, C. 1983. *Management et formation contenus (Management and training)*. Maastricht: European Institute of Public Administration.

Monjardet, D. 1972. Carrière des dirigeants et contrôle de l'entreprise (Career patterns of company presidents and control of the firm). *Sociologie du Travail* 14, (2):131–44.

Quilés, P. 1982. Quel changement pour les cadres? (What are the changes for the cadres?). *Le Monde*, February 23:3.

Rojot, J. 1978. Evolutionary trends in the French management group. *International Studies of Management and Organization* 8 (3):8–21.

———. 1985. France. In *Equality and prohibition in employment, bulletin of comparative industrial relations*, edited by R. Blanpain. 14:83ff.

———. 1986. L'Evolution de la politique des employeurs Francais vis-à-vis des organisations syndicale (The evolution of the politics of French employers toward trade unions). *Travail and Société* 11 (1):1–15.

Le salaire des cadres, 1984 (The salary of cadres, 1984). 1984. *L'Expansion*. 240–48 (22 June):132ff.

Savage, D. 1976. Patterns of access to business leadership in France. In *European industrial managers, east and west*, edited by J. J. Boddewyn. White Plains, NY: International Arts and Science Press.

9
Italy

CLAUDIO PELLEGRINI

In Italy, high-level managers and professional staffs are regulated by different laws, have separate unions and collective bargaining, and have had divergent histories. For these reasons, the issues relevant for the two groups will be treated separately.

In this report, the word manager will be used as the equivalent of the Italian *dirigente*. It is important, however, to note that the Italian term is more restrictive than the American one and includes only higher levels in each of the traditional management functions such as advertising, sales, financial analysis, and personnel. Employees such as professionals and technicians, who in the United States would be considered management, are defined here as cadres.

In Italy, managers have been treated differently from other employees.* This division was based on the actual job functions performed within the firm and was reinforced by legislation. However, particularly in the last decade, such differences have been blurred by transformations in the context of jobs, the size and structure of firms, and class and group identifications in Italian society. Differences in legislation remain, however.

Managers, who were once part of a small and elite group, have lost their previous status and prestige while gaining in numbers. Regarding their power, in the public industrial sector they lack autonomy because of unavoidable political interference, and in the private sector their role is also obscured by the active presence of owners. This is true in large private corporations (for instance FIAT, Pirelli, or Olivetti) and even more so in small enterprises that constitute the more active and innovative section of the economy.

---

*For a more detailed analysis of Italian industrial relations, see: Barkan (1984), Giugni (1981, 1984), Horowitz (1963), Kogan (1981), Lange (1977, 1982), Martinelli and Treu (1984), Pellegrini (1987), Regini (1982), and Treu (1978, 1983).

In Italy managers have played a minor role because of the late development of capitalism and continuation of the owners' leading role (Ferrarotti 1959). These factors have also prevented the development of a managerial culture and the absence of business school is a symptom of this situation. The extensive economic role played by the government has not created a substitute group of public managers with recognized professional abilities.

The rapid growth of the cadres, professional and lower-level workers, has been another major and continuous development in Italian industrial relations. A critical issue for this group has been the flattening of wage differentials caused by egalitarian policies and high inflation.

Finally, the economic environment of Italy, in which small, specialized firms are concentrated in certain geographical areas, has played an important role in industrial relations (Piore and Sabel 1984, 151–56). For instance, in the 1981 census, the average firm in the industrial sector had 4.6 employees, and 81 percent of all firms with 38 percent of total employees were operated by single proprietor managers.

Also, Italy has suffered from high levels of inflation for many years. Between 1976 and 1981, the average rate of price increases has been 16.6 percent versus 9.2 percent in the United States. In 1986, the consumer price index rose 5.9 percent and in 1987 increased less than 5 percent. Additionally, notwithstanding the economic recovery after 1983, there has been a high level of unemployment totaling 11 percent for 1986. The official data do not take into consideration the large Italian informal or clandestine sector that is estimated to be up to 20 or 30 percent of the GNP.

INDUSTRIAL RELATIONS OF DIRIGENTI

Numbers and Characteristics

Data collected by the Istituto Centrale di Statistica (ISTAT), Central Statistical Institute, merge managers with other white-collar employees. This larger group made up 16 percent of the nonself-employed (i.e., dependent) employees in 1951, 19 percent in 1961, 27 percent in 1971, 35 percent in 1981, and 42 percent (6.3 million) in 1985.

White-collar workers have gotten more numerous because of increasing employment in sectors with a greater representation of such workers and because blue-collar employment has declined. For instance, the number of dependent employees in the industrial sector diminished from 46 percent to 41 percent between 1977 and 1984, and the percentage of managers and white-collar workers grew from 17 percent to 21 percent. Outside the industrial sector, employment rose from 46 percent to 53 percent, and the white-collar employment went from 37 percent to 60 percent.

To give separate figures for managers, it is necessary to draw on other, less complete sources. In the annual analysis of family budgets for the Bank of Italy

(Banca D'Italia 1984), for example, managers constitute about 1.1 percent of the sample in 1983, or around 160,000. Independent research confirms the conclusion that managers on the average are between 1 and 2 percent of dependent employees. Naturally, a large variation exists among different companies depending on the activity and the policies followed by the employer. At the Istituto per la Ricostruzione Industriale (IRI), Institute for Industrial Reconstruction, the largest public conglomerate, in 1985 there were 480,000 employees and 7,500 managers with a ratio of 1 to 64; at the Ente Nazionale Idrocarburi (ENI), National Institute for Hydrocarbons, there were 2,500 managers and 110,000 employees with a ratio of 1 to 44.

According to Quirico (1983), who attempted to integrate the different sources of information, the total number was around 135,221 in 1981. Because economic activity is not evenly distributed geographically, 67 percent of all managers are in the economically more developed north, 22 percent are in central Italy, and 11 percent in southern Italy.

Managerial employment varies by sector. The ratio of managers to other employees is much higher in the manufacturing sector (an average of one manager to 83 employees) than in the service, insurance, and banking systems (one manager to 20 employees).

More complete data are available for managers in the industrial sector since 1954 (Table 9.1). The figures in Table 9.1 include all managers in the industrial sector that contribute to the Istituto Nazionale Previdenza Dirigenti Aziende Industriali (INPDAI), National Institute for Social Security of Managers in Industrial Firms, the organization that collects pension contributions for managers that employers must contribute by law.

Table 9.1 shows that in the last decades the ratio of managers to dependent employees in the industrial sector went from 1:230 in 1968 to 1:117 in 1975 to 1:62 in 1984.

There have been several causes of this growth. First, sectors with a higher ratio of managers, such as service and commerce, have gotten bigger. Second, within the enterprises managerial qualifications have increased their job functions and areas of responsibility. Third, there has been a change in the distribution of employees among enterprises of different sizes. Between 1971 and 1981, according to the census, the number of employees working in firms with more than 100 employees went from 45.5 percent to 28.97 percent. The decentralization of the economic structure enlarged the number of *dirigenti* necessary for the functioning of the smaller independent units. In small firms that meet certain legal requirements and are not in the artisan category, owners have some advantage in nominating themselves or their relatives to be *dirigenti* in order to have better pension and health plans.

Fourth, the increase in the number of managers is the result of a rigidity in the Italian compensation structure. Flattening wage differentials among employees caused employers to use the managerial designation as a way to increase compensation. (Cesareo, Bovone, and Rovati (1979) show that 42 percent of surveyed managers held this opinion.)

Table 9.1 Number of managers

Year	A	B	C	D	E
1954	12100	9515	79.6		
1955	12665	9676	76.4		
1956	14444	9802	67.9		
1957	14393	10234	71.1		
1958	15008	11029	73.5		
1959	15918	11983	75.3	5693	358
1960	17358	13044	75.1	5949	342
1961	19307	14465	74.9	6208	321
1962	21608	15813	73.2	6474	300
1963	24198	17386	71.8	6673	276
1964	26038	17846	68.5	6580	253
1965	27800	18488	66.5	6309	277
1966	29329	18652	63.6	6211	212
1967	31438	19220	61.1	6384	203
1968	32679	20027	61.3	6467	198
1969	35590	20790	58.4	6686	188
1970	38434	21402	55.7	6837	178
1971	40978	22896	55.9	6940	169
1972	44195	23640	53.5	6855	155
1973	46310	24692	53.3	6880	149
1974	50029	25174	50.3	7076	141
1975	52608	26587	50.5	7092	124
1976	58669	26945	45.9	6549	112
1977	61819	27293	44.1	6535	106
1978	66840	30940	46.3	6496	97
1979	71632	35918	50.1	6512	91
1980	76040	36984	48.6	6537	86
1981	80319	36750	45.7	6470	80
1982	83390	36120	43.3	6337	76
1983	85414	35701	41.8	6148	72
1984	86967	36012	41.4	5898	68

A = Managers in the Social Security Fund.
B = Manager members of the union FNDAI.
C = Unionization rate (B/A) × 100.
D = Total (in thousands) dependent employees in the industrial sector.
E = Manager per dependent employees (D : A).

Sources: D from ISTAT (Instituto Centrale di Statistica, Central Statistical Institute), *Annuario.* A and B from FNDAI *Documentazioni Statistiche,* 1983–84.

Demographic information regarding managers is not collected officially. However, it is possible to piece together a description from a few independent sources. Among these are: (1) *Dirigenti '80* by The Federazione Nationale Dirigenti Aziende Industriali (FNDAI), National Federation of Managers in Industrial Firms, based on the answers of 25,287 managers to a mailed questionnaire in 1980, the largest research ever done on managers; (2) research by

Cesareo, Bovone, and Rosati (1979) based on a 1978 sample of 400 middle-level managers in the area of Milan; (3) research by Quirico (1983) based on a sample of 15,902 managers (11.7 percent of the universe), collected in 1980; (4) research by Talamo (1979) based on a sample of 663 managers in the manufacturing industry, collected in 1970–72; (5) a 1986 survey by Santini and Conti (1986) and the Associazione Italiana per la Direzione de Personale (AIDP), Italian Association of Personnel Managers.

Based on these surveys, the average age of managers is between 47 and 49 years, and the average manager had been nominated to his position ten years earlier, but sooner in the smaller enterprises. The age of access to a managerial position has been growing in the last decade. In terms of education, 87 percent now have a university degree, continuing a long-term trend in the professionalization of managers (Derossi 1978). The majority are in engineering or economics-business; in Italy, there is no business school as such.

Italian managers display very low levels of inter- and intra-firm mobility: 67 percent have never changed firms and 16 percent have only been in two (*Dirigenti '80* 1981). The typical manager has been hired at age 26. Even within the same firm, 50 percent have never changed their area of activity, which to some extent is a reflection on the general practice of tying a large percentage of a manager's compensation to seniority. Permanence within the same firm is probably the necessary condition of access to the managerial role.

Even though there has been a growing trend in the number of small enterprises with a natural increase of managers working within them, the little research that is available overrepresents the managers working in large enterprises. In *Dirigenti '80* (1981), only 8.6 percent of all managers work in firms with fewer than 50 employees and the majority (54.8 percent) are concentrated in firms between 51 and 1500 employees, while 17 percent are in firms with more than 10,000 employees (*Dirigenti '80*, 1981). In terms of the number of managers in each firm, 45.8 percent are working in firms with fewer than 10 colleagues. This figure helps to explain why the career ladder is quite short. Only 20.7 percent of managers have four steps or more in their firms, while in 24 percent of cases there are no steps at all.

Drawing from the research of Cesareo, Bovone, and Rovati (1979), it is possible to describe the main features of managerial activity as seen by the managers themselves. Only a minority consider it as almost entrepreneurial (11.7 percent); this is a symptom of managers' current lack of authority and autonomy. In *Dirigenti '80* (1981), 32 percent answered that they were carrying out decisions made by others. More than 65 percent describe their activity in terms of responsibility, duty, and obligation, and only 3 percent in terms of competition; the loyalty itself is felt to originate from a sense of duty and only in small part (19 percent) from coincidence of interests with the employer. According to Cesareo, Bovone, and Rovati (1979), managers see themselves as being in a difficult spot because they believe the employer considers them to be an employee like other employees, while the employees see them as an employer. But interestingly, *Dirigenti '80* (1981) found that only 20 percent had entrepreneurial positions, such as president or members of the board of directors. In terms of their social origins, only 7.8 percent of managers had a working-class father and 12.2 percent a working-class grandfather. This aspect is also confirmed by Talamo (1979) and testifies to how class barriers are still present in Italy.

Finally, one must note in terms of political behavior (Cesareo et al. 1979) that the center parties had 80 percent of the managers' vote in 1976, when in that election those parties obtained only 46.7 percent of all votes; of the manager voters, 7.4 percent voted for the communist party and 8.6 percent for the socialist. These parties received respectively 34.4 percent and 9.6 percent of all votes cast in that year.

Legal Definitions

The first legal reference to managerial employees appeared in 1923 in law number 692/1923, concerning the restriction of working hours for blue- and white-collar workers in industrial and commercial undertakings. In that law, managerial employees, together with other employees, were excluded from the coverage. In the rules for the application of the law, managerial employees were defined as those in charge of the technical and administrative direction of the enterprise or of a section of it, with direct responsibility in the functioning of the activity.

Another reference to managers is made in decree 1825/1924, later transformed into law 562/1926, regulating the conditions of private white-collar workers. In this law, which basically repeats a 1919 text, the legislators gave certain rights to employees in the private sector to enhance their position while blue-collar workers were gaining certain rights through collective bargaining. In the law, the white-collar employees were basically defined as those involved in nonmanual activity. Managers were the top section of the private employees, and under the law were given a right to two months' notice in case of end of employment.

In 1926, after the consolidation of the Fascist regime, legislation 562/1926 was established giving a corporatist framework to industrial relations. It also was stated that the same top-level administrative categories identified by the previous law were granted separate union organizations. These organizations were to be part of the employer side within the institutional organizations (*corporazioni*) which were based on industrial sectors.

According to Fascist ideology, citizen participation should be channeled not through competing political parties that damage the unity of the State, but through the *corporazioni* where employer and employee organizations could cooperate toward the common goal of greater production. In practice, the workers had no freedom to choose their representatives and, even if they did, the unions had little room for bargaining without the right to strike and other ways of influencing the decision-making process. Finally, in the Civil Code approved in 1942, article 2095, all employees were divided into three groups:

administrative and technical managers, employees, and workers. In 1985, a fourth category of cadre was added to the law.

None of this legislation nor any of the other scattered articles where managers were mentioned gave a functional definition of managers. There were, however, a number of cases where litigation occurred between an employee and an employer because the former believed that he or she was performing a managerial job and should consequently receive the employment conditions stated in the management contract (See Nigro 1985, Salad Ghiri 1986, and Tosi (1974) for a review of this case law).

In case law, the judges have outlined a series of elements that define the manager's function. The constitutional court, in a case relating to the exclusion of managers from the law dealing with employment, law 121/6 July 1972, stated that the management function is characterized by the following elements: (1) immediate collaboration with the employer for the coordination of firm activity in its entirety or in an essential branch; (2) the fiduciary character of the activity; (3) the large and autonomous power of direction; (4) hierarchical supremacy over all the employees of the firm or of an important branch, even without disciplinary power but necessarily with organizational power; (5) the exclusive subordination to the employer or to a higher level manager; and (6) the existence of a power of representation outside or inside the firm.

The same approach, which tends to restrict the number of managers to the higher level of the hierarchy, has been confirmed several times by the courts at all levels. Managers are seen as the *alter ego* of the employer. In practice, however, changes in the organization of work and employer practices have caused an increase in the number of employees that have been granted managerial status by the employer. Employees who seek recognition of their managerial role from the court, against their employer's wishes, are not usually successful, because the courts stand by a restrictive legal definition of that role.

Conditions of Employment Established by Legislation

When legislation mentions managers, it usually does so to exclude them from protection given other employees. This is particularly noteworthy in the laws limiting hours of work. Legislation and the courts have adhered to the belief that the nature of managerial activity is such that it cannot be measured by the actual time spent on the job. Thus, limitations on the hours, overtime, and weekly vacations do not apply to managers.

Managers are also excluded from protection of employees against dismissal, an area in which legislation has severely restricted employer prerogatives. As a result, managers have sought to obtain some protection from collective bargaining. In addition, in order to hire a manager, the firm does not have to follow the regular practice of filing a request with the special commission that refers the unemployed.

Employment contracts in Italy usually do not have time limits, with the exception of certain types of work such as seasonal jobs. For managers, instead, the contract cannot be longer than five years and managers can leave after three years with notice (Article 2125 Civil Code).

At the end of the employment period, managers have the legal right to severance pay equal to 13.5 percent of their annual pay, which is payable to them at termination or to their heirs. Severance pay also is guaranteed in case of bankruptcy. Finally, the employer can establish noncompetition agreements after the expiration of a contract. These agreements have to be limited in terms of content, geographical area of applications, and time, and the employees have to receive compensation for them.

The government has transformed into law a number of collective agreements made in the early 1960s. The purpose of the law is to extend to all (*erga omnes*) certain rights that were gained by collective bargaining. In this way, even if the employer is not part of the association that signed the contract, the employees benefit from certain minimal standards of basic rights. For managers, the pertinent contracts were the ones signed in 1948 for the industrial sector (law 483/1962), as well as the contracts signed in other sectors by managers' unions.

Legislation also influences the pension system for managers. INPDAI, a public organization that is compelled to follow governmental guidelines, is in charge of managers' pensions in the industrial sector. It is particularly important to note that the amount of salary covered by a pension is set by legislation, and that managerial unions have been strongly critical of the limits set in the past.

Collective Bargaining

The Confederazione Italiana Dirigenti di Azienda (CIDA), Confederation of Managers Union, is the only organization for managers in Italy, and composed of six federations based on major industrial sectors. Each federation is in charge of collective bargaining at the national level in its sector and signs one or more agreements covering all the *dirigenti* (members and not members) in that sector. For instance, FNDAI signs the leading contract in industry with the private and public employer associations. The Confederazione Generale dell'Industria Italiana, National Confederation of Italian Employers in Industry (Confindustria) represents private employers (excluding small firms). For the public industrial sector the two leading organizations are Intersind, which represents firms that belong to Istituto per la Ricostruzione Industriale, Institute for Industrial Reconstruction (IRI), and Associazione Sindacale Aziende Petrolchimiche, Employers Association of Petrochemical Firms, (ASAP), which represents firms that are part of the Ente Nazionale Idrocarburi, National Institute for Hydrocarbons, (ENI). IRI and ENI are the two largest public conglomerates. Six similar contracts are also signed by FNDAI with the representatives of different groups, among them the representatives of the Confederazione Italiana Servizi Pubblici degli Enti Locali, Italian Confederation of Local Public Utilities and Transportation of Municipalities (CISPEL), the Ente Nazionale Energia Elettrica, National Electric Company (ENEL), and the Editors Associations. These contracts are not very different from the contract signed with Confindustria and the analysis below will be limited to that one.

Since 1932, ten agreements have been signed by FNDAI, eight of them since the end of World War II. The two contracts signed under the Fascist regime were concerned only with the regulation of notice and indemnity for dismissal. In 1937, the contract also established the formation of an institute in charge of social security with contributions from managers and employers (this later became the INPDAI).

More significant was the contract signed in 1948 which was later transformed into law. In this contract, such issues as probation period, vacations, leave of absence, pay during sickness and disability, and moving expenses were covered. In 1960, pay increases related to seniority were established, and in 1970, the unions gained a clause stating that the contract should cover all employees that actually performed the duty of the managers as stated in the contract. Previously, the employer had the unilateral right to designate which employees could be considered as managers and have the conditions established by the contract. This clause gave employees the right to go to the courts if they believed that they were performing managerial functions without receiving contractual recognition. Few employees, however, receive managerial recognition through the judicial process.

In the contract of 1970, the effects of the so-called "workers' statute" (law 300/1970) had an impact. It established basic rights for the employees and aided the growth of unions. On that basis, managers have the right to establish union representatives at the work place.

The most innovative contract was signed in 1975. The *scala mobile*, a mechanism for granting automatic cost-of-living increases, was established and an arbitration board was formed to examine dismissal cases.

The most recent set of contracts, signed in May 1985 and expiring in 1988, have broadly similar sets of provisions in each of the jurisdictions they cover. Apart from economic benefits (discussed below), these contracts confer on managers several other benefits, such as having terms of the individual employment contract given to managers in writing; the period of probation cannot be longer than six months; and, in case of sickness, managers have the right to maintain their jobs and salary up to twelve months and their jobs without pay for another six months.

Other clauses regulate sickness and/or accident insurance related to the job. In the case of a change of proprietorship, the established rights of managers have to be maintained. Moreover, managers may be transferred only for reasons related to organizational and productivity problems. Still other clauses deal with moving expenses and housing expenses. The contract also establishes the right to 35 days of paid vacation excluding Sundays and holidays, and to leave of absence with the duration varying from firm to firm. In addition, managers who travel for business have the right to be reimbursed for all documented expenses plus a bonus of 2 percent of their monthly salary per day.

In case of dismissal, the contract permits managers to have their cases heard by an arbitration board, which has the authority to fine an employer who improperly dismisses a manager, but it cannot order the manager's reinstatement. Between 1980 and 1984, managers initiated this procedure in 777 cases. In 42 percent of the cases, the board reached a solution through conciliation, and only in 17 percent of the cases was there an award. Seventy-five percent of the awards were favorable to the manager, and on average the employer was fined the equivalent of 11 months' pay. Twenty-two percent of the cases were not yet settled because the parties refused arbitration in favor of the judicial process.

It is interesting to note that the average age of dismissed managers has been decreasing. Dismissals tend to be concentrated in the first two years and are more likely to occur in the commercial area. Where the causes of dismissal are known (in 510 cases), 51 percent were for objective reasons, such as a change of ownership or bankruptcy.

In case of dismissal, managers have the right to an advance warning of eight months if their seniority is less than two years. The warning is increased half a month for every year of seniority up to four months. If a manager decides to leave, he or she has to give notice equal to one-third of the above period. Fines are set for violations.

In the case of dismissals for economic reasons, special legislative guidelines are often established. Managers who fall under these guidelines are entitled to supplementary payments

Collective bargaining also establishes a supplemental pension fund. By law, the contribution to INPDAI is equal to 23 percent of a minimum annual salary of 35 million lire or a maximum of 42 million lire. Because even the maximum figure is lower than the minimum contractual salary, and because the pension can be no more than 80 percent of the maximum, managers suffer a drastic decrease of income when retiring. The Fondo Integrativo Previdenza Dirigenti Aziende Industriali, Supplementary Fund for Social Security of Managers in Industrial Firms (FIPDAI), raises the maximum of 25 percent and establishes according to that figure a contribution of 2.7 percent (1.98 percent to be paid by the manager). On the average, this means a 25 percent increase over the pension that is paid is by law.

All pension systems in Italy are under a strain because of low contributions, higher average life, and policies that have favored retirement to avoid dismissal or create job opportunities. This is also true for the managers' pension system. Managers' unions strongly disagree with the adequacy of proposals to increase pension payments; in fact, pension inadequacy was the reason behind the first managers' strike lasting one day in December 1985. The issue is yet unresolved.

Finally, the contract also establishes medical benefits that provide additional coverage for expenses incurred outside the inefficient public medical system. The cost of Fondo Assistenza Sanitaria Integrativa (FASI), Integration Fund for Medical Assistance, is paid by the employer in the measure of 70 percent.

The contract signed in 1985 will be in effect through the end of 1988. Pay clauses, however, were supposed to be renegotiated at the end of 1986. This new salary agreement took more than six months to negotiate because the employers' and the managers' union positions were far apart. The union goal, according to Francesco Faccin, the general secretary of the managers' union, was to reduce the difference between contractual pay, set at 42 million lire, and actual average management pay, about 75 million lire. The union felt this gap gave employers too much power in these matters (Bonafede 1987). Employers estimated that the managers' union demands would raise their salary costs by 25 percent. Furthermore, employers were not eager to see an increase across the board to all managers. The new agreement establishes a monthly pay increase of 250,000 lire starting in January 1987 and an additional 170,000 starting in January 1988. The minimum is increased to 50 million lire yearly (*European Industrial Relations Review* 1987, 6).

Salaries

It is not easy to assess salaries for managers because there is very little information on the topic, and available data are conflicting. Moreover, both employers and managers are reluctant to release detailed information.

Collective agreements are one source of information. In the private sector they establish only the minimum conditions that each firm always betters. According to *Dirigenti '80* (1981), at least 60 percent receive increases beyond what is established in the contract; only 11 percent were receiving a salary equal to the contractual minimum, and 23 percent were declaring twice as much. While increases beyond the collective contracts are almost the rule in the private sector, they are rare in the public sector. Collective contracts also give us information about the structure of pay.

Analysis here will be limited to the industrial sector, because it plays a leading role for the other sectors. In July 1986, a manager with less than two years of seniority could receive a minimum of 3,332 million lire; with seniority of ten years, the pay is 25 percent higher, and with twenty it is 63 percent higher.

The main elements of the collectively bargained salary are a base minimum, a component for seniority, and a cost-of-living adjustment. The base is increased at each renewal of the contract and is used for calculating increases due to seniority. Seniority gives a 6.75 percent increase of the base minimum every two years for ten times. After twenty years, seniority constitutes 23.4 percent of the contractual pay.

Cost-of-living allowances, introduced in 1975, provide a 3,000 lire increase for every point increase in the price index. The adjustments are added to the pay twice a year, and in the past ten years have contributed about 45 percent to the total increases. Recently, the system of indexing wages to inflation has been under attack and is a source of controversy in industrial relations for all employees.

The practice of adjusting salaries for large increases in inflation has resulted

Table 9.2   Contractual pay in industrial sectors by seniority, 1986

Pay scale	Seniority (years)		
	0	*10*	*20 or more*
a) Base minimum	56.4	45.1	34.7
b) Seniority	—	12.2	23.4
c) Cost of living	32.9	26.3	20.2
d) Cost of living increase by seniority	—	5.7	11.0
e) Adjustment—12% increase over a,b,c,d	10.7	10.7	10.7
Total	100	100	100
Monthly salary in millions of Italian lire	3,332	4,169	5,424

Source: Data provided by FNDAI.

in a narrowing of the salary dispersion within seniority ranks. To deal with this problem, in 1979 an 8 percent increase was added onto all the elements of pay. In 1985, the percentage was increased to 12 percent.

Table 9.2 shows the weight of the elements of pay at different levels of seniority. Seniority plays a large role in contractual pay and directly or indirectly constitutes about 20 percent of pay after 10 years of service and 38.4 percent after 20 years.

Pay differentials between managers and other groups of employees have been studied by several research projects over the years. As summarized in Table 9.3, these studies show that managers' pay before taxes is between 3.8 and 4.5 times the level of blue-collar pay, and between 2.6 and 3 times the level of white-collar pay, with the exception of the sample from the Bank of Italy, which is unusually low.

To illustrate pay differences among managers, it is useful to report the results of *Dirigenti '80* (1981), Quirico (1983), and Santini and Conti (1986). According to Quirico (1983), average pay is higher in insurance (+23 percent),

Table 9.3   Ratio between managers' and blue- and white-collar pay

Sources	Managers	White collar	Blue collar
EEC Report 1978	380		100
Parliamentary Commission 1976	380	260	100
INPS 1979	450	280	100
Bank of Italy 1983	240	190	100
Quirico 1983 Gross	400	300	100
After taxes	320	240	100

Source: Quirico 1983.

the electric sector (+19 percent) and banking (+15 percent). In public administration, on the other hand, the average pay was much lower (−36 percent). According to *Dirigenti '80* (1981), higher salaries were to be found in the electronic and publishing sectors. For Santini and Conti (1986), the higher pay levels are in finance and marketing.

Dirigenti '80 (1981) and Quirico (1983) agree that in southern Italy levels of pay are usually lower (12 percent), and that the size of the enterprise (measured by number of employees) influences the level of pay, which is 9 percent lower than the overall average in firms with fewer than 100 employees and grows with the size of the enterprise. According to the Management Centre of Europe (1981), 52 percent of the variance in managers' pay is explained by gross earnings. According to Santini and Conti (1986), for middle-level managers pay levels are better in medium-sized firms and in multinational enterprises; for top executives, pay opportunities are better in multinational and large private Italian conglomerates. However, analyses based only on the monthly salary are misleading, for monthly pay in Italy is usually distributed in thirteen paychecks, with 28 percent of all managers receiving fourteen.

Managers are also distributed between two and four hierarchical levels or steps in 55 percent of the cases. When they are present, these step increases influence about 44 percent of the compensation without considering seniority. The overall effect of hierarchical levels is quite small, according to Quirico (1983), and seniority plays the leading role in wage differentiation. Evidently, the effects of collective agreements that stress seniority are maintained by policies adopted independently at the firm level, and the range found by Quirico is about the same as the one obtained using the contractual minimum.

In more recent years, the pay differentials among managers have been increasing. Table 9.4 shows the results of a survey conducted in 1986 by Hay Management Consultants in 241 firms (De Marinis 1987). According to this data, managers fall into three pay levels, and the differences between those three are quite substantial. The top pay level manager in the public sector earns 2.7 times the gross pay of entry level managers; the figures are 3.3 for the private sector and 3.2 for multinationals. Managers at the entry level in multinationals earn 8.3 percent more than their counterparts in the private sector; the figure is 3.8 percent for middle and top level managers.

If we consider the compensation profile according to age, increases are particularly high at the beginning of the career in the first ten years. Afterwards, they tend to flatten. The leading role played by seniority explains why managers tend to stay in the same firms, especially since merit increases play a minor role; these are estimated by the Management Centre of Europe (1981) to be between 7 and 9 percent of the salary. This situation may be changing, however, because in the latest survey by Santini and Conti (1986) 70 percent of managers had annual pay reviews, and 15.6 percent of the pay was linked to the achievement of the firm's goals.

According to Santini and Conti (1986), annual turnover for managers in 1985 was 5.7 percent. For 34.5 percent, a 20 percent pay increase was necessary

Table 9.4 Cadres and managers gross annual pay in 1986 (millions of lire)

Cadres	Public sector	Private sector	Multinationals
Level I Department head sales, programmer	28.9	26	28.5
Level II Project engineer, district	40.1	37.9	40.6
Level III Regional sales head, department planner	51.9	49.8	52.7
Managers			
Level I Production manager, head of accounts	57.9	57.9	62.7
Level II Divisional marketing manager Plant manager (about 1,000 employees)	84.6	88.8	92.2
Level III Top managers	155.4	190.8	198.2

Source: De Marinis 1987.

to consider a change, while for 38.1 percent, the increase should be around 30 percent. Females are a small percentage among managers in Italy, 2.6 percent according to Santini and Conti (1986), and *ceteris paribus* they were receiving 18.7 percent less on the average. According to the Hay Management Consultants (De Marinis 1987), turnover was higher, around 9.4 percent. The figure refers to the year 1986 and reflects a more dynamic market.

Regarding fringe benefits, it is important to understand whether the integration fund and supplemental medical insurance that are established by contract are considered fringes. According to *Dirigenti '80* (1981), 70 percent do not receive fringe benefits beyond those established by contract, while for Santini and Conti (1986), the percentage was only 24.6 percent.

Finally, one must examine the effects of social contributions and taxes on managers' income. The former equalled 6 percent and the latter about 25 percent of total income (Quirico 1983). Managers also receive public income allowances based on the number of family dependents, about 1 percent of the paycheck.

Developments in fiscal policy have been constantly criticized by managers and managers' organizations. In the last twenty years, there has been a dramatic change in the sources of government income from indirect to direct taxation. In this process, professionals, small employers, and merchants have largely been able to evade new income taxes. Dependent employees, however, pay taxes on all their income, and help to explain why 77 percent of managers in one study

Table 9.5 Percentage of taxes at various
income levels

Percent tax	Income in millions of lire
12	6
22	6–11
27	11–28
34	28–50
41	50–100
48	100–150
53	150–300
58	300–600
62	Over 600

Source: FNDAI, Dirigenti Aziende Inustriali, no. 3,
March 1986.

stated that while underground compensation in various forms was diminishing, it was still present (Santini and Conti 1986).

Another negative element to be considered is inflation that has pushed taxpayers into higher tax brackets and made them more vulnerable to tax collectors. The current fiscal structure is reported in Table 9.5.

Managerial Unions

As mentioned earlier, managers established their first union organization on the basis of the legislation of 1926. According to that law, managers were supposed to have a separate organization that had to be part of the employers' associations. At that time the union, to gain more members, had an inclusive definition of manager. In 1932, however, at the time of the first contract in the industrial sector, a more restrictive definition began to emerge (Lodigiani 1975, 12).

After the end of the World War II, the national federations of managers began to reorganize and, in 1946, the Italian Confederation of Managers (CIDA) was founded. While the Confederazione Italiana Generale del Lavoro (CGIL), Italian General Confederation of Labor, the major Italian union, split after 1948 along ideological lines and two other competing organizations emerged (Confederazione Italiana Sindacati Lavoratori (CISL), Italian Confederation of Workers' Union, and Unione Italiana del Lavoro (UIL), Italian Union for Work), the CIDA has remained the only managers' union and is the only one representing managers in those governmental bodies in which union participation is required.

CIDA has a total of 97,550 members including retired managers (in FNDAI the retirees are about 23 percent of the total membership). Membership in the six constituent groups is as follows: FNDAI constitutes 54.8 percent of the total membership. Federazione Nazionale Dirigenti Aziende Commerciali (FENDAC), National Federation Managers of Commercial Firms, has 14.5

percent, Federazione Nazionale Personale Direttivo Aziende di Credito e Finanziarie (Federdirigenti Credito), National Federation of Managerial Employees in Credit and Financial Institutions, has 24.5 percent for the banking and financial sector. FIDIA, FNDA for agriculture, and Federdirigenti Funzione Pubblica for public administration have about 1.4, 0.8, and 4 percent, respectively.

If we consider the total number of managers to be 160,000, the overall unionization rate is 47 percent, higher than for all the other employee groups, where it is estimated around 40 percent. For the FNDAI, it is possible to consider the trend in the unionization rate (see Table 9.1), which declined steadily from 74 percent in the 1950s to 44 percent in the 1980s. The decline probably results because, in the early period, managers were a smaller and more homogeneous group with similar interests and stronger social ties.

Finally, it should also be kept in mind that in Italy it is appropriate for professions to belong to a union; for instance, journalists and doctors belong in large numbers to unions. However, most of these groups do not belong to the leading workers' confederations (CGIL, CISL, and UIL).

Union membership among managers has grown. In FNDAI, membership has increased continuously except for the years 1981–83 when managerial employment was affected by a restructuring in Italian industry. A large increase in membership (16 percent) took place between 1978 and 1979 because only union members could benefit from a newly formed health insurance program. This provision was not maintained, however, in the following years because of opposition from employer associations.

Why should a manager join a union if, as in Italy, collective agreements are applied to all members of the bargaining unit without consideration of union status? Employees are induced to become members for many reasons: to make the organization stronger, because of peer pressure, or from the satisfaction of belonging to a group. It is also true that Italy is characterized by a high level of participation in the political and organizational life. Finally, union membership is important if an employee wants the union to prosecute his or her grievances vigorously.

Under the "workers' statute," union representatives (known as RSAs) are selected by employees in relevant national or local agreements. For managers, because there is a single union representing them, there is no competition for these positions. One union representative can be established where there are at least ten managers, and the number can increase with the number of managers in the work place up to seven, if there are more than 100 managers.

RSAs are protected by law against dismissal and transfer. Their role is to make sure that the collective agreements are applied; they deal with grievances at the first step of the grievance process. FNDAI in 1986 had 446 RSAs representing a total of 10,072 managers. A large percentage of RSAs (40 percent) were in publicly owned firms, where there are only 26 percent of the members. This is partly explained because the public corporations are larger, but it is also true that union activity is more concentrated in the public sector of the economy.

Managers' unions are supported by their membership through fees that are collected via a check-off system and are about .6 percent of contractual pay levels.

Participation in union activity is not very high. According to *Dirigenti '80* (1981), in 1980 only 13.2 percent participated in union activity.

PROFESSIONAL AND MANAGERIAL STAFF

For cadres, there has been a more dramatic change in the last decade. The number of such employees included in this category has increased significantly. Changes have also taken place in the legislation regarding cadres and their organizations, as well as the collective bargaining activities of those groups.

Quantitative Aspects

As in the case of managers, it is not easy to find data about the total number of employees that are cadres. This is made even more difficult by the fact that they have only recently emerged as an independent group in both legislation and union history (Lelli and Giannini 1984). Census information unfortunately reports data on managers and white-collar employees as one group.

Collectively bargained national agreements usually distinguish several categories of employees, of which the top two are made up of white-collar employees with professional and technical qualifications. From coverage data, we know that in the manufacturing sector around 500,000 employees are cadres. In the entire economy, the total number would be around 1.5 million, but some estimates go as high as 2.5 million (Cerretta 1986). To chart the distribution of employment in the different categories and their evolution, one can look at the situation in the metalworking sector, which is the leading industrial sector.

In 1981, at the top two categories (the sixth and seventh), there were only white-collar employees who were about 11 percent of all dependent employees and 39 percent of all white-collar sectors. In the most recent metalworking contract signed in 1983, the sixth category was assigned to technical or administrative employees who carry out management functions that require special preparation and professional ability with discretionary powers, the right to make decisions, and to take initiatives within the limits of general directions. Examples include accountants, analysts, laboratory technicians, project designers, and purchasing agents.

In the seventh grade are employees responsible for the coordination of services, offices, and productive units essential to the enterprise, or who are involved in activity requiring a high degree of specialization necessary and important for the development and fulfillment of the goals of the enterprise.

Examples include engineers, financial analysts, researchers, and specialists in firm planning.

Opinions vary as to whether all the employees in these categories can be considered cadres. Some may have been reclassified in these top categories so that they could receive a higher salary without changing job responsibilities. According to Guala Duca (1985), 31 percent of the employees that belong to the top two classifications did not have any people reporting to them.

The problem of delimiting the area of cadres has become even more difficult because of the intense technological and organizational transformations that have been taking place since the mid-1970s. The trend toward smaller firms has produced more professionals but fewer supervisors. At the same time, the number of new job titles has increased.

Classification System

Until 1973, collective agreements have grouped all employees except managers into two distinct units, one for white-collar employees and one for manual workers. The two groups had different contracts; in addition, significant differences existed in conditions of employment that originated from the special legislative provisions for private white-collar employees enacted in 1924, and which were reinforced by later contractual provisions. It is also important to mention that in Italy systems of job evaluation that applied to all employees never took hold, although in the early 1960s they were started in several sectors.

During the 1970s, the rigid separation between blue- and white-collar employment conditions became anachronistic. With the increase in the number of nonmanual workers, many were performing unskilled duties and were receiving a lower level of pay than the top blue-collar categories. At that point, it was inconceivable that they should receive overall better fringe benefits. Moreover, rigid barriers between the two groups were less visible in society. In the same period, the unions sought to give everyone the same basic rights and to end the long history of discrimination against manual work.

The result was a new classification system (*inquadramento unico*) in which blue- and white-collar categories were reduced to seven (European Trade Institute 1982). In 1972, 40.6 percent of all blue-collars were in the lowest two levels, but in 1982 that percentage was reduced for both levels to 3.7. In 1972, the fifth level was almost all white-collar, but in 1982 were 57 percent of it was blue-collar.

This new classification achieved the goal of integrating, to some extent, blue- and white-collar groups. However, the goal of changing the content of the job was not attained. The new classification, together with the wage indexation system that began in 1975 and provided equal increases for all levels, caused a narrowing of wage differentials during the period of high inflation level in the last decade. For instance, in 1975 the highest level was getting a salary that was 3.1 times the lower; in 1981 that ratio was equal to 2 (Santi 1982).

Cadres' Dissatisfaction and the FIAT Case

The classification and indexation systems that were agreed on in the early 1970s mirrored the situation in the mass production industries at a time when assembly-line workers were the largest group in the factories. In later years, however, technological innovation reduced their leading role. Employees in the upper levels felt that the wage differentials were too narrow and that the added responsibility and professional status of cadres should receive a premium. There was also dissatisfaction with the major unions because they had concentrated their attention on blue-collar groups.

The issues exploded at FIAT in 1980, considered a major turning point in Italian industrial relations (Baldissera, 1984). The conflict involved the contract between FIAT and the Federazione Lavoratori Metalmeccanici (FLM), the Metalworkers' Union Federation. The employer had a goal of reducing employment by almost 20 percent. The unions refused the plan, in part because in Italy there is no agreed-on seniority system for determining who should be laid off and who should receive unemployment benefits. Negotiations became a deadlock based on divergent principles among the largest private employer and the most militant workers' union. The FLM staged a strike that lasted 35 days, an unusually long time considering the Italian tradition of frequent but short strikes.

During the strike, a difference of opinion emerged between the more militant workers who had taken over the leadership of the strike and were in charge of picketing, and the other employees, especially the cadres, who did not identify with the strike's goals. In October 1980, the cadres (which at FIAT included the first-level supervisors) organized a street demonstration, which has become known as the "march of 40,000," even though FIAT employed only 8,000 cadres. The national union signed an agreement with FIAT the following day, signaling the shifting bargaining power between employers and unions.

The case also raised problems related to union democracy, rules about picketing, and representation right; however, the concern here is with the drive that the FIAT case gave to the mobilization of cadres as an independent group. As a result of the incident, the traditional unions began giving more attention to professionals' groups, independent unions gained strength among the professions, and the Parliament was motivated to introduce changes in the legal status of the cadres.

Legislative Recognition of Cadres

Law 190/1985, modifying civil code article 2095, established cadres as one of the major groups of employees. They were defined as employees who do not belong to the category of managers, but who perform significant functions for the development and fulfillment of the enterprise. The law also established that collective bargaining can establish rules to ensure that cadres are appropriately compensated for their technical and organizational skills. Employers also are required to insure cadres against damages they may inflict on third parties.

Even though the law was considered a victory by the organizations of cadres, it remains controversial. CIDA was afraid that a cadre organization would prevent the promotion of top-level white-collar employees into the ranks of management. The leading unions were afraid that the new law would bring about independent unions for cadres with the consequent loss in their membership. Employers feared that new unions for cadres would fragment bargaining power and cause strife at the work place. Indeed, even among leading labor lawyers, the law has been criticized because it perpetuates divisions among employees and contains inconsistencies (Giugni 1985, Pera 1985).

Collective Bargaining for Cadres

Since 1980 the major unions (CGIL, CISL, UIL) have tried to pay more attention to the problems of cadres. During collective bargaining in the major sectors, for instance, attempts have been made to enlarge wage differentials for cadres. After the legislation of 1985, all major unions have asked for recognition of the title of cadre for employees with certain characteristics and duties. The unions also request more flexibility in the hours of work for cadres, additional salary, and rights to insurance, information, and training programs.

While it remains to be seen what future contracts will be like, some major firms have already sought to deal with the problems of cadres. For instance, in the energy sector, at ENI and in gas and water, cadres' unions have been recognized but divided into different levels according to the level of their professional qualifications.

Cadres and Unions

In Italy, controversies over union representation are not resolved by the law but by practice and the power of parties. Within the blue-collar sectors, CGIL, CISL, and UIL have established a leading position. Among cadres or in certain sectors of public administration, the situation is not as clear-cut. In the industrial sector, cadres tend to have a lower unionization rate among the leading unions. In the public sector, which includes areas such as transportation, hospitals, schools, and municipal corporations, independent unions have a certain following with both workers and cadres. Among the cadres sampled by Guala Duca (1985), 17 percent were members of the three leading unions while 11 percent belonged to independent unions. Where several unions have members in a company, the employer usually meets with all the unions and may even bargain with them at the same table, if they agree. However, the leading role at the bargaining table has always been played by the unions belonging to the major confederations.

After several mergers and divisions among cadres' unions, two leading organizations have emerged at the national level: The Unionquadri, which tends to consider itself as mainly a professional organization and is not especially interested in collective bargaining, and Confederquadri, which has become the leading bargaining organization for cadres. Confederquadri claims to have 85,000 members, 35 percent of them in the industrial sector. Both organizations lobbied intensely for the passage of the new law. At the bargaining table, however, they have been less successful because employers prefer to deal with the well-established leading organizations, and because the latter have started to bring cadres' requests to the bargaining table. It is not clear which of the competing unions will gain the leading role in the future.

CONCLUSIONS

The traditional division established long ago between managers, white-collar employees, and blue-collar workers has been challenged by transformations that occurred in the early 1970s.

Managers are no longer a small elite selected by the employer; they have become a profession. Consequently, educational attainment and careers have become more standard. At the same time, market forces are more important in shaping work conditions.

In terms of gross pay levels, managers have been able to maintain their position compared with other employees. More unfavorable, however, have been the impact of inflation on tax burdens and pensions, both established by legislation. Regarding taxation, further changes will be likely, especially if the government succeeds in preventing tax evasion by autonomous workers, and if fiscal pressure could be spread more evenly. With respect to pensions, individual company plans will become more widespread and more effective in integrating the pension system established by legislation.

At the firm level, the increase toward training programs and specific benefit packages will increase, but collective bargaining will remain important in establishing minimum conditions of employment throughout the category. The unions will remain particularly important in lobbying toward legislative changes in the social security and fiscal area. Even though unions have a membership that is too small to have an electoral impact, they can exert political pressure and the parties in government are usually sensitive to managers' organizations.

Finally, managers' conditions will also be positively affected by the changes in public opinion more favorable now to the business community and to the management profession. This will make it easier to obtain changes in legislation, increase the prestige of the occupation, and attract more talented people into the profession.

The emergence and mobilization of professional groups signal a major development in Italian industrial relations. In the early 1970s, while differences between blue-and white-collar workers were being challenged and wage and benefits differentials were eroded by the effects of collective agreements and inflation, the growth of a larger group of managerial employees posed a new challenge to the Italian industrial relations system. The mobilization of cadres has already produced new legislation and changes in collective bargaining. It is difficult to say now if the leading workers' unions will be able to make up for lost time and regain the confidence of the cadres, or if the new organizations will emerge. In any event, issues posed by cadres will remain prominent in the collective bargaining agenda as well as in the political arena because of the large number of possible voters that are involved.

On the other hand, it is clear that the managers' unions are not willing to open their organizations to include cadres or find a way to represent them at the bargaining table, or even act together with the emerging new organization. This is impossible because it runs against the established separations. In fact, managers' unions do not look favorably on the establishment of independent organizations for cadres because the creation of an intermediate group could diminish the number of managerial ones and, consequently, affect union membership. These divisions between managers and cadres also prevent a larger role for management in the society as a whole.

For cadres it will be very important to make sure that the new category of employment that recognizes their existence results in collective agreements that address their needs. Among the emerging issues for these workers are efforts to define who is included in the occupational category, what career opportunities stem from being a member of the cadres, and whether their wages and benefits are in relation to other occupational groups.

Also, cadres are interested in ways of dealing with economic fluctuations and changes in the business. They have become involved in training and educational programs, and specialized labor market intermediaries help prepare them for employment and to find jobs. In this, as in other issues, cadres will be affected by collective bargaining results for all the other employees. By comparison, collective bargaining for the managers will not be affected by what happens in negotiations involving managerial employees.

Finally, it is not currently clear whether the cadres will select the existing confederations to represent them or join the independent unions. The choice of the cadres will probably have important implications for unionized blue-collar workers as well.

REFERENCES

Baldissera, A. 1984. Alle origini della politica della diseguaglianza nell'italia degli anni 80: La marcia dei quarantamila (The origins of the inequality policy in Italy of the eighties: The march of the forty thousand). *Quaderni di Sociologia* 31:1–78.

Banca D'Italia. 1984. I bilanci delle famiglie Italiane nell'anno 1983 (Budgets of Italian families in 1983). *Bollettino Statistico* 39:3–4.

Barkan, J. 1984. *Visions of emancipation: The Italian workers' movement since 1945*. New York: Praeger.

Bianchi, M., and L. Scheggi. 1982. Un sindacato per i quadri (A union for cadres). Supplement to no. 42 of *Il Mondo*.

Bonafede, A. 1987. Se il dirigente contesta il padrone (When managers protest against owners). *La Repubblica*, June 26:17.

Cerretta, M. 1986. A favore del carattere precettivo della legge sui quadri (In favor of the preceptive character of the law on cadres). *Il Diritto del Lavoro*, March–April:144–63.

Cesareo, V., L. Bovone, and G. Rovati. 1979. *Professione dirigente* (*The managerial profession*). Turin: Fondazione Agnelli.

Derossi, F. 1982. *The Technocratic Illusion*. Armonk, NY: M. E. Sharpe, Inc.

————. 1978. *L'illusione tecnocratica. Il potere dei dirigenti dell'industria Italiana* (*The technocratic illusion: The manager's power in Italian industry*). Milan: Etas Libri.

De Marinis, F. 1987. Quanto guadagna il manager (What managers earn). *La Repubblica*, June 5: *Business Section*, pp. 4–5.

Dirigenti '80. 1981. In *Notiziario FNDAI* 7 (5):1–110.

European Industrial Relations Review. 1987. (164) September:6.

European Trade Union Institute. 1982. *The unionization of professional and managerial staff in Western Europe*. Brussels: G. Kopke.

FNDAI. 1986. *Dirigenti Aziende Industriali* (*The Manager of Industrial Firms*), March.

Ferrarotti, F. 1959. Management in Italy. In *Management in the industrial world: An international analysis*, edited by F. Harbison and C. A. Myers. New York: McGraw-Hill.

Giugni, G. 1981. Italian system of industrial relations. In *Industrial relations in international perspective: Essays on research and policy*, edited by P. B. Doeringer. New York: Holmes and Meier.

————. 1984. Recent trends in collective bargaining in Italy. *International Labour Review* 123 (5):599–614.

————. 1985. Quadri: Una legge inutile (Cadres: A useless law). *L'Opinione* 1 (10):8–10.

Guala Duca, R. 1985. *I nuovi colletti bianchi: Dagli impiegati ai quadri* (The new white collars: From white collars to cadres). Milan: Angeli.

Horowitz, D. L. 1963. *The Italian labor movement*. Cambridge, Mass.: Harvard University Press.

Kogan, N. 1981. *A political history of postwar Italy: From the old to the new center-left*. New York: Praeger.

Lange, P. 1977. *Studies on Italy 1943–1975: Selected bibliography of American and British materials in political science, economics, sociology and anthropology*. Turin: Fondazione Agnelli.

Lange, P., G. Ross, and M. Vannicelli. 1982. *Unions, change and crisis: French and Italian unions' strategy and the political economy 1945–1980*. London: Allen and Unwin.

Lelli, M., and M. Giannini. 1984. I quadri nella divisione del lavoro: La riflessione sociologica (Cadres in the division of labor: Sociological thought). In *Sociologia del Lavoro*, vol. 22.

Lodigiani, F. 1975. *Manuale del dirigente industriale* (*A manual for the industrial manager*). Milan: Angeli.

Management Centre Europe. 1981. *Executive remuneration in Italy 1981*. Brussels: The Executive Compensation Service.

Martinelli, A., and T. Treu. 1984. Employers associations in Italy. In *Employers associa-*

tions and industrial relations: A comparative study, edited by J. P. Windmuller and A. Gladstone. Oxford: Clarendon Press.

Nigro, B. 1985. *Dirigenti d'azienda* (Firm managers). Rome: Buffetti.

Pellegrini, C. 1987. Italian industrial relations. In *Comparative industrial relations,* edited by G. Bamber and R. Lansbury. London: Allen and Unwin.

Pera, G. 1985. La legge per i quadri (The law for cadres). *Rivista Italiana di Diritto del Lavoro* 2, April–June:270–85.

Piore, M. J., and C. F. Sabel. 1984. *The second industrial divide: Possibilities for prosperity.* New York: Basic Books.

Quirico, P. 1983. *La retribuzione del dirigente: Mistificazioni e realta* (*Manager pay: Myth and reality*). Milan: Angeli.

Regini, M. 1982. Changing relationship between labor and the state in Italy: Toward a neo-corporatist system? In *Patterns of corporatist policy-making,* edited by G. Lehmbruch and P. Schmitter. London: Sage.

Salad Ghiri, M. 1986. *Le categorie dei lavoratori: Dalla tripartizione tradizionale al riconoscimento legislativo dei quadri intermedi* (*Categories of workers: From the traditional tripartite division to the legal recognition of middle-level cadres*). Milan: Giuffre.

Santi, P. L. 1982. I differenziali retributivi professionali negli anni '70: La situazione europea e il caso italiano (Professionals' pay differentials: The European situation and the Italian case). In *Inflazione, struttura del salario e contrattazione* (*Inflation, wage structures and collective bargaining*). Milan: Angeli.

Santini, G., and C. Conti. 1986. Come si paga il manager (How managers are paid). In *Class,* 1 (7), 1986.

Talamo, M. 1979. *I dirigenti industriali in Italia. Autorita, comando e responsabilita sociali* (*The industrial manager in Italy: Authority, power and responsibility*). Turin: Einaudi.

Tosi, P. 1974. *Il dirigente d'azienda* (*The firm manager*). Milan: Angeli.

Treu, T. 1978. Italy. In *International encyclopedia for labour law and industrial relations,* suppl. 5, edited by R. Blanpain. Deventer: Kluver.

——. 1983. Collective bargaining and union participation in economic policies: The case of Italy. In *Organizational democracy and political process,* edited by C. Crouch and F. Heller. New York: Wiley.

IV

JAPAN

10
Japan

VLADIMIR PUCIK AND MYRON J. ROOMKIN*

There is hardly a book or article on Japanese business and management that does not deal with the working life of Japanese "salarymen"—the stereotypical middle-aged overworked Japanese male, employed in a managerial position by a large firm in downtown Tokyo. He commutes to his job on the crowded train and does not return to his small suburban house until late at night, after an evening in Ginza with his colleagues. To what extent is this perception of the typical Japanese manager realistic? What are the actual employment conditions affecting managerial careers in Japan? And even more important, what kind of changes in human resource management and the employment system can be observed in the late 1980s that may have an impact on Japanese middle managers? Which direction will these changes take in the future?

The relevance of these questions is underscored by the critical role played by Japanese middle managers in the decision-making and implementation process inside Japanese business firms (Nonaka 1985). Their continuous commitment, loyalty, and dedication are considered essential if the Japanese economy is to maintain its generally favorable performance. Yet it is claimed that the increasing difficulties in obtaining promotions, the reduction of salary differentials between managers and other employees, and the rapidly growing number of managers facing "voluntary retirement" from previously secure jobs are taking their toll on managerial attitudes and morale, thus endangering the traditional "harmony" of Japanese business organizations (*Far Eastern Economic Review* 1985; *Fortune* 1987).

*The authors have based this chapter partly on a report about managers in Japan compiled by Takeshi Inagami. He, however, does not share in the responsibility for the contents of this chapter. Minoru Sakurai also provided valuable advice and Kiyohiko Ito helped with capable research assistance.

255

After fifteen years (1958–73) of rapid economic growth, the Japanese economy has faced a rather turbulent environment. The initial oil crisis of 1973 was followed by another in 1979, along with a rapid revaluation of the yen. Access to foreign markets in traditional export industries was subjected to "voluntary export restrictions," while domestic demand was constrained by the government's tight fiscal policies. In this respect, the economic adjustments resulting from the recent yen revaluation, including changes in the employment system, are a part of a long-term trend, not its reversal.

In addition, the employment system has been strained by the aging of the Japanese work force. As a result of the postwar baby boom followed by a dramatic drop in birth rates, the population pyramid shifted dramatically. Between 1950 and 1985, the proportion of the Japanese population over the age of 65 doubled. The most numerous population group today is that of 35 to 39 year olds. The aging of the Japanese labor force, combined with the economic slowdown in many key industries, resulted in a surplus of middle managers. This surplus is especially large for those recruited during the booming 1960s who are now reaching the midpoint of the middle management career ladder. While the compensation of contemporary Japanese middle managers is substantially better than that of their predecessors, their chances of reaching the coveted higher level managerial positions are severely restricted.

Many of the changes we are now seeing in Japanese employment practices are to a great degree shaped by the employers' needs to cope with the clogging of the career tracks and the resulting frustration among middle managers. However, as in the case of the restructuring of the economy, such policies represent more of a continuous adaptation than a dramatic shift in direction or a radical break with tradition.

BASIC ATTRIBUTES OF JAPANESE MIDDLE MANAGERS

The term middle manager is ordinarily used to denote persons below the level of corporate directors or officers *(torishimariyaku)* and above the first or the second level (in the manufacturing area) of supervision. Though many more titles are used, the three most common middle management ranks are general or department manager *(bucho)*, manager or section chief *(kacho)*, and supervisor or assistant section chief *(kakaricho)*. The actual occupational hierarchy in most firms is generally more complex.

Middle managers have been the fastest growing occupational category and an important component in the white-collarization of the Japanese labor force. The share of middle management among all occupations reached 4 percent by 1985, about twice the share of 1980. According to the *Japan Statistical Yearbook* (1986), the number of middle managers in private corporations has increased from 910,000 in 1960 to 2,110,000 in 1985, an increase of 230 percent. In the same period, the number of blue-collar workers increased only 1.5 times. The rate of growth was most rapid from 1965 to 1970, nearly flat in the next five years, and increasing thereafter.

In 1986, close to 80 percent of all middle managers were employed by firms with more than 100 employees. Middle managers in large firms (over one thousand employees) accounted for half this number. Most of the subsequent discussion will pertain to these two managerial groups. The ratio of the number of persons employed in three middle management groups to all regular workers, according to the Ministry of Labor (1986), was as follows.

Employee group	All firms	More than 1,000
Bucho	2.2%	1.7%
Kacho	5.4	5.6
Kakaricho	5.8	6.4
Total	13.2	13.7

Moreover, the proportion of middle managers in the firm increases with size. The *kakaricho* group is the most numerous.

Table 10.1 provides data on the basic characteristics of the *bucho, kacho,* and *kakaricho* groups as reported in annual editions of Ministry of Labor's *The Basic Statistical Survey of Wage Structure* from 1970 to 1985. Separate statistics are provided for managers of firms with more than one thousand employees. Among the major findings reported by these tables are the following:

1. Nearly all managers are male; the higher the rank, the lower the number of women managers employed. The few women who have been or are now managers are employed mainly in small and medium-sized firms.
2. The typical middle manager *(kacho)* is getting older and is now about 45 years of age. The average age of all three groups of managers increased by about two years since 1970.
3. The increase in the average age also indicates that promotions in all three middle management groups are taking place at a slower rate.
4. The length of service has increased even more rapidly than the average age. This indicates that managerial mobility in Japan is still extremely low. A typical middle manager has been with his current employer for about twenty years or more.
5. For middle managers, the number of monthly working hours has stabilized, after falling in the early 1970s. Managers in smaller firms work longer hours than their counterparts in larger firms and all lower ranked managers work about three hours longer during the week than their superiors.
6. Managerial compensation (monthly wages and bonuses) has increased more than threefold since 1970, while wage differentials among the three levels of middle management have narrowed. Wage differences due to the size of a firm increased marginally.

7. By 1985, the total compensation of a typical Japanese middle manager reached 7 million yen ($46,700 at $1 = Y150. In comparison, a rank-and-file worker of similar age earned slightly over 4 million yen.
8. In the last 25 years, the educational level of Japanese middle managers has increased substantially. As would be expected, the proportion of university graduates among managers is higher for larger firms and for the higher status managerial ranks.

The picture of middle management that emerges is one of an occupational group has grown in size, is better educated, and is older than middle managers twenty-five years ago. However, at the same time, there have been important changes in the ways that firms train, appraise, compensate, and motivate managerial employees. While, as discussed, there have been adequate reasons for these changes, they have not taken place without costs. One has been greater competition among managers in companies that have endeavoured to maintain cooperative corporate cultures.

Table 10.1 Attributes of middle managers, 1970–84

Occupational group/attributes	1970ᵃ	1975ᵇ	1980ᶜ	1984ᶜ
Bucho				
All firms	91,140	143,230	224,620	272,210
Ratio of male manager (%)	—	—	99.0	98.9
Average age	47.3	48.0	49.1	49.7
Duration of service (average years)	19.1	21.4	21.2	22.5
Monthly working hours	188	179	178	180
Monthly wage (thousand yen)	150.4	295.1	401.1	478.6
Annual bonus (thousand yen)	885.7	1,823.9	2,153.0	2,450.5
Ratio of those college-educated (%)	48.1	51.2	53.4	55.5
Firms with 1,000 employees and more	52,830	78,580	86,260	98,140
Ratio of male manager	—	—	99.4	99.5
Average age	48.1	48.7	49.6	50.2
Duration of service	22.1	23.8	24.7	25.5
Monthly working hours	182	171	169	171
Monthly wage	166.1	324.9	465.7	552.0
Annual bonus	1,068.1	2,163.3	2,908.0	3,400.7
Ratio of those college-educated	56.7	61.1	69.7	74.1
Kacho				
All firms	248,840	372,840	533,310	671,070
Ratio of male manager (%)	—	—	98.7	98.5
Average age	42.1	42.6	43.6	44.4
Duration of service (average years)	17.5	18.7	18.8	19.8
Monthly working hours	187	176	176	177
Monthly wage (thousand yen)	112.4	232.8	320.6	382.7
Annual bonus (thousand yen)	598.3	1,328.9	1,644.2	1,938.9
Ratio of those college-educated (%)	39.8	43.5	44.1	46.7

Table 10.1 (*Continued*)

Occupational group/attributes	1970ᵃ	1975ᵇ	1980ᶜ	1984ᶜ
Firms with 1,000 employees and more	160,570	229,240	240,360	285,020
Ratio of male manager	—	—	99.4	99.3
Average age	43.2	43.7	44.1	45.0
Duration of service	19.6	20.8	21.0	22.2
Monthly working hours	182	172	168	170
Monthly wage	122.3	252.0	368.5	440.4
Annual bonus	687.1	1,500.4	2,094.0	2,528.9
Ratio of those college educated	43.7	48.6	57.5	59.2
Kakaricho				
All firms	315,160	446,280	617,040	684,880
Ratio of male manager (%)	—	—	96.9	96.0
Average age	38.3	38.9	39.2	40.0
Duration of service (average years)	16.1	16.9	16.2	16.9
Monthly working hours	197	181	174	176
Monthly wage (thousand yen)	90.4	190.3	271.8	321.7
Annual bonus (thousand yen)	394.4	937.5	1,185.9	1,371.1
Ratio of those college-educated (%)	29.0	30.0	32.3	35.0
Firms with 1,000 employees and more	221,450	306,300	296,900	310,210
Ratio of male manager	—	—	97.7	97.5
Average age	39.7	40.2	40.2	40.8
Duration of service	18.1	19.0	18.5	19.1
Monthly working hours	194	178	167	169
Monthly wage	95.9	200.1	305.6	362.2
Annual bonus	434.7	1,016.2	1,430.7	1,690.1
Ratio of those college-educated	30.2	31.2	37.9	39.6

Source: Ministry of Labor, *The Basic Statistical Survey on Wage Structure* (each year).

ᵃIncludes the firms with 500 employees and more in mining, construction, and manufacturing industries, and those with 100 employees and more of other industries, except service industry.
ᵇDenotes firms of all industries except service industry with 100 employees and more.
ᶜIndicates firms with 100 employees and more of all industries.

WHITE-COLLAR EMPLOYMENT PRACTICES

In most Japanese firms, the hiring of middle managers with previous work experience is unusual. Nearly all promotions to middle management jobs are from within the organization, although some managers may arrive from affiliated firms or, in large firms, from government agencies. The potential middle managers are hired fresh out of college under the implicit assumption that they will remain with the company until they reach compulsory retirement at about 60 years of age. During most of their career, in addition to merit-based raises, employees are granted annual pay increases related to their tenure in the firm. Dismissals are exceptional, and the maintenance of so-called "life-time employment" (a somewhat incorrect but widely used term) is one of the principal concerns of corporate executives (Pucik and Hatvany 1983).

Such employment patterns are best described as an internal labor market. In Japan, these practices have developed gradually since the early 1900s and became fully institutionalized during the postwar growth years as a response to economic and social constraints imposed on Japanese employers (Shimada 1983). Although many aspects of the employment system may now be subject to revisions as a result of changing environmental circumstances, the reliance on the internal labor market as the dominant employment mechanism is expected to continue basically unchanged (*The Journal of Japanese Trade & Industry* 1986).

An important feature of Japanese internal labor markets is that entry is limited mainly to new school graduates. Most of a manager's professional life then evolves within a cohort of peers who all joined the company at the same time and share similar demographic characteristics (gender, age, educational background). During their early professional years, most promotion and compensation decisions are taken within the context of the peer group. This is important not only from the organizational point of view. The peer group is also the principal reference group for individual managers, heavily used for information gathering and decision-making within the firm (Rohlen 1974; Yoshino and Lifson 1986).

The internal labor market in many Japanese firms, especially the large established corporations, is based on a dual career system for white-collar employees. One set of distinctions reflects the status rank *(shikaku),* the other designation is for job classification *(shokukai).* Promotion to a given rank opens eligibility for a range of jobs, but the match between ranks and titles is often imperfect. There are also firms, mostly smaller companies, that use only one hierarchical ladder, and also those that use three complementary ladders, adding position or salary class (Pucik 1984a). The *shikaku* classification, commonly referred to as "employee qualification system" is used extensively to guide most personnel policies, from wage and promotion determination to career planning and development. In this regard, an employee's standing in the *shikaku* ranking is the most relevant indicator of his or her position within the organization.

An example of a typical dual career system in a large-scale manufacturing firm is shown in Table 10.2. It should be pointed out, however, that the use of specific titles varies by firms and even within a single organization, and the terms used to label individual grades within the rungs of job hierarchies are often not exclusive. The well-known term *kacho* (section chief or manager) is used frequently to describe a specific status rank as well as a position class or a job title, but not all employees with *kacho* status are assigned to *kacho* positions. To complicate the matter even further, each company develops its own vocabulary with its own firm-specific order of ranks and positions.

Within the structure of the internal labor markets, seniority *(nenko)* has an impact in some firms on certain career outcomes, such as retirement benefits, basic salary, or eligibility for promotion to higher managerial rank. However, the effect of length of service on Japanese employment practices is often exaggerated. Educational background and company size are more important factors (Mouer and Sugimoto 1986). In particular, the impact of size on employment

Table 10.2 Distribution of status ranks and position classes in a large manufacturing firm

Position	Bucho	Kacho	Kakaricho
Senior manager	336	142	—
Manager	15	1047	83
Specialist	—	196	—
Supervisor	—	—	941
Unclassified	—	—	88

Source: Pucik 1984a. Reprinted with permission of John Wiley and Sons, Inc.

practices seems to be more pronounced in Japan than in other advanced industrialized countries. By contrast, Japanese seniority patterns in compensation or promotions can be readily observed elsewhere (Koike 1983; Mouer and Sugimoto 1986).

Japanese internal labor markets are also characterized by the existence of enterprise unions. However, most managers are not members of labor unions. In general, unions are virtually prohibited under Article 2 of the Trade Union Act from organizing managers who represent the interests of the employer. Excluded are employees in supervisory posts having direct authority to hire, fire, promote, or transfer workers, workers with access to confidential information relating to the employer's labor relations policies so that their official duties directly conflict with their loyalties and obligations as members of the trade unions concerned; and other individuals who represent the interests of the employer. Employers and unions use collective bargaining to determine whether a particular employee is barred from union membership by this article, but today less than a quarter of the existing unions actually have members drawn from lower-level supervisory and professional ranks.

However, given the enterprise-based rather than craft-based unionism dominant in Japan, in unionized firms, nonmanagerial white-collar employees are nearly all union members. The employment practices that impact on the early stages of managerial careers, in particular compensation, are thus frequently covered by union agreements. Also, while managers are not represented by any unions, many managers and even executives are former elected union officials. It is estimated that nearly two-thirds of large Japanese firms have some board members that served in the past as union officers. Altogether, about fifteen percent of executives have labor union backgrounds, many of them assigned to personnel and labor relations jobs.

RECRUITMENT AND CAREER DEVELOPMENT

Most established firms in Japan recruit new employees once a year. The same starting date (April 1) applies to both blue- and white-collar workers. Preferably, new employees are hired directly from schools. As a consequence of the educational boom in postwar Japan (about a third of college-age youths attend a university), graduation from college is generally considered a prerequisite for a managerial career. However, this pressure is somewhat tempered by the fact that recent job openings for new university graduates have outnumbered the supply by more than a two-to-one ratio.

The recruiting process is subject to "administrative guidance" from the Labor and Education ministries. Employers are not supposed to contact students or invite them for screening tests before specified dates each year. However, it is not uncommon for a company to get a jump on competition and select prospective employees informally even before the official recruiting season begins. It is estimated that up to 40 percent of college graduates reach informal employment agreements before the beginning of the official recruiting period (*Japan Times* 1987). As the competition for capable students heats up, some firms even attempt to shield their "catch" from competitors by offering overseas trips or resort vacations.

College students are recruited on the basis of their majors, either in technical areas (*gijitsukei*) or in nontechnical fields considered appropriate for careers in administration (*jimmukei*). This establishes a pattern of differential treatment for technical and administrative employees that is found in other areas of personnel practices. However, the qualification systems and related compensation are the same for both groups.

For candidates seeking administrative positions, selection is based on a series of interviews, although it is common for those who have passed the interviews to take a formal written entrance examination, usually on the first day of the official recruiting period. However, this examination is largely a formality, since the invitation to sit for an exam is a de facto offer of employment and taking the exam indicates an acceptance of the offer. The emphasis put on interviews seems to be well justified. According to an internal study of Kobe Steel, one of the largest steel companies in Japan, the performance ratings of college graduates after ten years with the firm correlated most closely with interview results. Written examination scores were second-best predictors of success, followed by university grades (The Institute of International Business Communication 1987).

The most promising employees in technical areas are identified and evaluated with the assistance of their professors, who work closely with company recruiters. The firm asks for a certain number of recommendations from the university and these are issued to qualified students on their request. Once a recommendation is issued, the employment offer and acceptance are considered morally binding and should not be rescinded except for the most serious reasons. Technical graduates who do not request or receive recommendations are hired through a similar recruiting process as the administrators, although the "informal" interviews will generally include tests of their professional knowledge.

Until recently, large firms hired managers with previous work experience only in exceptional circumstances to fill emergency manpower needs. Many of the mid-career hires *(chuto saiyo)* are specialized professionals who seldom progress very far within their new employer's corporate hierarchy (Pucik 1986). However, exceptions to this trend can be found in rapidly growing firms that are forced to rely on outside recruitment as a key source of managerial talent, and in occupations where demand is much greater than supply. The most recent examples are traders in the financial industry and electronics and software engineers *(Japan Economic Journal* 1987a; *Japan Labor Bulletin* 1986a).

In general, however, the hiring of managers with previous work experience is still limited mainly to medium- and small-sized firms that find it difficult to compete for fresh school graduates. Foreign-owned firms often fall into this category. The inability to recruit young graduates has a severe impact on the competitiveness of smaller firms. As wages rise with age, the higher average age of employees in smaller firms forces the employer either to offer lower wages, thus limiting its ability to attract superior staff, or to incur higher employment costs.

The preference for new school graduates to the exclusion of employees with prior experience also allows a firm quickly to assimilate each employee into the environment of the company. This begins immediately with a period of initial training lasting several weeks to several months geared to familiarizing new employees with the company. Periods of resocialization take place each time an employee begins a new position. This emphasis on intra-company education is especially important given that the university system is modeled on the European pattern and master's degrees are granted mainly in technical fields. The specialized business education on a post-graduate level (for example, the MBA curriculum) is limited to only a handful of institutions.

Most learning occurs on the job. During their careers, Japanese workers rotate through a variety of positions to gain experience in a wide area of the business. The rotation patterns have been described in detail for banks (Rohlen 1974), manufacturing firms (Pucik 1986; Sakakibara and Westney 1985), and trading firms (Yoshino and Lifson 1986). Among white-collar workers, rotation is especially frequent during the first ten to twelve years of their employment in a firm. On average, young employees move to a new section every two or three years, although the frequency of mobility differs by industry as well as by individual firms.

Even within a single firm, not all managers experience an equal amount of exposure to or rotation among jobs. Managers in the administrative track have broader mobility across functional areas and organizational subunits than managers on the technical track (Pucik 1986). Differences in promotion prospects may also influence the career path pattern. Those considered promotable to higher positions in middle management or to executive positions continue to rotate along a generalist career path, while others, in rapidly growing numbers, become increasingly specialized.

The new emphasis on specialization during the later career stages is partly driven by the employer's need to develop managers with a sufficient depth of experience within narrow functional areas. This trend is especially pronounced among the *gijitsukei* managers slated to rise within narrow technical ladders in R&D and engineering. Nevertheless, in comparison to U.S. managers, both classes of Japanese managers experience significantly higher mobility across functional boundaries.

The cross-functional mobility is expected to increase as such career development programs offer several benefits to the employers: Horizontal mobility can alleviate some of the stress and frustrations caused by lack of promotional opportunities; because of cross-training, managers can be assigned to new jobs with a greater flexibility; frequent job rotations enhance communication linkages in the firm, thus supporting the organizational ability to change (Nonaka 1985).

THE PROMOTION PROCESS

During the first five or six years of employment, employers try not to make great distinctions between pay or status to maintain competitiveness and morale among the young workers. Nevertheless, appraisals of all white-collar employees are made several times a year in connection with decisions on base salary, periodic bonuses, and promotion. In these appraisals, companies seek to distinguish a worker from the peer group, usually his or her cohort of entering white-collar employees. Managerial attention to the appraisal process is strictly enforced.

The content of the appraisal is not much different from Western practices, although more weight is generally given to an employee's behavior and attitudes, not just to the outcome of his or her performance. A great emphasis is placed on cooperation and getting along with others. According to Tawara (1979), formal feedback from the appraisals is not commonly given to an employee. The employee's ability to solicit feedback informally is considered a mark of his or her understanding of how informal communication channels operate; this is also a good way to avoid confrontations in the work place.

Not much variance in ranking is evident among younger workers in the nonmanagerial positions for at least ten years after they are recruited. Once white-collar employees reach their mid-thirties, career differences become more pronounced. Some are judged promotable to a managerial position; others are given responsibilities as a professional or specialist in a staff capacity. Up until their late fifties, some of those originally promoted to managerial positions may still be given staff jobs when their upward mobility becomes sidetracked.

The distinctions between managers are based on merit. In the past, during the period of rapid growth, the abundance of managerial positions allowed firms to promote virtually anyone even minimally qualified to do the job. As the rate of growth slowed down in the mid-1970s, promotions became more selective. In 1970, nearly 73 percent of employees with a university education could look forward to retirement from a position of *bucho* (see Table 10.3). By 1985, that proportion had shrunk to less than 58 percent. Similar patterns can be observed for other status ranks and age groups.

Table 10.3   Distribution of college graduates in large manufacturing firms[a,b,c]

	Bucho				Kacho				Kakaricho			
Age	1970	1975	1980	1985	1970	1975	1980	1985	1970	1975	1980	1985
25–29					0.3	0.2	0.1	0.1	8.2	4.2	2.4	1.8
30–34	0.5	0.2	0.2	0.2	8.3	5.0	1.5	2.4	35.9	37.8	22.9	26.6
35–39	5.7	2.1	0.8	0.5	50.0	45.5	33.8	13.3	19.4	27.1	33.5	28.9
40–44	29.0	26.3	13.1	4.8	51.3	54.5	57.8	49.8	4.7	3.4	8.1	14.6
45–49	64.7	63.4	56.5	25.9	17.3	20.4	22.1	45.5	4.1	2.4	1.2	5.9
50–54	72.7	70.4	64.7	49.5	14.4	10.4	10.5	25.3	NA	1.4	2.1	3.8

Source: National Institute of Employment and Vocational Research 1982a. Ministry of Labor, *The Basic Statistical Survey on Wage Structure* 1985.

[a]All college graduates in the cohort equal 100%.
[b]The large firms indicate those with 1,000 employees and more.
[c]1970–80 data are from *The Basic Statistical Survey on Wage Structure* conducted by the Ministry of Labor and reaggregated by the National Institute of Employment and Vocational Research.

A "fast-track" employee becomes a *kakaricho* after about ten years with the firm. Promotion to *kacho* follows after another four years. The speed of subsequent promotions varies greatly from firm to firm, but *buchos* in their late thirties are still unusual in large firms. Even with the economic slowdown, the speed of promotion has not changed much for the fast-trackers. However, for an average manager, who before could expect promotions with a reasonable degree of probability, it is more and more difficult to climb the hierarchy of a typical Japanese firm. In addition, even those who are promoted must often wait longer to obtain upper-level positions, a new phenomenon occuring especially after 1975. In comparison to the mid-1970s, promotions to middle management positions are delayed by three to four years (Association for the Promotion of Older Workers Employment 1983). Further delays in promotion are anticipated by both public and private sources (Ministry of Labor 1986).

For most firms, delays in promotion are a significant problem because of the importance attributed to managerial status in Japanese society. Some firms are seeking to deal with this issue by increasing the number of managerial jobs through additional differentiation of managerial ranks, without actually assigning any specific line responsibilities. Others prefer to give those in the eligible age brackets a promotion in name, but not in responsibility.

The complexity of promotion processes in Japanese firms can be illustrated by personnel practices in a large trading company (Pucik 1985). Managerial jobs at the trading firm were classified by status as well as titles. The company made a further distinction between a line manager and a staff manager; managers do not usually cross the line/staff boundaries. An assignment into a staff position could have a long-term negative impact on an employee's career. Moreover, the promotion process, at least at Company T, was not like a smooth ride on an escalator. Rather, career progress could be halted, leaving many behind as the escalator moved on.

Three types of career timetables were evident. A group of elite managers with mostly line experience reached the top grade of general manager after twenty-seven years in the firm. In a second group of line managers, a few also reached the top level with some delay, but most retired having obtained the level of deputy general manager. A third group, mostly staff managers, tended to retire in the lower managerial grades or were transferred into one of the numerous subsidiaries. The company made an early assessment of managerial potential and facilitated the development of promising managers by giving them the more desirable assignments and promotions. Once a manager slipped in ranking, the chance for recovery was slim. For Western firms, such a promotion system was described as the "tournament model" (Rosenbaum 1979).

The rigidity of the promotion system was caused by personnel regulations stipulating a minimum service time for each rank and grade before the next promotion. In traditional firms, such as the trading company observed, seniority in a grade still plays an important role in determining eligibility for promotion. In other words, seniority functions as a necessary but not sufficient promotion criterion. However, the impact of grade seniority is smaller in firms facing rapid environmental change or those dependent on technical innovation (Sekimoto and Hanada 1986). Delays in promotion at one career stage can be compensated by a shorter stay in the grade; thus recovery, while infrequent, is nevertheless possible.

The product or the area in which managers are employed may also cause differences in promotional opportunities, especially in large established firms (Pucik 1986). For example, in a large steel and engineering company, managers employed in the core steel business had greater chances of advancement than those employed in engineering. In an electrical machinery firm, managers who originally entered the mature mainstream divisions had better promotion chances than managers who entered emerging businesses, although the growth rates of the latter were by far superior. The career progression structure clearly lagged behind the development of the business.

COMPENSATION PRACTICES

As illustrated in Table 10.1, middle managers benefited from a considerable income gain between 1970 and 1985. At the same time, middle managers' wages declined relative to the income of blue-collar workers and white-collar workers in nonmanagerial positions (see Table 10.4). Much of this decline occurred during the early 1970s; since then, the wage ratio has remained relatively stable. Still, as Koike (1983) has shown, at least in the manufacturing sector, wage differentials in Japan between white- and blue-collar workers are the smallest of the major industrialized nations.

For middle managers, as for all other regular employees, compensation includes four principal components: the basic salary, semiannual bonuses, a retirement allowance tied to the basic salary, and a monthly special allowance tied to particular employment conditions (position, place of work, family status). The compensation system of Japanese middle managers is often referred to

Table 10.4 Annual income by employee categories*

Employee category	1970	1975	1981	1986
Junior high school all levels = 100	100	100	100	100
High schools all levels	121	123	117	113
University graduate *Kakaricho*	160	158	164	155
University graduate *Kacho*	204	199	204	190
University graduate *Bucho*	250	210	222	215

Source: Ministry of Labor, *The Basic Statistical Survey on Wage Structure* (each year).
*All firms, 40–49 age group.

as *nenko* or seniority system. In reality, the salary administration is more complex and, as pointed out earlier, the importance of seniority in salary determination for white-collar employees is often overstated.

Table 10.5 illustrates compensation differences due to age, position, and firm size for middle managers with a university education. Within each subgroup, the peak compensation is reached in the 50 to 54 age bracket, but merit and company size are far more significant for the absolute amount of pay. There is a difference in compensation of more than 100 percent between a 50-year-old *kacho* in a medium-sized firm and a *bucho* of the same age employed by a large firm. Two thirds of this gap is due to size-related salary differentials and one-

Table 10.5 Annual income of middle managers*

	Bucho					
	Firms with 100–499 employees			Firms with more than 1,000 employees		
Age	Monthly salary	Bonus	Total	Monthly salary	Bonus	Total
35–39	458.7	1753.5	7257.9	539.6	2513.1	8988.3
40–44	461.0	1909.9	7441.9	520.0	3048.1	9288.1
45–49	489.0	2246.5	8114.5	560.5	3642.7	10368.7
50–54	491.3	2343.6	8239.2	613.0	3973.4	11329.4
55–59	508.4	2305.2	8406.0	625.5	3839.1	11345.1

	Kacho					
	Firms with 100–499 employees			Firms with more than 1,000 employees		
Age	Monthly salary	Bonus	Total	Monthly salary	Bonus	Total
35–39	331.5	1448.2	5469.4	418.5	2478.7	7500.7
40–44	371.1	1723.1	6176.3	460.2	2740.4	8262.8
45–49	405.9	2072.6	6943.3	499.2	2937.6	8928.0
50–54	426.9	2266.4	7389.2	517.5	2994.0	9204.0
55–59	406.7	2112.8	6993.2	470.9	2502.1	8152.9

Source: Ministry of Labor, *The Basic Statistical Survey on Wage Structure* 1986.
*Male university graduates (thousands of yen).

third to the promotion lag. Similar comparisons can be made for other age groups and positions.

Even within a single firm, seniority is not the key determinant of pay for managers. It is true that, as the length of service with the firm increases, base salary rises. However, at the same time, the proportion of salary attributable to seniority declines and the proportion given for merit rises, so that employees with more than twenty years of service with the firm receive virtually no annual increment due to service. As a result, in large companies such as Nippon Steel, on average only 60 percent of managerial compensation is partially influenced by seniority; the remaining components are merit- or job-driven (Oda 1983).

Managerial salaries are generally subject to review once a year. In any given year, a manager can receive up to three kinds of salary raises. First, most managers receive a salary "base-up" similar to raises granted to nonmanagerial employees as a result of collective bargaining. The average "base-up" percentage is adjusted plus/minus 10 to 15 percent based on individual performance. In the case of younger managers, they may also be eligible for an incremental increase based on seniority. Finally, each managerial rank has its own salary curve so that each promotion also results in an upward shift into a higher curve.

In addition to base salary, managers receive positional allowances and other supplementary payments related to their specific situation (such as family and commuting benefits). All together, these allowances compose about 20 to 25 percent of the monthly pay. Most companies also provide a modest expense account for entertaining subordinates or clients, a natural part of the Japanese manager's job. In 1980, such amounts averaged Y110,000 per month, 40 percent less than the actual expenditures (*Japan Economic Journal* 1980a).

It is important to recognize that even among young employees, salary increases each year contain some variance for merit which, although very small in absolute amounts, convey appropriate messages to employees and impart status differences within the group. After twenty years, the wage gap between the highest and lowest earners amounts to about 30 percent of the average salary. These inter-rank differences in salaries are relatively small in comparison, for example, with the United States (Pucik 1984b).

Figure 10.1 compares salary distributions for a cohort of managers with twenty years' seniority in two large automotive firms: American (Company A) and Japanese (Company J). In the American case, just over 50 percent of the cohort is ranked in the two lowest salary grades and their salaries are less than 40 percent of the amount paid to managers in the top grade (bonuses excluded). In the Japanese case, most managers are lumped in the top half of the scale and the difference between the top and the average is similarly reduced.

Twice, in December and in June, managers as well as all regular employees receive their semiannual bonuses. The amount of bonus is related to the basic pay and expressed as a multiple of the monthly salary. Customarily, managers receive a bonus of similar magnitude to nonmanagerial employees for whom the level of the bonus is negotiated by the union. In recent years, annual bonuses for managers in medium-size and large firms equaled 4.5 to 6 months' pay. Fluctua-

Company A

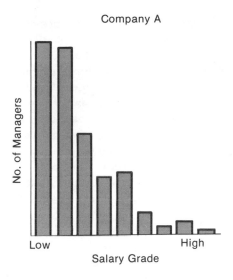

Company J

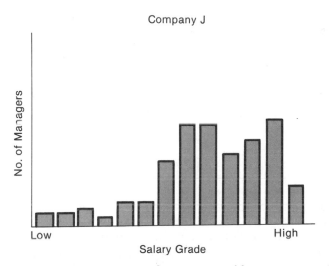

Figure 10.1 Salary grade distributions for managers with twenty years of experience (*Source:* V. Pucik 1984b, 92).

tions in bonus level are related to the business performance of the firm. In this sense, bonuses function as a group profit-sharing plan (Freeman and Weitzman 1986), providing a buffer for employment as well as basic wages and salaries. When the performance of the firm suffers, executives and upper-level middle managers are expected to take the biggest cuts. Such adjustments are customary, before any additional entrenchment measures (such as temporary layoffs or voluntary retirements) are introduced.

Japanese middle managers also receive a whole array of social benefits, ranging from company payments for social security and medical insurance (statutory benefits) to retirement bonuses and housing loans (voluntary benefits). The weight of benefits in total compensation cost for a firm is seldom greater than 20 percent. However, this relatively low number can be attributed more to the low cost of key benefits (such as national insurance) than to the scope of services provided to the individual. In most cases, benefit plans for middle managers are equal to benefits provided to all regular employees.

The most significant benefit is the retirement allowance. A 1987 survey of 2,100 large firms estimated the average lump-sum retirement allowance of retiring college graduates (nearly all of them middle managers) was approximately 25 million yen (*Japan Economic Journal* 1987b). In small firms, the retirement allowance is often less than half that amount. The accumulated retirement allowance is paid out also in the case of voluntary separation, adjusted for the number of years worked in the company. In the case of an "early retirement" requested by the company, the regular retirement benefit is augmented by an additional premium.

With an increased number of employees close to retirement age, many firms are deeply concerned about the accumulated retirement liability. To reduce the expected cash outflow, companies are introducing annuity-type pensions, in most cases replacing part of the lump-sum allowance. Today, a majority of large firms has set up retirement plans that provide monthly pension payments supplementing social security pensions usually for a period of ten years after retirement.

COPING WITH THE SURPLUS OF MIDDLE MANAGEMENT

Since the oil crisis in 1973 and the resulting slowdown in the economy, more and more Japanese firms find it difficult to accommodate the swelling ranks of middle managers. In spite of the slowdown in promotion rate discussed earlier, the rise in middle managerial positions is lagging more and more behind the number of potential candidates. The situation is most severe in mature established firms where large cohorts of employees hired during the peak boom years of 1968–72 are now reaching an age when promotion to the middle management ranks is expected. Already by 1980, one out of three such Japanese firms reported a surplus of middle managers (*Japan Economic Journal*, 1980b). With the yen revaluation, such a pressure has further increased. Today the major issue facing Japanese human resource managers is how to adjust to the new conditions without dismantling the employment system that served so well in the past.

So far, several steps have been taken, in particular by the large firms that were most severely affected by middle management surplus (Table 10.6). According to the Ministry of Labor, among firms with more than five thousand employees, 44 percent have introduced a new "specialist" system for employees

Table 10.6 Introduction rate of new personnel policies*

	Firm size		
Personnel policy	Over 5,000 employees	1,000–5,000 employees	300–999 employees
Specialist system	41.5	32.9	28.1
Early resignation system	34.5	29.9	18.5
Early retirement system	50.1	39.8	17.1
Temporary transfer system	91.6	77.0	49.4
The proportion of transferred employees over 45 years old	31.1	36.4	34.1
Retirement transfer system	34.2	23.1	10.4
The proportion of transferred employees over 45 years old	68.7	50.7	45.4

Source: Ministry of Labor, Rosei Jiho, 1987, No. 2844 (August 7).
*Firms that instituted the new policy as a percentage of all firms.

in managerial ranks without supervisory responsibility; 34 percent ask managers to resign their line positions several years before actual retirement from the firm; 46 percent have in-place programs encouraging voluntary early retirement of senior employees. At the same time, 92 percent of the large enterprises report sending employees on temporary assignment to other firms *(shukko)*. One-third of employees in this category are over 45 years old. Thirty-four percent of all large firms also use *shukko* for permanent assignments outside of the parent firm, with the majority of such transferees being senior employees (Rosei Jiho 1987).

The "specialist" system was introduced to Japan during the 1960s under the influence of U.S. managerial theories to develop employees with sufficient depth of knowledge in narrow professional fields (such as marketing research or computer systems). However, the original intent to provide a dual career ladder for valuable professionals was soon compromised in many firms by the assignment of "specialist" positions to senior employees who did not receive line management promotions. Consequently, the number of large firms with the specialist system in place have tripled since 1979 and employees in these positions account for nearly a quarter of all middle managers (Ministry of Labor 1986).

In most cases, the title of specialist does not have much professional value outside of the firm, as many of the employees assigned to a specialist position often perform usual routine jobs. Their compensation is similar to that of managers in a comparable qualification grade, but their opportunities to be promoted to higher grades are generally constrained. In theory, employees can move from a specialist to a managerial position, but in practice, such moves are increasingly infrequent the longer an employee remains in a specialist slot (Pucik 1985). It is not surprising, therefore, that an assignment as a specialist is not much appreciated and that over 40 percent of firms with more than a thousand employees reported problems and dissatisfaction with the system, while less than 10 percent were fully satisfied (Rosei Jiho 1987).

The extension of the traditional retirement age from 55 to 60 further aggravated the strains caused by the middle management bulge. As illustrated in Table 10.6, many firms attempt to open the blocked path to advancement by instituting mandatory resignation age for middle managers and by encouraging early retirement. In the case of mandatory resignation, the company stipulates at what age (usually between 55 and 58) a manager must resign his or her line position and move into a specialist status with no subordinates, or accept an assignment into a similar or higher line position in a subsidiary or in an affiliated firm. In other words, a resignation from a managerial position comes several years prior to retirement from the firm, unless an employee chooses to retire voluntarily.

However, most voluntary retirement programs are targeted for employees in their forties and early fifties. For younger employees, such programs are in effect only for a limited period of time (between ages of 42 and 45). In other cases, employees may choose an early retirement option at any time between the minimum eligible age and the mandatory retirement date. Under both kinds of programs, which are generally made available to all qualified employees in the firm, those who retire early receive full retirement benefits and occasionally an additional early retirement bonus. The payment of the latter is generally essential when the early retirement is solicited by the firm, for example, during a prolonged business slump. The amount of the allowance may also depend on whether the company arranges for another job in a subsidiary or an affiliate. In 1986, in all firms about thirty thousand employees (17 percent of all retirees) chose the early retirement option, but this proportion rises to nearly 40 percent for firms with more than five thousand workers (Rosei Jiho 1987).

Other important devices to cope with a surplus of potential middle managers are temporary transfers and retirement transfers (*ichiji shukko* and *taishoku shukko*) into subsidiaries or affiliated firms. Retirement transfers have a long history in the Japanese employment system (Clark 1979), but they have increased in frequency since the first oil crisis in 1973–74. Their purpose is twofold: to provide managerial skills or technical assistance to the related firms and subsidiaries, and to guarantee longer employment opportunities for older employees, mostly managers, of the parent firm.

In contrast to early retirement, during *shukko* the original employment relationship remains intact and the dispatched manager continues to receive the same compensation and benefit package as managers of equal rank working within the parent firm. In effect, the parent company is subsidizing a part of the dispatched manager's compensation because in many cases the pay level is lower in the subsidiaries or the wage subsidy is a part of the acceptance package demanded by the receiving organization. When *shukko* is used to remedy problems related to the surplus of managers, its intended effect is more to relieve the scarcity of managerial positions than to save on compensation costs.

Some subsidiaries are created for no other reason than to have an outlet for surplus managerial and regular staff. Many small firms providing ground maintenance, security, and other auxilliary services for a large corporation are staffed nearly exclusively by retirees from the parent firm. However, the recent changes in commercial law force firms to report consolidated earnings that include most of their direct subsidiaries. Under these conditions, the income statement of the parent firm cannot be manipulated by transferring surplus staff to subsidiaries, which was a standard practice in the past.

In large firms, temporary *shukko* is about four times more frequent than retirement *shukko*. Over 1.6 percent of all employees in firms with more than five thousand workers were temporarily assigned to other firms in 1986. Many are middle managers since temporary assignments to subsidiaries are often a part of regular managerial job rotation. It is not unusual that a majority of upper-management positions in a subsidiary are occupied by managers transferred from the parent. However, as subsidiaries increase the scope of their business activities and grow in size, transfers of managers from the parent firm meet mounting resistance from employees hired into the subsidiary. Naturally, they perceive the retirement policies of the parent as a hindrance to their own promotional opportunities.

MANAGERIAL VALUES AND SOCIAL CHANGE

While Japanese managers are known for their commitment and loyalty to the firm, and although managerial careers in Japan have been traditionally characterized by a relatively low degree of interfirm mobility, the frequency of job changes has increased since the early 1980s and is likely to increase in the future. At the same time, it is important to recognize that in absolute terms the number of managers switching employers in any of the recent years is quite small. The total amount, including managers permanently dispatched to affiliated firms and those whose job switch is related to an early retirement program, is not much more than 1 percent of the total managerial work force (Rosei Jiho 1987).

The lack of career mobility does not imply that all other middle managers are content with their job situations. In fact, a number of opinion surveys indicate a growing frustration over delays in promotions and doubts about company commitment to lifetime employment in the face of difficult economic conditions (*Japan Times* 1984). However, this job dissatisfaction rarely leads to a decision to change jobs. As pointed out earlier, *chuto saiyo* careers seldom result in upper-management jobs. In addition, because of the existing structure of wages and retirement benefits, most job changes entail a significant income loss. On average, a young middle manager changing jobs at the age of 35 can lose up to Y58 millions (25 percent of expected lifetime income) by changing employers (*Japan Economic Journal* 1986). As in the past, there are always some willing to take the risk, hoping to join the next Honda or Sony, but their numbers, at least so far, are not growing very rapidly.

In some instances, switching employers can be quite profitable. Managers in the *bucho* rank joining foreign-owned firms generally receive a superior compensation package compared to that of similar Japanese firms (The Institute of

International Business Communication 1987). A move from a manufacturing firm to the financial industry can also be advantageous; recently, banks and trust banks have been hiring large numbers of midcareer managers in response to the growing need for persons with expertise in international banking operations, securities operations, and systems engineering (*Japan Economic Journal* 1985). Nevertheless, such opportunities, while receiving wide press coverage, are still limited.

Managerial job mobility will continue to be restricted as long as there is only a limited demand for external hires. Most employers are far more interested in outplacement of their existing middle managers than in recruiting new ones. A majority of so-called career counseling and placement firms have been established to find ways for reducing the existing work force, not to recruit new managers. Even the well-known executive search firms conduct 80 percent of their business with foreign-owned companies; the other 20 percent is mostly assignments to staff Japanese-owned operations abroad.

The environment that faces Japanese middle managers willing to change jobs can be described as a quasi-external labor market at best. If there is a significant increase in managerial job mobility in the future, it will probably result from the urgency many Japanese firms feel to reorganize their middle management infrastructure and reduce the managerial work force. Also, in some rapidly changing technical professions (such as software development), employers may find that the lifetime employment contract is a rather inefficient way to staff organizations. In particular, the continuous growth of the service industry will attract managers looking for new opportunities. Nevertheless, the publicity given to the new mobility patterns is still more an indication of their exceptionality than of a fundamental change in managerial values and, even more important, in alternative employment opportunities.

With limited promotional opportunities, shrinking income differentials in comparison to nonmanagerial employees, and diffusion of traditional managerial authority through various participation schemes, the benefits of pursuing a managerial career are diminishing. Given that leaving a firm is not a viable alternative for most middle managers frustrated by their work conditions, we might expect they would have a renewed interest in collective action and would organize to improve their bargaining power. However, there has been no indication of this happening on any significant scale.

We might also expect that decline in union membership may motivate some unions to add to their ranks by enlisting "specialists" and other managerial-class employees removed from lines of direct authority. However, such attempts are also rather infrequent. At most, unions try to cope with the problem of forced interfirm transfer by negotiating detailed rules about how and when an employee can be moved to another enterprise and by coordinating their activities with other company unions operating within the same quasi-intrafirm labor market. Most of this affects managers only indirectly, as regulation of interfirm transfers is binding only for unionized employees.

By far the largest change in managerial employment practices of the future will come from the implementation of the Equal Opportunity Legislation enacted in 1986, after considerable domestic and international debate. This legislation brings Japan into compliance with international convenants concerning nondiscrimination to which Japan is a signatory. The law, which does not incorporate any penalties for its violations, requires equal treatment for men and women in all aspects of personnel policies, including promotion to managerial positions.

At the time when the new law went into effect, less than 7 percent of Japanese middle managers were women, most of them concentrated in small and medium-sized firms in the service sector (International Labor Office 1986). Many factors account for low female participation in management. To begin with, numerous organizational practices discouraged women from aspiring to managerial positions. Before the new legislation was enacted, only a handful of large industrial and financial firms actively recruited female four-year college graduates. Even in those firms that did, they were put on restricted career tracks that prevented most young women from acquiring the experience and training needed for promotion. Legal restrictions or established norms, such as a ban on night work and limitations on overtime and intracompany transfers, created additional promotional barriers. Heavy emphasis on after-work, male-oriented socialization among managers is another contributing factor (Carney and O'Kelly 1987).

Restrictive policies limiting the managerial promotion of women often were justified in terms of their high turnover rates, which make investment in training and development uneconomical. At the same time, one of the main causes of high turnover among female employees is the realization that their career opportunities are limited. Yet, even in the presence of unbiased employment policies supported by the new law, the obstacles facing the 40 percent of graduating female seniors that hope to become managers (*Business Week* 1986) are considerable. Japanese women still feel strong social pressure to put their roles as wife and mother ahead of job responsibility. In fact, a majority of Japanese women, including those holding a job, see the fulfillment of the traditional family role as more important than career advancement.

Nevertheless, the changing economic conditions facing Japan are forcing a gradual widening of women's access to managerial positions. Japanese firms have to meet a shortage of skilled professionals in a number of rapidly growing high technology sectors such as software development or biochemistry, while the supply of well-educated women is increasing. Shifts in the industrial structure from manufacturing to service industries also enhance promotional opportunities for women who form the bulk of the labor force in the tertiary sector. As a result, in 1986, the placement ratio for women graduating from four-year colleges reached 73.4 percent, only 5.5 percent below the male rate and the highest level ever (*Japan Labor Bulletin* 1986b). By the year 2000, many of these young women may be in middle management.

SUMMARY AND FUTURE PROSPECTS

Despite the successful performance of the Japanese economy, large numbers of middle managers are facing troubled times as the employment system continues to evolve and adjust to the changing environment. Through the increasing use of the "qualification" and "specialist" systems, the status position of middle managers was uncoupled from positions of real managerial responsibility. Early retirement and retirement transfer policies make tenure with a single firm less predictable. In most firms, promotions at all middle management levels are delayed as a consequence of the middle management glut. At the same time, companies have responded to this problem by becoming more explicit in their evaluation of middle managers' ability and performance. With constrained resources, it is no more feasible to assign even symbolic positions of responsibility to those who would otherwise not qualify on merit.

The newly instituted personnel policies, which increasingly differentiate the managerial work force, make even more apparent the severe internal competition that always characterized the careers of Japanese middle managers. In the past, this had been carefully hidden under the traditional veneer of the corporate family, but it is now coming to the surface with yet-to-be-seen consequences for social harmony in the work place. What makes the situation more difficult is that the increasing severity of the competition is not accompanied by increasing rewards. Most Japanese middle managers have to run harder to stay even.

Yet the current situation should not be overdramatized. The living standards of Japanese middle managers have risen substantially and many of the economic problems they are facing, such as exorbitant cost of housing, affect the whole population. In addition, as companies continue to digest the vast cohorts of pre-1973 hires, the relationship between the demand for managerial jobs and the available positions will stabilize. From the mid-1990s, the promotion odds in many firms are bound to improve if for no other reason than favorable organizational demographics.

Other macro-level variables will continue to force further adjustments in employment practices. The continuous expansion of the service sector, exploding technological changes, and the increasing internationalization of the Japanese economy are creating new demands on companies and their managers in terms of job skills, flexibility, and ability to manage differentiation. How will changes in employment conditions affect Japan's international competitiveness? While these may be challenges that the country has not faced before, Japan's impressive record in managing change during the whole postwar era may give a reasonable clue as to what can be expected.

REFERENCES

Association for the Promotion of Older Workers Employment. 1983. *Survey concerning personnel management, aging and extension of the retirement age.* Tokyo (in Japanese).

Business Week. 1986. Look whose sun is rising now: Career women. August 25:50.

Carney, L. S., and C. G. O'Kelly. 1987. Barriers and constraints to the recruitment and mobility of female managers in Japanese labor force. *Human Resource Management* 26 (2):193–216.

Clark, R. 1979. *The Japanese company*. New Haven, Conn.: Yale University Press.

Far Eastern Economic Review. 1985. Japan at work: Who are the workers? December 19:49–80.

Freeman, R. B., and M. L. Weitzman. 1986. *Bonuses and employment in Japan*. Cambridge, Mass.: National Bureau of Economic Research, Working Paper No. 1878.

Fortune. 1987. Japan's troubled waters. March 30:21–53.

The Institute of International Business Communication (IIBC) 1987. *Foreign affiliates in Japan: The search for professional manpower*. Tokyo: IIBC.

International Labor Office (ILO). 1986. *Yearbook of labor statistics*. Geneva: ILO.

Japan Economic Journal. 1980a. Company expense account for entertaining clients is not enough, section chiefs say. May 20:15.

———. 1980b. One firm out of every three is troubled with problem of middle aged, old workers. February 12:11.

———. 1985. More Japanese are now leaving "lifetime" jobs for new careers. November 23:8.

———. 1986. Changing jobs costs heavily for Japanese workers. August 30:24.

———. 1987a. Harsh business climate sends workers job jumping. March 28:8.

———. 1987b. College graduates want monthly pension allowance, not just severance bonus. April 11:21.

Japan Labor Bulletin. 1986a. City banks hire persons in midcareer. 25 (9):3.

———. 1986b. 73.4% of female college graduates employed in 1985. 25 (1):2.

Japan Statistical Yearbook. 1986. Tokyo: Statistics Bureau, Management and Coordination Agency.

Japan Times. 1984. White collar values are changing: Poll. March 7:2.

———. 1987. Next year's graduates look for work as job season opens. September 6:2.

Journal of Japanese Trade and Industry. 1986. Ongoing transformation in Japanese management, no. 4:46–49.

Koike, K. 1983. Internal labor markets. Workers in large firms. In *Contemporary industrial relations in Japan*, edited by T. Shirai. Madison: University of Wisconsin Press.

Ministry of Labor. 1986. *Labor white paper*. Tokyo: Japan Institute of Labor (in Japanese).

———. 1970–1985. *The basic statistical survey of wage structure*. Tokyo: Ministry of Labor.

Mouer, R., and Y. Sugimoto. 1986. *Images of Japanese society*. London: KPT Limited.

Nonaka, I. 1985. *An evolutionary theory of the firm*. Tokyo: Nihon Keizai Shinbunsha (in Japanese).

Oda, M. 1983. *Compensation and promotion: The plight of middle managers*. Tokyo: Sophia University, Institute of Comparative Culture Business Series, Bulletin No. 95.

Pucik, V. 1984a. White-collar human resource management in large Japanese manufacturing firms. *Human Resource Management* 23 (3):257–76.

———. 1984b. White-collar human resource management: A comparison of the U.S. and Japanese automobile industries. *The Columbia Journal of World Business* 19 (3):87–94.

————. 1985. Promotion patterns in a Japanese trading company. *The Columbia Journal of World Business* 20 (3):73–79.

————. 1986. *Careers and internal labor markets: Determinants of career achievement among managers in large Japanese firms.* PhD diss., Columbia University.

Pucik, V., and N. Hatvany. 1983. Management practices in Japan and their impact on business strategy. In *Advances in strategic management,* edited by R. Lamb. Greenwich, Conn.: JAI Press.

Rohlen, T. 1974. *For harmony and strength.* Berkeley: University of California Press.

Rosei Jiho (Labor Policy Bulletin). 1987. Analysis of current state of personnel systems and personnel mobility. August 7, no. 2844 (in Japanese).

Rosenbaum, J. E. 1979. Tournament mobility. Career patterns in a corporation. *Administrative Science Quarterly* 24:220–41.

Sakakibara, K., and D. E. Westney. 1985. Comparative study of the training, careers, and organization of engineers in the computer industry in the United States and Japan. *Hitotsubashi Journal of Commerce and Management* 20:1–20.

Sekimoto, M., and M. Hanada. 1986. The analysis of employee commitment: Survey of 4539 workers in 11 firms. *Diamond-Harvard Business Review,* no. 1:53–62.

Shimada, H. 1983. Japanese industrial relations—A new general model? In *Contemporary industrial relations in Japan,* edited by T. Shirai. Madison: University of Wisconsin Press.

Tawara, J. 1979. *Career patterns of white-collar employees.* Tokyo: Center for Human Development.

Yoshino, N., and T. B. Lifson. 1986. *The invisible link. Japan's sogo shosha and the organization of trade.* Cambridge, Mass.: MIT Press.

Index